Lecture Notes in Computer

Edited by G. Goos, J. Hartmanis and J.

Springer
Berlin
Heidelberg
New York
Barcelona
Hong Kong
London
Milan
Paris
Singapore
Tokyo

Reidar Conradi (Ed.)

Software Process Technology

7th European Workshop, EWSPT 2000
Kaprun, Austria, February 21-25, 2000
Proceedings

Springer

Series Editors

Gerhard Goos, Karlsruhe University, Germany
Juris Hartmanis, Cornell University, NY, USA
Jan van Leeuwen, Utrecht University, The Netherlands

Volume Editor

Reidar Conradi
Norwegian University of Science and Technology
Department of Computer and Information Science
O.S. Bragstads pl. 2 E, Gløshaugen, 7491 Trondheim, Norway
E-mail: conradi@idi.ntnu.no

Cataloging-in-Publication Data applied for

Die Deutsche Bibliothek - CIP-Einheitsaufnahme

Software process technology : 7th European workshop ; proceedings
/ EWSPT 2000, Kaprun, Austria, February 21 - 25, 2000. Reidar
Conradi. - Berlin ; Heidelberg ; New York ; Barcelona ; Hong Kong ;
London ; Milan ; Paris ; Singapore ; Tokyo : Springer, 2000
(Lecture notes in computer science ; Vol. 1780)
ISBN 3-540-67140-4

CR Subject Classification (1991): D.2, K.6, K.4.2

ISSN 0302-9743
ISBN 3-540-67140-4 Springer-Verlag Berlin Heidelberg New York

Springer-Verlag is a company in the specialist publishing group BertelsmannSpringer
© Springer-Verlag Berlin Heidelberg 2000
Printed in Germany

Typesetting: Camera-ready by author
Printed on acid-free paper   SPIN 10719813   06/3142   5 4 3 2 1 0

Session 3: Applications, Part 1

Session 4: Distributed Processes / Process Modeling Languages

Session 5: Experimental Software Engineering

Session 6: Industrial Experiences, Part 1

Table of Contents

The program committee for this workshop has consisted of:
- Sergio Bandinelli, ESI, Bilbao, Spain
- Reidar Conradi, NTNU, Trondheim, Norway (chair)
- Jean-Claude Derniame, University of Nancy, France
- Letizia Jaccheri, NTNU, Trondheim, Norway
- Even-Andrè Karlsson, Q-Labs, Lund, Sweden
- Manny Lehman, Imperial College, London, UK
- Carlo Montangero, Università di Pisa, Italy
- Nazim Madhavji, McGill University, Canada
- Henk Obbink, Philips, The Netherlands
- Markku Oivo, VTT, Oulu, Finland
- Wilhelm Schäfer, University of Paderborn, Germany
- Marv Zelkowitz, University of Maryland, USA

The organizing chair was Mehdi Jazayeri, Techn. Univ. of Vienna, Austria.

The workshop was organized in 11 sessions:
- PIE project
- Keynote by M. M. Lehman, "Thirty Years in Software Process"
- Methods
- Applications, Part 1
- Distributed Processes / Process Modeling Languages,
- Keynote by Victor R. Basili: "Experimental Software Engineering"
- Industrial Experiences, Part 1
- Industrial Experiences, Part 2
- Keynote by Robert Balzer: "Current State and Future Perspectives of
    Software Process Technology"
- Applications, Part 2
- Wrap-up and Future Directions (no papers)

We hope you enjoyed the workshop and will enjoy the proceedings.

Trondheim, January 2000
Reidar Conradi

Preface

The European Workshop on Software Process Technology celebrates its 10th anniversary in the year 2000.

The goal of the workshop is to assemble researchers and practitioners in the area of Software Process Technology. Issues such as process modeling, process enactment, and process improvement are central, as are empirical studies of such technology. We are happy that at EWSPT'7 about 40% of the papers reported on practical experiences.

This workshop series has, for most of the time, been supported by the PRO-MOTER/PROMOTER2 ESPRIT Basic Research Working Groups, coordinated by the University of Nancy.

The year 2000 workshop will be a combined workshop with the European PIE project. PIE stands for Process Instance Evolution and constitutes an ESPRIT IV Framework Long Term Research project number 34840 (not to be confused with the ESSI Process Improvement Experiments, PIEs). The aim of the PIE project is to study, to investigate, and ultimately to demonstrate what kind of services are needed to support change and evolution in human organizational processes.

Twenty-one out of 44 submitted papers were accepted for the combined workshop. The accepted papers, including 4 PIE papers, will be presented and discussed. There will also be three keynotes.

The following, related workshops have taken place in the past:
- EWPM'1 in Milan, Italy, 30-31 May 1990,
    eds. Vincenzo Ambriola, Reidar Conradi, and Alfonso Fuggetta, AICA Press.
- EWSPT'2 in Trondheim, Norway, 7-8 Sept. 1992,
    ed. Jean-Claude Derniame, Springer LNCS 635.
- EWSPT'3 in Villard-de-Lans (Grenoble), France, 7-9 Feb. 1994,
    ed. Brian Warboys, Springer LNCS 772.
- EWSPT'4 in Nordwijkerhout (Leiden), The Netherlands, 3-5 April 1995,
    ed. Wilhelm Schäfer, Springer LNCS 913.
- EWSPT'5 in Nancy, France, 9-11 Oct. 1996,
    ed. Carlo Montangero, Springer LNCS 1149.
- EWSPT'6 in Weybridge (London), UK, 16-18 Sept. 1998,
    ed. Volker Gruhn, Springer LNCS 1487.

The PIE Project: An Introduction

Pierre-Yves Cunin

LSR – IMAG, ACTIMART, bâtiment 8, Avenue de Vignate, 38610 Gières, France.
Pierre-Yves.Cunin@imag.fr

Note

This paper is a brief presentation of the PIE (Process Instance Evolution) ESPRIT project. It is not supposed to be a research paper but to provide overall information about the project and its objectives. It should be considered as an introduction to the research papers (see section 4) presented by the partners of the project.

1 Objectives

The objective of the PIE project is to investigate and demonstrate what "computer-assisted services" are needed to support human intensive processes.[1] Such processes are usually long lived (possibly as long as the company that holds them), distributed (among the various participants), made of heterogeneous components (with various levels of autonomy) and always subject to dynamic evolution (real-time re-engineering: enhancement, adaptation, refinement, correction) to cope with industrial and market pressure. For example, the concept of the "virtual" enterprise requires the efficient mastering and support of these types of processes (and their evolution).

Initial research in the process technology field was focused on process modeling formalisms and process engines to execute process model instances ("enactment") concurrently with real processes ("performance"). It did not fully consider evolution of processes, which were supposed to be defined statically in a homogeneous and centralised way. Since then particular aspects of process evolution have been intensively studied within academia. The primary motivation of the PIE project is to go a step further towards generic methods and techniques that assist industry (seeking to exploit process technology) in carrying out process evolution with the benefit of maximum efficiency and flexibility.

The project relies on concrete scenarios proposed by the industrial partners on the basis of real requirements derived form their current needs.

Based on these requirements, the project intends to produce three major results:

- A methodological framework for process evolution which involves approaches and methods aiming at defining proactive monitoring plans, analysis and decision making, as well as effective changes.

- A set of tools to support the definition, execution, monitoring, and dynamic modification of ongoing processes.

---

[1] Processes where humans and software systems interact to achieve a common goal, and where humans play a crucial and active role.

- A platform to federate the heterogeneous tools and components involved in a process, allowing them to interoperate consistently, possibly under various levels of control and automation.

The selected applications are used for the evaluation/assessment of the proposed methods and techniques.

2 Administrative description

The PIE project is a LTR (Long Term Research) ESPRIT IV project, n°34840. A first feasibility phase lasted 6 months in 1998. The main stream started in February 1999. It has a two-year duration for a total effort of 23 person years.

The partners are:

- Université Joseph Fourier – Grenoble 1 (Coordinator)
- The Victoria University of Manchester
- Universitaet Dortmund
- Inter Unec – Université de Savoie
- Politecnico di Milano
- Xerox The Document Company
- Teamware Group Ltd
- Dassault Systèmes

Further information can be found at the following URL:
http://www.cs.man.ac.uk/ipg/pie/pie-e.html

3 Process evolution problems

Process Evolution has become a research topic in the process technology field. It covers a wide variety of problems ranging from e.g. adding a characteristic or making minor corrections to a product involved in a running process, to large scale changes such as a new business venture within the organization, or setting-up new tools in a distributed process environment.

A lot of effort has been put into solving these problems, but the support provided for the process change has often been misdirected to the implementation of ad-hoc mechanisms to support modifications of the process. These techniques focus on the modification of the process itself, but not how to identify and predict the need for change.

3.1 "Functional" view

The process evolution services the project wants to provide in response to industry expectations and problems are:

- *Dynamic on-line evolution for "critical" enterprise processes.* By critical processes, we mean processes that cannot be stopped at any time. For this kind of process (which tends to be the norm), dynamic on-line changes must be supported. Either the process model instances are changed on the fly or the process model is changed and a strategy that determines how the change is propagated to enacting instances of that model has to be defined and implemented. These changes have to be done in conjunction with the real process (changes) and they must be validated and controlled (change control).

- *Scope of a change.* The scope of a dynamic change is not necessarily confined to the running process, but most often, it has to be reconsidered (evolution strategy) for other process fragments or for future projects (instances), enabling therefore reuse of experience learned from previous projects. To this end, there must be functions enabling the conveyance of changes applied at the real process level and at the model instance level to the model level.

- *Detection of the need for change.* Events (or sources) that necessitate a process change fall into two categories: *internal* and *external* events to the running process instance. External events may arise for different reasons, such as, change in the environment in which the process operates, market pressure, or technological trends. They are perceived by decision makers (e.g. project manager) who initiate the change process. The detection of internal events will be conducted automatically through process monitoring. Generally, methods for monitoring projects are based on quantitative measures whose purpose is to express to what extent process performance can deviate from the existing process model. Proactive monitoring can propose corrective actions to reconcile the real process and the model instance.

- *Support for risk analysis.* Methods for risk analysis and decision making must be defined to help project managers in selecting the "right" change that meets the targeted objective in situations where several alternatives for real process change can be envisaged. This is in relation with the previous item *"Scope of a change "* because it is partly based on reuse of experience. Such facilities may be used on-line at the model instance level or off-line at the model level.

- *Implementation of the change itself.* Besides the detection and selection of the change, performers must be supplied with active help in implementing it. The action of change must be conducted by keeping the overall process in a consistent state. The problem is to control and implement the complete impact of a change, particularly when it concerns distributed process fragments.

- *Managing multiple types of change.* This issue is related to changes that may emanate from different sources, internal or external. The project will investigate and develop strategies for managing changes (e.g. ordering with respect to priorities). It is expected this service may also cover other aspects such as changes of the evolution environment (e.g. introduce a new implementation of the change action that corresponds to a tool replacement). Such change strategies belong to the core of the company and are themselves manifest in different company "ways" (processes, know how) of doing things, which may themselves evolve or develop over time. The process support environment should provide services to deploy them and to make them evolve in a flexible and dynamic way.

Fig. 1 represents graphically how these functionalities fit together.

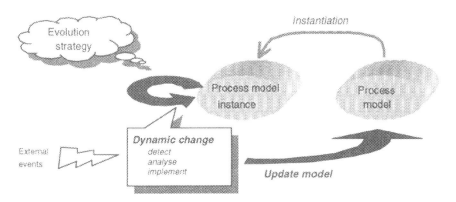

Fig. 1. Main functions for dynamic process evolution

This list of problems and functionalities is based on the experience that the project partners have gained in previous work and on the requirements stated by the industrial partners. In addition they have identified application fields where process evolution support would be essential for their business (e.g. large business insurance activities, deployment of large software systems, ...).

3.2 "Non functional" view

A main interest of the application fields, selected by the industrial partners, lies in their nature to exhibit a representative set of "non functional" requirements and constraints that large-scale process-sensitive systems must fulfil today if they are ever to be helpful. New architectures and technologies for adaptable support platforms have to be explored and proposed so that it becomes possible to implement the previous functionalities, and thereby to come up to users' expectations. Among this new set of requirements, we focus on the following:

- *Cooperation*: although the tasks included in almost all business processes are developed individually from the performer's point of view, they are highly co-operative. All users' and teams' interactions must be taken into account in order to better determine how profound the impact of a (local) change could be over all the tasks of the involved actors.

- *Distribution*: the process is not necessarily monolithic, but can be composed of numerous process fragments, each one running in a remote site and has to inter-operate with the other processes. This issue becomes more critical when considering mobility of the participants, enabled today by the emergence of new technologies like the world-wide-web, the high performance of laptops and mobile phones, etc.

- *Heterogeneity*: tools are neither homogeneous nor all proprietary. They can be COTS (Commercial Off The Shelf) tools embedding some process concepts and fragments and they can be widely disseminated on different platforms. Practitioners are unwilling to change the tools they are used to. Support systems and platforms have to cope with interoperation of such tools.

We claim that these aspects belong to the process evolution domain. In effect, any process evolution support technology has to take care of the evolution of the infrastructure and the working environment on which the execution of the process relies. The lack of adoption of software process technology within industry may be partly due to the lack of support of those aspects in the software process systems developed so far.

4   Project main streams

The project is structured in several workpackages, which reflect the different classes of problems we consider as strategic.

1. The interoperability support platform. Evolution of and within such platform is a difficult challenge: e.g. adding or removing tools or components, mobility of participants who may act from different places depending on their tasks and responsibilities, distribution of the components over a network which may change during the execution of the process.

2. The change and decision support services. This includes proactive monitoring and concerns the various facets of changing an ongoing process, anticipating deviations between the model instance and the executing process, proposing preventive and corrective actions and facilities for decision support systems.

3. The evolution strategy support. This level concerns the capability of a company to master and manage its (business) processes. The ability to define strategies for process evolution, to model them and of course to make them evolve depending e.g. on high level company decisions, is seen as a major improvement with respect to the support of human intensive processes.

The three presented papers illustrate this structure. The first paper entitled: "Support for Software Federations: the PIE Platform" explains the rationale behind the unique approach adopted by the project, the relationship between the core Foundation and PIE Middleware technologies, and the services that are to be developed in the project as the PIE components.

These components are described in the other two papers: "Advanced Services for Process Evolution: Monitoring and Decision Support" describes two of the technologies that provide services to the federation and illustrates their application in the scenario drawn from industry; and "A Support Framework for Dynamic Organizations", which describes the Evolution Strategy service. This framework is on one hand a PSS (Process Support System) component of the PIE architecture, and on the other hand it defines the relationships between other relevant components (both static and dynamic relationships) from the point of view of the user and the organization.

A Support Framework for Dynamic Organizations

Mark Greenwood, Ian Robertson, Brian Warboys

Informatics Process Group,
Department of Computer Science,
University of Manchester, Manchester M13 9PL, U.K.
{markg, ir, brian}@cs.man.ac.uk

Abstract. This paper describes a framework that is intended to provide an infrastructure for the delivery of support for business processes – including design processes, software development processes and procurement processes. This framework has to be capable of supporting quasi-independent process model instance evolution, and to provide seamless support in this environment for the non-expert Process Manager to exploit this capability

1 Introduction

Many organizations see benefit in, and will provide resources for, the modelling and analysis of their processes. However very few see that benefit extending to the use of software process technology to support and enact these selfsame processes. This state of affairs is in marked contrast to that of the workflow community, which is characterized by a number of application-driven initiatives and relatively widespread adoption. There may be a number of reasons for this: greater interest by tool manufacturers, the focus on simpler processes, or the availability of "better" technologies or modelling formalisms. As yet there is no clear consensus regarding the issues on which research should focus in order to remedy the situation and the questions remain open.

The core justification for this work is the belief that process technologies, to be successful, must be capable of supporting the inherent complexity of human-intensive processes. The kinds of complexities that affect support technologies are: inconsistency in views, incomplete views, and the ongoing state of flux. This work brings into focus the need to support organizational processes to a greater extent and to a better degree than has hitherto been seen as necessary – complexity in structure and behaviour (arising from evolution) has not yet been addressed by contemporary modelling and enactment systems.

The approach described in this paper is based on the concept of structuring software development processes in particular, and business processes in general, in a manner that is analogous to the way in which systems (software systems and others) are designed and implemented in the real world. It aims to support and exploit the diversity and richness of the different methods used by organizations to achieve their goals, yet be able to accommodate the dynamic nature of such organizations.

The following section describes the context of this work in the PIE project, with related work in section 3. A key aspect of this project is its emphasis on evolution, so there follows in section 4 a brief discussion of relevant evolution issues. Section 5 describes the framework that is proposed as the basis for addressing certain core problems identified for the project. Section 6 provides an overview of the Process*Web* technology in which the framework is currently implemented. An example application of the framework is briefly described in section 7, and conclusions are expressed in Section 8.

2   Context

This paper describes the aims of the Evolution Strategy (ES) workpackage of the Esprit PIE[1] project together with the architecture and technology which, it is believed, will be capable of contributing significantly to all of the major results of the project but in particular to a) the framework for process evolution, and to b) the development of tools to support definition, execution, and dynamic modelling of organization processes [7].

Evolution Strategy is one of the services needed to bring the goal of the project within reach. Its focus is on the organization and its processes, and it acts as a mediator between the PIE Middleware infrastructure to be provided by other workpackages [6] and the services available from the components of Monitoring and Decision Support (MS and DS respectively) [1], and ultimately also a Change Support (CS) component. From another viewpoint it is acting as a mediator between the user and the technologies available to the user via the PIE Middleware.

It operates at the same level as these components because, although certain evolution in an organization can be imposed top-down, there are many coordinations and adaptations that are developed and implemented at local levels in contexts that are quite isolated from high level concerns. Therefore Evolution Strategy is viewed as a component just as the other services are components, and as other process support systems are components recognized by the PIE infrastructure.

In undertaking this mediation role, the ES component has some specific aims which are laid down in the objectives of the project, and enhanced where appropriate by the emerging requirements being determined by the project's industrial partners. The results are intended to allow a non-specialist Process Manager to:

- Treat a very complex process model, composed of numerous model components or fragments, as if it were monolithic.
- Use preferred methods for the modelling and evolution of process models, be they on-line or off-line.
- Evolve very large and complex process models, such as those for software development, in a responsive manner (involving feedback) in a compact time frame.
- Evolve them taking cognisance of the fact that their implementations in different businesses may be on different platforms, and indeed may be paper-based.
- Focus attention on particular process model instances in a concurrent fashion by means of software components that support monitoring, decision-making and change, and to be able to tailor these components to suit contextual needs at run time.

---

1. Process Instance Evolution (PIE), a Framework IV LTR project.

- Add models incorporating successful changes to a library, thus supporting organizational learning. These models would initially be specialized process models, and ultimately they could be generic.
- Accommodate changes being applied to the Process Manager's domain through different Evolution Strategies located elsewhere in the business (or even outwith it).

The Framework is an architecture implemented as a process model. This process model can generate a network whose nodes represent products and processes of the organization (or placeholders for these). In addition, other process models or PIE Components, referred to as methods, can be invoked through operations of the nodes to support product and process evolution. The PIE Components help identify the need for process model evolution (MS), determine alternative models and select the most appropriate(DS), and implement this model in a running process model instance (CS). They are controlled by means of a meta-process that is built into the framework.

The workpackage is split into two tasks, each covering one year. The first is concerned with developing the mediation framework, the essence of which is described in this paper, and the second is concerned with supporting concurrent evolution, i.e. when a process model instance is subject to evolution from a number of unrelated sources. Both tasks are driven by user requirements and the industrial case study prepared by the industrial partners (introduced in [1]).

3 Related Work

Supporting a business process through technology often provokes changes to that process. In part this is a direct result of the attention given to the process to decide how it ought to be supported. However, this merely accelerates the natural tendency of business processes to evolve as new requirements and opportunities emerge. Early experience with a software development environment illustrated that a process support system's long term effectiveness is restricted if it is difficult to adapt to new methods and tools [15].

The need to support processes over time is illustrated by the research on meta-processes, processes which deal with other (operational) processes [5][8]. Our implementation experience [17] is that while meta-processes support evolution there is still a complexity problem. A complex meta-process to support the evolution of a complex operational process can be very unwieldy.

This framework exploits a hierarchy to manage complexity. This is based on previous work in managing large specifications [14], and software systems [10]. The framework provides a process architecture to complement a meta-process in supporting evolution. The expectation is that many changes will not involve changing the overall system architecture, though the meta-process does understand the architecture enough to do this if required. The implementation gives a generic process system which is adapted to the business process being supported.

The notion of a process system which has the ability to adapt to new demands is not unique. The Endeavors system keeps an internal model of itself which can be used by enactable models supporting the development, installation, customizing and reconfiguring of the system [3]. Amber has experimented with a meta-linguistic approach, where callbacks to instance specific code is used to modify the system's default enactment behaviour [11]. However, most emphasis has been on configuring a process system to specific demands of one model, rather than supporting ongoing adaption over a sustained period of time. Similarly WebFlow [2] has mechanisms to support the evolution of a process model at the micro-level but does not address the broader, policy issues involved in supporting the evolution of complex processes.

4   Structuring Evolution

A common theme running through this work is the phenomenon of evolution and, before describing the framework on which the solution will be based, the issue of evolution will be expanded upon.

Evolution is a transformation. It is adaptive change with a time dimension, which implies that:

- the changed system is based on the earlier system,
- there exists a structure to maintain equilibrium between the system and it environment,
- there are issues relating to successive and concurrent system changes.

Evolution can be directed or spontaneous, that is, it can be externally imposed or internally driven. An example of directed evolution would be the shift of a business in a new direction such as retailers expanding into the banking business. An example of spontaneous evolution could be local initiatives of process improvement. Directed evolution is not always top-down, for example the propagation of a new software technology throughout an organization can be orthogonal to the normal hierarchy of line responsibility. Different kinds of evolution can coexist, so process support needs to be able to accommodate changes arising from a number of sources, possibly concurrently.

Evolution in organizations is at the same time both focused and diffuse. Much of evolutionary change is a result of purposeful strategic decision, for example to enter a new market, to change a product line, or take-over by another business. On the other hand it is diffuse in that a) strategic evolution is implemented by many minor evolutions, and b) minor evolutions can take place on a local basis that may well have no impact on business strategy. It cannot be said that evolution is entirely externally constrained, nor that it is isolated, and this leads to the notion of "quasi-independence" which will be discussed later in section 5.4.

In looking at systems that include many related process model instances, the issue of "co-evolution" has to be considered. This refers to the situation where the evolving system has a dependency on another system. The consequence is that evolving one system might result in an inconsistency between the two systems, and this inconsistency has to be addressed. This has to be either a corresponding evolution of the second system, a reversion in the first system, or a tolerance of the inconsistency. There are three common situations for process co-evolution, and this work is concerned about all three:

- Co-evolution between two related process models.

- Co-evolution between the definition domain and the enactment domain [9].
- Co-evolution between enactment and performance domains.

One consequence of recognizing the time dimension is that the relative duration and frequency of changes becomes significant. The duration of a cycle of evolution, from initial feedback to applied change, is related to the life expectancy of the process model instance and the responsiveness expected of it. The frequency with which it is possible to apply changes means that there is unlikely to be a 1:1 relationship between reported inconsistencies and applied changes, and the evolution process will need to deal with aggregation of feedback.

In order to separate out the different issues that must be addressed, and to give an indication of evolvability, we use the term "mode" to identify, where possible, distinct and orthogonal models of evolution processes. It is explained in section 5.4.

Evolution can also contribute to the maturity of an organization if the results of experiences can be incorporated into models of process behaviour that can be usefully exploited on future occasions.

5   The Framework

The framework is referred to as the Product Evolution Tower (Peltower) and consists of three core features: nodes, their structure, and evolution. The structure relates one node to another, and all features are subject to evolution.

The Peltower is generic and can be specialized in two ways: first of all, certain specific behaviours can be identified in the node, and secondly, the structure can be defined as a particular kind of hierarchy, where child nodes have a specific relationship to the parent. It has so far been implemented in two particular examples–the Hdev (Hierarchical Development) tower [10], and the OPM (Organizational Process Modelling) tower [16]. The former is used as the basis for the PIE investigations and development.

Such hierarchical structures are commonly evidenced in system design to represent the relationship between design components. In order to implement a specification (either as a design or as an artefact) it is necessary to decompose or refine the specification into manageable units, i.e. where they can be transformed into design artefacts with appropriate modularity properties, or can be directly implemented by a known process. Thus each node represents a part of the product that can be usefully encapsulated and interfaced with other nodes. The decomposition of the specification is determined by known technologies.

Although based on a software development process [10], it is believed that such a generic approach can usefully support the kind of process activity evidenced in dynamic organizations. The framework makes no claim to be able to support all aspects of activities, but it is intended that off-line coordination will be accommodated by the structure. The framework aims to support all process aspects of business activity whether the outcomes of these processes are products or services. It is envisaged that a population of Peltowers could in effect represent all the models and instances of processes and meta-processes used in some particular context such as an organization, whether it is real or virtual.

5.1 Node

A node is characterized by three properties: specification, product and type. A specification represents a solution to a problem. It is a definition expressed in terms of behaviours and technologies which, if designed and implemented as a system, and executed, would resolve the problem. The specification property in the node is a representation of this. Likewise the product may be in a variety of media and the product in the Peltower framework is intended to represent the actual product that will probably exist in some other medium. This product is not intended to be solely a data object. It can represent both data and behaviour as does a conventional software system, or essentially behaviour, as does a process model. In fact at its most general, it represents *any* result that satisfies the specification.

The use of the terms is intended to be relative rather than specific. A product in one context can be a specification in another. For example, the output (product) of a requirements analysis process is a specification for use in a development process.

As well as the specification and product properties, a node consists of a number of key behaviours that are referred to as operations. These are primitive mechanisms that utilize behaviours defined in methods. Operations, like methods, are characterized by a type signature that defines inputs and outputs and which is also used to provide resources to the method. Methods are discussed further in section 5.3.

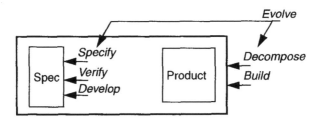

Figure 1 Hdev type of Peltower node

There several node types, and a node type is characterized by the available operations on Specification, Product and Node. As well as the Hdev and OPM types that constitute the already-mentioned Hdev and OPM towers, there is a Root type to facilitate the bootstrap of the framework in an implementation. There is also a Developer type to enact a model written in a Process Modelling Language (PML) [4] in order to develop (code) enactable models in the same language. The following operations are available in the Hdev node (see figure 1).

Specify. Operates on the specification to change it. A specification can be provided when the node is created, or it can be prepared subsequently. This operation is related to the Verify operation which is discussed in the following section. A change to a specification, and its consequent development into a new version of the product provides one of the modes of evolution discussed further in section 5.4.

Develop. This operation relates the specification to the product in any kind of system or part of a system. It can be a design process, where the product is a design artefact that can be used in turn as a specification for a manufacturing process to produce a tangible artefact, or a procurement process or a software development process. The framework does not specify the behaviour of Develop other than to indicate that it causes a transformation of the specification and results in a product. The actual behaviour that supports this activity is called a method, and it is context-sensitive. A full explanation of methods is provided in section 5.3.

Evolve. This can be applied to *all* operations except itself and, as currently defined, allows for one particular method definition to be substituted for another. Thus for example the process by which the product is developed can evolve. The method for this particular operation is loaded with the system, and it is not evolvable. This was a decision taken to constrain the complexity of the current implementation. The evolution process is discussed further in section 5.4.

The other operations of Verify, Decompose, and Build shown in figure 1 are related to a network of nodes and will be explained in the following section on structure.

5.2   Structure

It is usually impossible to develop complex artefacts such as a software system directly from a high level specification. As mentioned at the beginning of this section, an essential prerequisite for development or implementation is for the specification to be refined or decomposed into more manageable units of appropriate modularity that can be developed by an individual or a small team. The parent–sibling relationship in this decomposition is 1:N "part-of"[14]. This means that the specifications of all the siblings can be combined in such a way as to be equivalent to the parent specification, and this indicates how the child products can be combined to satisfy the original specification. The following description of the remaining node operations applies to the Hdev structure.

Decompose. This operation generates one or more child nodes of the same type as the parent and establishes certain links between them. The child inherits the parent's methods. Decompose implies some kind of refinement of the specification, and indicates cooperation between nodes. There is no limit to the number of times the Decompose operation can be invoked: if the first decomposition is incorrect, further children can be added or a child can be terminated. Terminating (thus deleting) a child has no effect on the parent or any of the other children, but terminating a parent results in all its children (and children's offspring) being terminated. The only inhibitor to termination in this case is if an operation is executing a method. In this case, termination will not proceed on the node until the method has concluded.

Verify. This is an operation that checks the consistency of specifications between a parent and a child, and is a key operation in one of the modes of evolution. It can be invoked after a decomposition when any inconsistency arising would need to be corrected in the child specification. More importantly however it would be invoked after any change in specification at any node. In figure 2 for example, a change might be made to specification of node 1.2 for some reason. After the change, the specification would be verified with respect to its parent (1) and its children (1.2.1 and 1.2.2). If the result revealed inconsistency with the children's specifications, then they would also need to be changed. With regard to the parent, if the verify revealed no inconsistency, then the remainder of the tower would remain unchanged. If inconsistency was revealed, then the change would be propagated elsewhere in the tower.

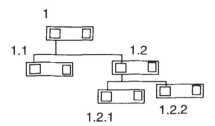

Figure 2 Peltower as a Hdev hierarchy

Build. This operates on a parent node, and combines the products of its children into a system complying with the parent specification and associating the result with the product property of the parent node. Just how it combines the child product depends on the particular method that is bound to the operation. It is, in some respect, the corollary of decompose.

5.3 Methods
A key concept in this framework is the separation of behaviour into "mechanisms" and "policies". By this we mean that mechanisms are core behaviours for some basic transformation that has to take place, and policies define a) the way that these mechanisms are used or b) provide the detailed behaviour for such mechanisms at run time [12]. The latter approach has been adopted in this work. Just how a transformation is effected is governed by the method (i.e. the policy) that is used by the operation (i.e. the mechanism). Invocation of the operation will call on a method that defines exactly how the operation will be carried out. For every operation there might be several alternative methods, one of which would be a default.

In essence, methods (and thus operations) are relatively easy to evolve at run time. This means that, for example, system developers would have at their disposal a choice of methods to carry out actual development, and they could be changed by an evolution process which at their disposal. Feedback from the success or failure of different methods could be a focus for organizational learning.

Much of the thinking underlying the Peltower framework has gone into putting as much behaviour into methods as possible, and as little into the operation mechanism as possible. In so doing it has enhanced its potential for evolution.

Methods so far defined for Peltower implementations have been simple although they may conceivably be quite complex and need to be evolvable. Thus the same principles that apply to the Peltower should also apply to the method, so logically they should be structured by another Peltower and re-used where and when needed. This thinking also extends to the other PIE components. It is intended that a method structured as a tower will be used to encapsulate such ad hoc software technologies in order to provide services needed by the users through the process model in a much more effective and context-sensitive way than has so far been possible.

5.4   Evolution

Evolutionary change can take place in a number of ways in the Peltower structure. The cyclic behaviours that bring them about are referred to as modes, and two are involved: the Specify and Verify operations together, and the P2E meta-process (they are explained later in this section).

When discussing evolution, a core question is, *what* evolves with respect to *what* [13]? Classically, the object is said to evolve with respect to its environment, and, in our context, the object is part of a software system. Peltower objects for which evolution support is provided are[1] listed below. In each case evolution is initiated by a user.

- Product. The combination of the specify and verify operations together provide for the Product mode of evolution. A change in specification results in a change in product. However, more importantly, change in specification can be ripple throughout the hierarchy, thus propagating product evolution wherever it is needed. This is quasi-independent evolution, by which we mean that the specification property of a node can evolve independently but only to the extent that its neighbours can accommodate such change.
- Operation. This is change in the behavioural definition of the particular method associated with an operation. As one of the operations is responsible for defining the structure of the tower (Decompose), it also handles structural evolution. The mode used is the meta-process known as P2E (see below). It is model evolution.
- Node. When applied to a node instance (via the P2E mode) the node instance type is changed, and thus its pattern of operations evolves.

The Specify/Verify evolution mode has already been introduced when discussing the operations that are possible on a node. The second mode is P2E, the Process for Process Evolution [8][16]. In this framework the P2E is a latent mode. By "latent" we mean that it is not instantiated until it is needed, i.e. until there is a need for operation or node evolution. When instantiated, it is parameterized for the operation whose method is to be evolved, and the node type. (This aspect will be reviewed in the light of emerging requirements of the PIE project.) It is the mode for evolving both methods and nodes.

Figure 3 shows the basic relationship between a P2E and its node. There are two interactions. One, from the node to the P2E, is "sensory", a form of feedback that provides information to the P2E about the node's type, and about its operation whose method is to be changed. The other interaction is "motor", one that imparts change. The Re-

---

1. It is envisaged that method evolution would take place in the Peltower whose products are themselves methods.

alizing component of the P2E mode applies a definitional change to the node instance so to implement the desired change and conclude the cycle of evolution.

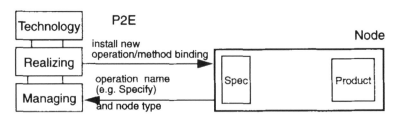

Figure 3 Evolving a node operation

The use of the P2E mode allows the support for humans participating in the evolution process. The P2E itself has operations, such as ObtainMethod for finding methods. This operation resides in the Technology component of the P2E and tries to find a class definition that matches the type specification of the particular operation. The framework recognizes that a suitable method might not be available, so it allows for a further cycle of evolution to determine a suitable method for the development of method. See figure 4.

The new P2E, on instantiation, is passed the name of ObtainMethod and the type of the parent Technology. Its own Technology finds or determines a new way to implement ObtainMethod, and installs this new definition in Technology as new method. An example of this is where we, instead of *finding* a method, want ObtainMethod to provide the means of *creating* one. The instantiation of a second cycle of evolution is a process of abstraction.

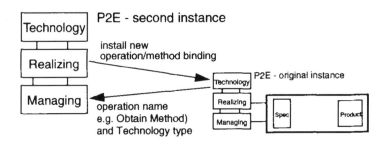

Figure 4 Evolving a P2E operation

There is nothing in the framework to inhibit concurrent evolution, however implementation details may impose constraints. In the Hdev implementation, product and operation modes allow concurrency. Others require instances of P2E to bring about the evolution, and only one instance of P2E can be associated with a node instance at any one time. There is no restriction on evolution between different node instances.

6   Technology - Process*Web*

All the PIE components - Evolution Strategy, Monitoring and Decision Support [1] - share where possible the common architecture illustrated in figure 5. This has been done *in order* to facilitate a) the addressing of common problems, b) a level of integration, and c) evolution. The architecture will be explained by reference to the Process*Web* [17] technology.

Process*Web* combines TeamWARE's ProcessWise Integrator (PWI) with a Web server so that users interact with the system through the familiar medium of their Web browsers. The ES component comprises an instance of Process*Web* running a Peltower framework process model, and PWI's process engine and the Peltower model are located in the Kernel of the architecture.

The GUI layer is a web browser. The Process*Web* system calculates and assembles html pages as required by the execution of process model instances. These pages include links or standard Web CGI (Common Gateway Interface) forms, through which users provide input. This user interface communicates through the PWI external application interfaces (API in the architecture). Thus ES departs slightly from the common architecture which proposes a direct connection between Kernel and GUI layer.

The same PWI application interface allows communication with databases or other software tools at the "global" Process*Web* level, and in the context of the PIE project, for communicating via a Communications Layer with the PIE Middleware.

The Persistent Layer for Evolution Strategy is conceptual. This is because the language used to program Process*Web* is persistent – there are no explicit commands to write or read data from a persistent file or database. The PML language implementation ensures that a consistent state is regularly written to a persistent store, and also manages reading data from the store to memory as required.

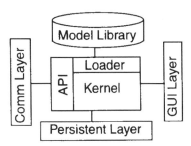

Figure 5   The PIE Common Component Architecture

The Loader makes use of a PML primitive which allows run-time compilation of PML code. This allows the methods which are located conceptually in the Model Library to be evolved independently of the Peltower implementation.

Basic constructs in PML include a Role (a thread of behaviour with its own local data), and Interaction (an asynchronous buffer which is used to communicate messages between roles). PML is a class-based language with single inheritance and incremental compilation, where a source PML class definition is compiled in the context of a set of existing classes.

An Hdev node is implemented as a network of PML roles and interactions. The key Hdev role includes the specification, the product, and the name, type and class definition of each operation, within its local data. The behaviour part of the Hdev role can express any constraints on the operations, e.g. that the develop operation cannot happen if there is no specification. There is a corresponding HdevUI role which deals with the presentation of the current state of the node. It has interactions with a UserRole which is a standard Process*Web* role for interfacing with a user. This design provides a clearer separation between the coding for the Hdev node and the coding for the user interaction. For example, two HdevUI roles could be used to enable two users to work concurrently on a node, conflicts between them being handled by the Hdev node.

The methods are also implemented as PML roles and contained in the Kernel model, however conceptually they are maintained in a Model Library. This is another example of the approach that separates policies from mechanisms (see section 5.3). When an operation is invoked, a role of the appropriate class ('"loaded" from the type space) is created and initialised with the operations input parameter. The method role is also given interactions which enable it to communicate with the UserRole, and hence the user, and also an interaction which it uses to return its result to the node which created it. Implementing methods as PML roles enables the Hdev tower implementation to use the PWI error handling facilities to inform the node if there is an error in the method code. It also means that more complicated methods can be implemented as networks of roles and interactions.

The P2E is similarly implemented as a network of roles and interactions. A P2E connected to a node (see figure 3) may be created in response to a request to evolve an operation, a request to evolve the node type, or because an existing method has failed reporting an error. Once the source PML class definition for the new method has been found, using ObtainMethod, then this definition is compiled to check for errors and consistency with the other PML class definitions which the node is using. Finally the new method class definition is installed in the node, updating its local data, updating its local data for the appropriate operation. Where a node type is evolved, there may be several new methods to obtain. In this case the implementation creates a new node, and transfers to it the specification, product, and the interactions which are its connections with other nodes in the hierarchy.

7   Example

This framework is being implemented in the context of the "Hood and Headlights" scenario that is being defined in the PIE project, and which has been introduced in [1]. The context is set by the Peltower being populated by motor car specifications, designs and design process instances. For example, the specification for a car body can be decomposed into a number of specifications that relate to the body shell, doors, headlights and hood etc. The body is represented by a node, and the sub-components by children of that node. Some of the process model instances will be running in another process support system, and the Peltower representation will then be a placeholder allowing communication with the actual instance.

Each node contains a process for developing its specification into a design. They are usually design processes, but equally they may be procurement processes. They are all supported by process technologies. The scenario envisages the situation where designs for the hood and the headlights are found, on an integration test, to be in conflict, and this conflict cannot be handled by that activity. The associated P2E instance then supports the determination of a conflict resolution process (involving new instances) and integrates the other PIE components where appropriate. On conclusion of that process, the integration test can be resumed.

8 Conclusions

8.1 Managing Workflow Applications

One consequence of the success of workflow technologies has been a proliferation of applications without any means of supporting their systematic evolution. Until now, this has not been seen as a serious problem although workers are attempting to address the evolution issue on a technology-specific basis. This trend, together with the natural desire to support more complex and longer-lived processes, will expose the shortcomings in evolution support. This work has shown that such failings can be overcome by use of software process technologies supporting a framework such as is described in this work together with the other Components being developed in the PIE project.

8.2 Managing the Evolution Process

We are now beginning to appreciate the true nature of concurrency in evolution cycles, and the likely need to be able to support the aggregation of feedback and consolidation of changes.

A "case-based" approach might be appropriate to manage a number of potential change cases within an evolution process. This would allow progression of potential changes at different rates, and for the combination of prospective changes at any time up to the point of installation of the change.

Two modes have been identified for handling evolution in the framework. It will be interesting to see if more are required, or, conversely, if Specify/Verify is simply a particular specialization of P2E.

8.3 The PIE Project

The advantage of handling evolution through P2E is that it is itself based an intuitive process and is therefore appropriate to supporting the non-specialist. The results from the earlier first phase of PIE confirmed the appropriateness of this approach.

The PIE approach endeavours to consider models, tools, applications, and support systems intended to support human activity in a more consistent way, and an interesting aspect of the project is to blur the distinction between process model and tools. Their common purpose is support for organizational process-based activities, but to do this there needs to be integration at the appropriate level. This closer integration with software components may lead to more effective support for process workers, i.e. to bring tools, process and participant behaviour together seamlessly

In the same way the Peltower framework reflects this philosophy, in that process models and applications are simply methods for dealing with problems, and problem-solving is a core activity for managers and professionals everywhere in industry.

8.4   The Peltower Framework

The Peltower framework provides a promising approach to better address the true complexity of the real organizational behaviour. It does this by establishing a simple relationship between different process models that cooperate to define organizational behaviour. In addition, it provides a proper context for process evolution, recognizing that evolution is multi-faceted and this must be understood if support for evolution is to be a realistic aim.

It is accepted that most organizations are hierarchical in the way that they are set up in terms of responsibility, but evidence has yet to accumulate to justify our assertion that the framework can usefully represent the aggregation of process behaviour in *any* context.

Operational processes are not simply procedural: there is no reason why they should not be capable of changing and evolving in certain constrained ways, if such evolution does not affect another process. If it does, then the Peltower structure needs to be used to handle the co-evolution.

The potential relationship between Peltower hierarchies can be complex. Reference has already been made to the use of the Peltower to structure methods, and that these methods can largely be software systems. Other hierarchies are conceivable, for example an Abstraction/Specialization tower relating an abstract or generic process model to specialized and instantiated models (also known as template–customized–enacting).

Modelling techniques tend to assume that a process exists in isolation. The Peltower framework offers the possibility of a more comprehensive support to dynamic process activity.

References

[1]   I. Alloui, S. Beydeda, S. Cîmpan, V. Gruhn, F. Oquendo and C. Schneider. "Advanced Services for Process Evolution: Monitoring and Decision Support." In R. Conradi ed. *Proceedings 7th. European Workshop on Software Process Technology EWSPT'00*, Kaprun, Austria, 2000.

[2]   J.-M. Andreroli, C. Fernström and J.-L Meunier. "A Coordination System Approach to Software Workflow Process Evolution." *Proceedings of the 13th. International Software Engineering Conference ASE'98*, Honolulu, USA, 1998.

[3]   G. Bolcer and R. Taylor. "Endeavors: A Process System Integration Infrastructure." *Proceedings of the Fourth International Conference on the Software Process*, Brighton, UK, 1996.

[4]   R. Bruynooghe, R. Greenwood, I. Robertson, J. Sa, R. Snowdon, and B. Warboys.
        "PADM: Towards a Total Process Modelling System." In A. Finklestein, B. Kramer and
        B. Nuseibeh, eds. *Software Process Modelling and Technology,* Research Studies Press,
        Taunton, UK., 1994, pp. 293-334.

[5]   R. Conradi, C. Fernström, and A. Fuggetta. "Concepts for evolving software processes" In
        A. Finklestein, B. Kramer and B. Nuseibeh, eds. *Software Process Modelling and Tech-
        nology,* Research Studies Press, Taunton, UK., 1994.

[6]   G. Cugola, P. -Y. Cunin, S. Dami, J. Estublier, A. Fuggetta, F. Pacull, M. Rivière and H.
        Verjus. "Support for Software Federations: The PIE Platform." In R. Conradi ed. *Proceed-
        ings 7th. European Workshop on Software Process Technology EWSPT'00,* Kaprun, Aus-
        tria, 2000.

[7]   P.-Y. Cunin. "The PIE Project: an Introduction." In R. Conradi ed. *Proceedings 7th. Eu-
        ropean Workshop on Software Process Technology EWSPT'00,* Kaprun, Austria 2000.

[8]   J.-C. Derniame, A. Kaba and D. Wastell, eds. *Software Process: Principles, Methodology,
        Technology,* Lecture Notes in Computer Science, Vol. 1500, Springer Verlag 1999, pp. 53-
        93.

[9]   M. Dowson and C. Fernström. "Towards Requirements for Enactment Mechanisms." In
        B. Warboys ed. *Proceedings 3d. European Workshop on Software Process Technology
        EWSPT'94,* Villard de Lans, France 1994.

[10]   R. M. Greenwood, B.C Warboys and J. Sa. "Cooperating Evolving Components - a rigor-
        ous approach to evolving large software systems." *Proceedings 18th. International Con-
        ference on Software Engineering,* 1996.

[11]   G. Kaiser, I. Ben-Shaul and S. Popovich. "A Metalinguistic Approach to Process Enact-
        ment." *Proceedings of the Fourth International Conference on the Software Process,*
        Brighton, UK, 1996.

[12]   R. Morrison, D. Balasubramaniam, M. Greenwood, G. Kirby, K. Mayes, D. Munro and B.
        Warboys. "A Compliant Persistent Architecture." *Software Practice and Experience.* To
        appear.

[13]   I. Robertson. "Evolution in Perspective." *International Workshop on Software Evolution,*
        Kyoto, 1998.

[14]   J. Sa, B. Warboys and J. Keane. "OBM: A Specification Method for Modelling Organisa-
        tional Process." *Proceedings of the Workshop on Constraint Processing CSAM'93,* St Pe-
        tersburg, 1993.

[15]   B.C. Warboys. "The IPSE 2.5 project: Process modelling as the basis for a support envi-
        ronment." *Proceedings of the First International Conference on Software Development,
        Environments and Factories,* Berlin, Germany, 1989.

[16]   B.Warboys, P. Kawalek, I. Robertson and M. Greenwood. *Business Information Systems:
        a process approach,* McGraw-Hill, London 1999, pp. 37-54 and 182-198.

[17]   B.S. Yeomans. *A Process-Based Environment for the Evolutionary Development of Large
        Software Systems,* M.Res Thesis, University of Manchester, 1997.

Advanced Services for Process Evolution: Monitoring and Decision Support

Ilham Alloui[1], Sami Beydeda[2], Sorana Cîmpan[1],
Volker Gruhn[2], Flavio Oquendo[1] and Christian Schneider[2]

[1] University of Savoie at Annecy, ESIA LLP, 41 avenue de la Plaine B.P. 806, 74016
Annecy Cedex, France
{alloui,cimpan,oquendo}@esia.univ-savoie.fr
[2] University of Dortmund, Computer Science Department, Software Technology,
44221 Dortmund, Germany
{beydeda,gruhn,schneider}@ls10.cs.uni-dortmund.de

Abstract. Process support environments (PSEs) are widely used for modelling, enacting and analyzing human intensive processes. The benefits of a PSE become apparent when processes to be supported are long lived and distributed and contain heterogeneous components. Generally, such processes are subject to dynamic evolution, i.e. they have to be changed during their execution. Unfortunately, virtually none of the existing PSEs consider dynamic evolution of processes. This article explains the concepts and techniques underlying a set of components developed in the ESPRIT Project Process Instance Evolution (PIE) that support the dynamic evolution of processes. These concepts and techniques are demonstrated using a real-world scenario from the automotive industry.

1 Introduction

Generally, processes[1] are embedded in real-world environments such as a company producing goods for a particular market. As indicated by the saying "the world is changing", every real-world environment is subject to evolution which implies the evolution of the embedded processes. For instance, change in market requirements could trigger the evolution of the company process to produce goods that have more appropriate properties. The process support environment (PSE) used by an organization for the effective management of its processes has also to consider the evolution of these processes. This means that the PSE has to provide not only guidance and automation of tasks, but also it has to maintain the evolution of the processes it supports. An evolution support component should therefore be integrated into any PSE.

Evolution support offers controlled mechanisms for:

- identifying the need for process evolution;
- determine evolution alternatives and select one alternative to implement;
- implement the selected alternative.

---

[1] An exact definition of the used terminology can be found in [15, 24].

In the PIE project [13, 28], these tasks are addressed by different components; monitoring support (MS), decision support (DS) and change support (CS). The evolution strategy support (ES) handles the overall strategy employed by the evolution process [18].

The objective of MS is mainly to identify the process-internal reasons for process evolution. The reasons for process evolution can be classified into two main groups: *process-internal* and *process-external*. A process-internal reason for process evolution can be for example an unacceptable value for the observed progress of the process, i.e. the process manager could decide to modify a process that cannot meet the deadlines. Furthermore, the MS within the PIE framework possesses proactiveness. Proactiveness refers to the ability of identifying trends. The process manager should be informed not only about a process that has already been delayed, but also whether a process will be late in the future.

After identifying the need to evolve a process, the next tasks concern the generation of solutions and the evaluation of these solutions. The DS component assists the process manager in carrying out both tasks. The process manager can request the component to generate alternative modifications of a single process instance, or the underlying process model. She then has to decide which modification to carry out. In both cases, the DS component provides support in exploring and evaluating the alternatives. Based on probability distributions of throughput time and total costs, the component determines the alternative with the highest utility for the process manager.

After exploring appropriate alternatives, the next task of the process manager is to implement the most promising alternative. The objective of the CS component within the PIE framework is to provide the project manager with detailed information about the implementation of a particular modification. The information provided should help the project manager maintain consistency in the modified process instance. For example, if the project manager has decided to skip an activity in order to improve throughput time, CS has to assist the manager in connecting predecessor to successor activities. However, this article is focused on MS and DS, this means we do not consider CS.

This article explains in detail MS and DS. Section 2 introduces a case study from the automotive industry, which is used to demonstrate the applicability of the various concepts. Section 3 explains the concepts underlying MS. The concepts underlying DS are described in section 4. Section 5 presents a scenario related to the case study proposed in section 2. This scenario can be used to highlight some of the functionalities of the MS and DS. Finally, section 6 contains our conclusions.

2   Case Study

The case study we will use throughout this paper is currently used in the PIE project, and is taken from the automotive industry [14]. It relates to (part of) the process of designing a sport variant of an existing car. The output of the process is a CAD representation of the new sport variant. It is a process that involves creativity and an extensive use of computer means. This characteristics make it similar to a software proces.

For the part of the process we are interested in, there are three departments involved in the development of the new sport variant: the *style department*, the *body-in-white²* *department* and the *packaging department*.

The style department provides sketches of the hood for the sport variant, based on the hood of the existing car platform.

The body-in-white department modifies the hood design, starting from the previous designs and the sketches from the style department. The outcome of their work is the hood design for the sport variant, a CAD version.

The packaging department checks the integration of the hood design with its environment, i.e. the other elements of the body design such as the headlights.

Each of the departments follows its own process in order to provide its outputs. We do not detail the processes followed by the style and design departments, but regarding the packaging department, that part of the integration tests that concerns the fitness of existing headlights with respect to the new hood design is described.

A scenario linked to this case study is presented in section 5.

3   Monitoring Support (MS)

The need for measuring processes and analyzing the data collected on them is by now accepted and the Capability Maturity Model [21] with its forth and fifth maturity levels ("managed" and "optimized") offers a suitable methodological framework to do it.

We present in this section a MS and its underlying modelling formalism. The section is organized as follows: section 3.1 presents the related work with respect to the monitoring issue, section 3.2 presents the monitoring approach while section 3.3 presents an example of monitoring analysis, the conformance factors.

3.1   Related Work

Looking at the software process literature, the first observation with respect to the monitoring issue is that the scope and the features are very broad. All studied cases use certain means for data collection, but the analyzes made on collected data as well as the scope are very different.

The analyses employed vary from no analysis at all, as is the case in the Hakoniwa system [22] to the use of statistics and probability [7,11,12] and classification trees [31].

With respect to the scope, the monitored processes vary from short term repeatable processes in which case analyses are made on the entire process, as in the Balboa system [11], to long term and complex processes in which only parts of a process are

---

² Body-in-white (BIW) designates in automobile companies the subdivision of the design office that designs the external shape of the vehicle from specifications issued by the styling department.

monitored, as is the case in the monitoring prototype experiment undertaken at the AT&T Bell Laboratories [7].

3.2 Monitoring Approach

All the mentioned systems make the assumption that precise and certain information is available for collection. The prototyping experiment has some means for handling imprecision in the form of granularity (measurements are made on a daily basis, even though finer grain information would give a more accurate information). This approach is meant to reduce experiment costs and to make it less intrusive.

The need for precise information increases the costs of data collection, thus limiting the usage of the monitoring system that becomes too costly and intrusive. In this context, the existence of a monitoring mechanism that handles imprecise and uncertain information would reduce the costs of monitoring and would increase its acceptance, as it would be less intrusive.

The monitoring mechanisms proposed in this paper use fuzzy set theory [32,33] for representing the data, which allows expressing imprecise and uncertain information. Of course the system handles precise data in the classical way, as fuzzy sets theory is an super set of the classical sets theory.

The system architecture allows integration in a process support environment leading to a reduction of data collection costs, as most of such data can be automatically collected, without much interference in the subject process. The proposed monitoring is open to evolution, i.e. new analysis techniques can be added. This feature increases the flexibility of the support provided to the user.

The monitoring system uses monitoring models maintained in a Model Library. We distinguish between different kind of models:

- *Basic model*: this model allows to indicate what information to collect and what analyses or transformations to make on the collected data. The motivations behind the selection of a certain information to be collected is up to the modeler. A GQM approach can be used to decide what metrics to apply [5].
- *Sensor model*: indicates where from the data is to be collected.
- *Display model*: indicates what information to display to the user.
- *Publication model*: indicates what information to publish for the other components in the environment of the monitoring.
- *Trace model:* indicates what information to trace, i.e. what information is to be kept for use in the future.

For a given basic model, different sensor, display, publication and trace models may be defined for the integration in different environments. When the monitoring is launched, the models to be loaded are indicated. This component complies with the PIE Common Component Architecture which is described in [18].

A formalism for defining monitoring models has been developed in the PIE framework [8]. A detailed presentation of the formalism is out of the scope of this paper, only some characteristics of the formalism will be presented.

The theory on which the formalism is based is the fuzzy set theory, which was developed by Zadeh in order to represent mathematically the imprecision related to certain object classes [32,33,6]. It also responds to the need for representing symbolic knowledge, in natural language, subject to imprecision or presenting a vague character. A fuzzy subset A of a reference set X is characterized by an application from X to $[0,1]$. This application called *membership function* and noted μ_A allows to represent how much the elements x of X are also members of A. If $\mu_A(x)=1$ the value x is completely a member of A and if $\mu_A(x)=0$ it is not at all a member of A. In the particular case when $\mu_A(x)$ only takes values equal to 0 or 1, the fuzzy subset A is identical to a classical subset of X.

The formalism provides means for the representation of numeric as well as symbolic information, in a precise and certain as well as imprecise and uncertain form. The formalism also provides operators to handle such type of information. Thus there are arithmetic operators for working with fuzzy numbers, meaning functions to pass from numeric to linguistic universes, aggregation tables for combining symbolic information etc. A presentation of this formalism can be found in [8].

The existence of a formalism for defining monitoring models makes the MS open to evolution. The formalism allows to define new monitoring models, thus new analysis techniques.

The monitoring can also be used to monitor the monitoring of the subject process. This reflexive way of using the monitoring allows the tuning of the system [2,3]. Examples of tuning are the modification of fuzzy membership function and aggregation tables.

In order to better illustrate the functional and operational aspects of the MS, we will present an analysis technique employed by the MS, namely the conformance factors [9,10]. This example also allows us to illustrate the use of the fuzzy sets theory.

3.3 Conformance Factors: an Analysis Technique

The conformance factor analysis technique is used in order to compare the conformance, for a given aspect, between the process enactment (what happens) and the process instantiation (or process plan, what is supposed to happen). Examples of aspects of the process are progress, cost, effort consuming, chance of success, etc. In the following we will illustrate the conformance factor related concepts using the progress aspect. Aspects can be associated with process attributes. Following [16], the measure of attributes values can be direct (corresponding to raw data collected by the monitoring) or indirect (corresponding to monitoring analyses results).

Each of the attributes are represented under a given universe of discourse (domain). Such a universe may be numeric or linguistic. For the progress, the considered universe is linguistic, and contains the terms *{missed, almost missed, extremely late, very late, late, slightly late, on schedule, slightly ahead, ahead, very ahead, extremely ahead}*. This means that the progress of a process fragment will be expressed using these terms. The linguistic universes given as examples here are ordinal, but linguistic universes where an order is not defined can also be considered.

For a considered attribute, a *goal* is set by the process manager indicating the values considered as target, i.e. what are the values one would like to observe during enactment. For the progress conformance factor, an example of goal is to be *on schedule*. This is a restrictive goal, and fits processes where the deliver in time is the prior concern. A more relaxed one is to consider the goal as *slightly late, on time* or *slightly advanced.* The goals presented are crisp goals, as they represent classical subsets of their universe of representation. The goals may also be represented as fuzzy subsets of the universe.

The *observed value* for an attribute is obtained by analyzing data collected from the actual process. Its expression is a (fuzzy) subset of the universe in which it is represented. For the above progress example, the observed progress is expressed in terms of membership degree to each of the linguistic terms. The progress is obtained as combination of two attributes: *completeness* (how much of the planned work is actually completed) and *moment* (the position in time with respect to schedule). These attributes are also linguistic, and their combination is made by means of symbolic aggregation [9,10].

By comparing the goal and the observed value for a given attribute, the corresponding conformance level is computed, its values being placed in the interval *[0,1]*. A value of *0* for the conformance corresponds to *no conformance at all*, while a value of *1* corresponds to *total conformance*.

In addition, a *threshold* is set by the process manager for the acceptable level of conformance. An example of threshold may be *0.8*. Every conformance level lower than *0.8* would then indicate an unacceptable deviation, and an alarm would be set by the MS.

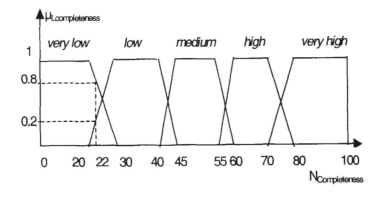

Fig. 1. Correspondence between numeric and linguistic universes of completeness using of meaning functions

As mentioned earlier, the observed value for *progress* is calculated by means of symbolic aggregation between *completeness* and *moment*. The completeness has two universes of representation (see Fig. 1):

- the interval $[0,100]=N_{completeness}$ for a representation in terms of achieved percentage,
- the linguistic universe $L_{Completeness}$ composed by *{very low, low, medium, high, very high}* for a linguistic representation.

The membership functions indicated in Fig.1 are subject to tuning , in order to adjust them to certain context of use.

Let us consider the process fragment in the design department for producing the new hood design (see section 2). If this process is monitored for progress, the design department would be systematically asked for the completeness of their work. Depending on the availability of this information, the design department can provide this data in a precise and certain form, for instance 22%, or in a imprecise manner, using the linguistic representation , for instance *small* or *very small*. If the value given by the design department is a linguistic one, it will be used as acquired in the symbolic aggregation in order to obtain the progress. If the data provided is a numeric one, the MS uses the meaning functions in order to pass from the numeric representation to the linguistic one. For the value of 22% the following linguistic representation is obtained[3]:

$$\mu_{Lcompleteness}(22) = \{0.8/very\ low,\ 0.2/low,\ 0/medium,\ 0/high,\ 0/very\ high\}^4 \qquad (1)$$

The interpretation of this result is that the value of 22%, and by that the completeness of the *new hood design*, can be described to certain positive degrees as *very low* and *low*. This linguistic representation is obtained using the membership functions in Fig.1. If the membership functions are changed (by tuning) then the results also change.

The *moment* has also two equivalent representations; one in the interval *[PlannedStartingDate, PlannedEndingDate]* and one in the linguistic universe $L_{Moment}=\{very\ beginning,\ beginning,\ middle,\ end,\ very\ end\}$. The correspondence between the two universes is made by similar meaning functions. The moment corresponds to the elapsed time.

The value of the progress attribute is obtained using the symbolic representation of *completeness* and *moment*.

The observed value for progress obtained after the symbolic aggregation is a fuzzy subset of its universe of representation. The symbolic aggregation uses rules associated with a pair of linguistic terms (one from the completeness universe and one from the moment universe) from the universe of progress. An example of such a rule is the following:

If completeness is low and moment is beginning then progress is on time (2)

Starting from the membership degrees of the observed completeness and moment to the different linguistic terms of their corresponding universes, the observed progress is computed. The following formula is used in order to compare it with the user defined goal:

$$C(goal, observedValue)=1-min\{1, \Sigma_k max \{\mu_{Lk}(observedValue)- \mu_{Lk}(goal),0\} \qquad (3)$$
$$L_k \in L_{monitoredAspect}$$

When the membership degree of the observed value to some term is greater than the respective membership degree for the goal (indicating elements that are not

---

[3] The observed completeness is represented as a fuzzy sub-set of the completeness linguistic universe

[4] $\mu_{Lcompleteness}$ stands for the membership value

included in the goal sub-set), the difference is decreased from the maximum conformance value (*1* in our case). The more the value of conformance is closer to *1*, the more the actual behaviour of the process conforms to the defined goal, so the deviation is smaller. When the conformance is *1* there is no deviation and the enactment conforms to the process plan and the user-defined goals.

Similar examples to the one for progress can be considered, for instance by combining the completeness and the effort. The progress example is a simple one, and it was chosen for illustrative purposes. The monitoring formalism allows to represent other types of analyses.

4   Decision Support (DS)

After identifying the need to modify a process instance or its model, the process manager has to carry out two tasks. Firstly, the process manager has to identify solutions to the problem identified by either MS or the user. Secondly, these solutions have to be analyzed with respect to their impact. Of course, the second task is only required when more than two alternatives, including the alternative of doing nothing, are available. The objective of the DS component within the PIE framework is to assist the project manager in carrying out these tasks.

In this section, we present our approach for these two tasks. The structure of the section is as follows: section 4.1 gives a brief overview of the literature on decision and risk analysis, section 4.2 contains an approach for identifying alternative modifications to a process model while section 4.3 includes a description of the technique which is used to analyze a process instance and to determine possible changes to a process instance.

4.1   Related Work

Almost every decision problem is adhered with risk due to the uncertainty of the real world. Despite its importance, the term *risk* is not exactly defined and its interpretation depends on the context [17, 25, 23]. In the context of the PIE project, we interpret the notion of risk in accordance with Moskowitz and Bunn [26] as the likelihood of an unfavourable outcome.

Researchers have long considered risk analysis and decision problems under uncertainty. Bernoulli and Bayes developed a formal framework two centuries ago which was further developed by Ramsey [30], von Neumann and Morgenstern [27], Arrow [4] and others. The method used within the PIE project is based on this formal framework.

Unfortunately, in the context of process technology, risk and decision analysis have received little attention, and in the PIE project, we attempt to investigate approaches and techniques for those important issues.

4.2   Proposition of Alternatives

Levels of Modifications to a Process

Generally, a process can be modified at two levels: the instances of the process model and the process model. For example, a process instance being too late in producing particular goods can be improved by providing each activity affecting the throughput time with additional resources such as manpower. By providing additional resources, the activities can be executed more effectively which generally leads to a decreased throughput time of the instance. The same objective can also be achieved by re-designing parts of the process model affecting the throughput time. The difference between these two levels of modifications is that a modification of the process model affects every instance generated after the modification, whereas a modification of an instance has no effect on subsequent instances. Specifically, single instances are often modified in cases where they deviate from the process model. Deviations of process instances from their corresponding models can be determined using the approach of Cook/Wolf [12].

We have two different approaches for identifying those alternatives that contribute to an improvement of the process. While changes to a single process instance can be determined using the technique for analyzing the process instances, changes to the process model require special considerations, as it is explained in the next subsection.

Identifying Possible Modifications to the Process Model

Generally, modifying a process at the level of its model requires semantic information. In the simplest case, the semantic information would have to include the importance of each activity. This would allow determining which of the activities could be skipped in cases of restricted resources and which one may not be skipped.

One of the concerns in the PIE project is the integration of different PSEs that would support the subject process and would allow the independence of the system from the meta-model used by such PSEs. This is why we in PIE use a generic meta-model called *common meta-model* whose concepts are mapped to the ones used by different PSEs. Only the PIE evolution components have knowledge of the common meta-model, which is rather general and does not take into account any semantic information.

Thus, modifications at this conceptual level can only be carried out by a human process manager. The process manager has to determine those modifications that are most likely to lead to the intended goal. After having determined alternatives, the process manager can use the analysis facilities provided by the DS component, which are explained below, to identify the most promising alternative. This cycle of determining and analyzing alternatives generally leads to a gain of experience.

Fortunately, by storing this experience, the DS component could assist the process manager in finding possible solutions in the future. Modifications proposed by the process manager can be stored in a database, called *experience database*, together with the results of the analysis in order to reuse these solutions in similar situations. Therefore, some means are needed to determine the similarity of such situations.

The methods used by the DS component employ the *delta-analysis* approach proposed by Guth and Oberweis [19] to compare the current situation with those occurred in the past. In the approach of Guth and Oberweis, two models are compared to identify their differences. After having identified the differences between the two models, a ratio, called *delta*, is calculated. Two models are said to be *similar* if the corresponding delta value is below a particular threshold. Thus, in order to find similar models in the database maintained by the DS, the delta value is computed for each of the models in the database. Those models that have a delta value below the threshold are tested with respect to their applicability to the current situation using the analysis facilities provided by the DS component.

4.3 Analysis of Process Instances

As mentioned above, our technique for analyzing process instances can be used for two different tasks. Firstly, this technique is capable of identifying those activities that substantially contribute to the throughput time as well as to the total costs. Both the throughput time and the total costs can be improved by improving these activities. Thus, the proposed technique can be used for optimizing process instances. Secondly, the technique can determine probability distributions of the time and the costs of executing the process instance. These probability distributions can be used to compute simple risk measures such as the *expected value* and the *variance* [1] of the distribution or the more complex *value-at-risk measure* [23] used in the finance area. These measures can be used to compare a pair of alternatives.

Representation of a Process Instance

Our technique for analyzing a process instance operates on a representation of this instance as a graph with the following properties. Nodes in the graph represent activities of the process instance. Each node possesses two attributes. One of the attributes represents the costs of the resources required for the execution of the activity. The other attribute attached to a node represents the additional time needed to finish the activity under consideration. The graphical representation of a process instance also includes special nodes referred to as *exit nodes*. Exit nodes indicate the completion of the execution of the process instance.

Control flows within the process instance are represented by edges connecting the nodes. Since an activity can have different outcomes and the succeeding activity may depend on the outcome, a node can have more than one outgoing control flow edge. In these cases, each outgoing edge is augmented with a probability to indicate the likelihood to take a particular branch. Obviously, the sum of the probabilities attached to the outgoing edges of one activity has to be exactly 1 and in the case of only one succeeding activity the probability attached to the edge corresponds to 1.

In our approach, an instance of a process model is represented by a set including the currently executing activities. Each activity A in this set is attached with a parameter A_t indicating the time to finish. Thus, if T is the current time, a currently executing activity A_i will finish at time $T+A_t$. Activities which are not contained in this set are not executing and are considered to be idle. Each activity in the set of executing activities possesses two parameters. One of these parameters indicates the costs caused by the process prior to the execution of the activity. Note that this parameter does not include the costs incurred by the activity till the current time. The other parameter indicates the probability of entering the activity. Thus, the cost and the probability parameters attached to an exit node give the corresponding values for finishing the process instance at that particular node.

```
Algorithm processInstanceAnalysis;
Input      processModel;
           SetOfExecutingActivities;
output     processInstanceTimeSchedule;
           setOfWaitingActivities;
begin
   T=currentTime();
   setOfWaitingActivities={ };
   while setOfExecutingActivities not empty do
      for all activities A ready to start in setOfWaitingActivities do
         delete A in setOfWaitingActivities;
         insert A in setOfExecutingActivities;
      determine that activity A in setOfExecutingActivities finishing next;
      delete A in setOfExecutingActivities;
      instId=A_instId;
      for all B in setOfExecutingActivities do
         B_t=B_t-A_t;
      T=T+A_t;
      m_t=T;
      if A is an exit node of processModel then
         m_c=A_c;
         m_p=A_p;
      put m in processInstanceTimeSchedule;
      for all successor S of A in processModel with S_p*A_p>p_{thres} do
         S_c=S_c+A_c;
         S_p=S_p*A_p;
         S_{instId}=instId;
         instId=newInstId();
         if S_{instId} ≠ A_{instId} then
            for all B in setOfExecutingActivities with B_{instId}=A_{instId} do
                  C=copy B;
                  C_{instId}=S_{instId};
                  put C in setOfExecutingActivities;
            for all B in setOfWaitingActivities with B_{instId}=A_{instId} do
                  C=copy B;
                  C_{instId}=S_{instId};
                  put C in setOfWaitingActivities;
         if all resources and products are available for the execution of S then
               put S in setOfExecutingActivities;
         else put S in setOfWaitingActivities;
      if processModel does not contain a successor S of A with S_p*A_p>p_{thres} then
         for all B in setOfExecutingActivities with B_{instId}=A_{instId} do
               delete B in setOfExecutingActivities;
         for all B in setOfWaitingActivities with B_{instId}=A_{instId} do
               delete B in setOfWaitingActivities;
   return (processInstanceTimeSchedule, setOfWaitingActivities);
end
```

Fig. 2 Algorithm for analyzing process instances

Determination of the Process Instance Time Schedule

The next step in our analysis involves the elaboration of a process instance time schedule. A process instance time schedule is a set consisting of marks which indicate the end of an activity execution. Besides, there are special marks indicating that the entire process instance has finished, i.e. the last activity of the process has finished. These special marks are attached with the total costs and also with the probability to finish at that time. The algorithm for generating the time schedule is given in figure 2.

The basic idea of the algorithm consists of considering every possible execution thread of the process instance simultaneously. Starting with the set of executing activities characterizing the process instance under consideration, the currently concluded activity is deleted from the set of executing activities and its succeeding activities are inserted, depending on the availability of the required products and resources, in the set of executing or waiting activities. Each time an activity is deleted from the set of executing activities, a mark indicating this event is inserted in the time schedule. If the entire process instance is finished, the mark then includes information concerning the total costs and the probability of that event. After finishing the execution of an activity, the set of waiting activities is searched for activities that have become ready to start, i.e. the required products and resources have become available. This loop is executed until the set of executing activities is empty i.e. there are no possible threads of execution in the process instance. A non-empty set of waiting activities indicates a deadlock situation. The probability attached to each activity in the non-empty set gives the likelihood of the particular deadlock situation.

Computation of Probability Distributions and Risk Measures

The output of the above explained algorithm, i.e. the time schedule for a particular process instance, can be used to determine the probability distribution of both the throughput time and the total costs of the instance. In order to obtain the probability for a particular time or cost value, the time schedule is queried for that value. If the time schedule contains several entries with this particular value, their probabilities are summed up to compute the probability of this value.

After having identified a probability distribution, statistical measures can be used to define appropriate risk measures. As mentioned above, the expected value and the variance [1] of the distribution or the more complex value-at-risk [23] defined on the basis of the distribution can be used as risk measures. Based on such risk measures, a *utility function* [29] can be defined taking into account the preferences and the risk aversion of the process manager. Thus, selecting an alternative involves computing the utility of all the available alternatives and then selecting that alternative which dominates all the others.

Process Instance Optimization

The results of the algorithm can be used for three kinds of optimizations. Firstly, the set of waiting activities of an optimal process instance should always be empty. Generally, a waiting activity indicates that by synchronizing predecessor activities the throughput time of a process instance can be decreased. Secondly, optimizations can be achieved by analyzing the set of executing activities. A process instance can be effectively improved with respect to the throughput time and total costs by improving those activities that appear frequently in the set of executing activities. Thirdly, the parameters of a process instance which determine the shapes of the probability distributions for throughput time and total costs are known. Thus, the shapes of these probability distributions can be formed as intended by altering these parameters. Specifically, this optimization can be automated if symbolic expressions are computed for the various probabilities.

5   Illustrative Scenario

This section presents a scenario and illustrates how the evolution support presented in this paper is used. The scenario is related to the case study presented in section 2, and deals with the study of a design variant that causes a "deviation process" to be put in place [14].

Let us consider that the Body Design Manager (BDM) is monitoring the Body Design process in terms of progress. The MS raises an alarm. Although the process deadline has not been reached yet, using its proactive features the MS observes that the process is likely to be late. BDM requires the MS component to provide more information about the progress and state of the composed sub-processes, i.e. the packaging and the hood design processes. The data given by the monitoring component indicates that the progress of both sub-processes corresponds to *late* and there is a clash issue in the packaging process. A clash is associated to an unexpected situation, that might imply the blocking of the process, some rework or supplimetary work to be made. An inquiry made by the BDM reveals the problem: although the specification for the new hood was that the shape of the headlights should not change, digital mock-up shows that this is not the case. The front shape of the headlights fits perfectly with the external part of the hood, but this is not the case internally, where the rear part of the headlight now interferes with the new hood shape. This clash corresponds to a rework, as the design of the hood has to be remade.

Given the situation in the body design process, i.e. the process is late and there is a clash issue, the BDM launches the DS asking for alternatives. The DS uses simulation techniques to identify those activities within both sub-processes whose modification will most likely lead to an improvement of the progress. It also queries its local database to solve the clash issue. Since such a clash has never appeared before, querying the database does not produce any results. DS proposes two alternatives to the BDM in order to solve the clash: do nothing and accept the clash issue (which in this case will no longer be considered a clash) or design a new deviation process.

As the clash is too important, the BDM decides to put a deviated process in place. The new process is called "sport version hood vs. headlight reconciliation process". In this process, the headlight design has to change in order to resolve the interference with the rear part. This change also implies the necessity of considering a sub-process for procuring a new bulb generation that would fit together with the new headlight. The modification of the hood design is also going on as a backup solution.

BDM uses the MS in order to monitor the two alternative processes with respect to two attributes: the progress and the chance of success. The chance of success is used in the procurement process any time there is an offer to supply a new headlight to find out if the offer is worth considering. It is also computed in an aggregated form at the procurement sub-process level to indicate the chance of success of the procurement process and rank the different offers. The hood and the headlight design sub-processes also use the chance of success factor to see what their chances of success are.

The monitoring model takes into account the following information (process attributes) when calculating the chance of success:

- Level of agreement with respect to time;
- Level of agreement with respect to the cost (in the procurement process this is indicated by the price of the bulbs, while in the other sub-processes this is included in the cost of the design);
- Trustworthiness – in the procurement process this corresponds to the trustworthiness of the suppliers, while in the design case, to the trustworthiness of each team.

The target values for the some of the above attributes are established, i.e. what is the price the process manager is prepared to pay and what delivery delays are acceptable.

In the procurement process the suppliers' offers are collected and the conformance factors for cost and delays are computed (corresponding to the level of agreement). The two factors obtained are combined in order to obtain the level of conformance of the offer as a whole (as there might be offers that satisfy one aspect, but not another). The trustworthiness coefficient is then applied to the level of agreement in order to obtain the chance of success, which has values in the interval *[0,1]*, where *0* corresponds to *no chance of success*, while *1* corresponds to *total chance of success*.

Based on the data monitored, the MS computes the chance of success of the offers and display them for the BDM. At a given point, the MS reports an offer that has a chance of success equal to *1*. The supplier agrees to provide the bulbs within schedule and at a good price. The supplier is known as a trustworthy one: every time he has made a commitment, the products were provided as agreed.

At this point the BDM launches the DS for a risk analysis of each of the parallel processes. It looks that the procurement process is promising, and the reported progress of headlight design is *on schedule*.

The DS carries out the risk analysis for both processes. It computes probability distributions for both processes with respect to time and costs. The computation of these probability distributions takes into account uncertain events expressed by trustworthiness. Since the BDM is risk averse, i.e. she prefers the process that is less risky even if another process might have better results, she decides to carry on with the headlight-procurement process, since the other process is late and there are conflicts with the style department, as some modifications in the style are also required.

The MS is used in order to make the change in the deviated process.

The BDM decides to stop the hood design process immediately, thus saving costs to the company.

6 Concluding Remarks

We have presented a combined monitoring and decision support for evolving software-intensive processes.

The monitoring support proposes a set of evolving services for on-line process measurement and analysis, and constitutes one of the key features in the support for process evolution. The existence of feedback and analysis in the process enactment offer a basis for evolution. The system provides evolved analyses, such as a measure of the conformance for different aspects between the process enactment and the process plan.

The presented application of fuzzy sets theory in the monitoring of software-intensive processes allows us to deal with the uncertain and imprecise aspect of the information gathered from the process enactment. The use of the same theory in the comparison of process enactment and process plan provides us with the possibility of quantifying the deviation between these processes.

We believe that the possibility of handling imprecise information makes the monitoring system less intrusive, as the effort that is often required in the collection of precise and/or certain information can be reduced. We also believe that the less the system is intrusive, the higher are its chances of being adopted.

We are aware that system efficiency depends on the adequacy of the analyses it employs (meaning functions, aggregation methods, etc.), thus the role of the person that constructs the analysis techniques is crucial.

The existence of a formalism for modeling the monitoring process makes the monitoring system very flexible and adaptable. The separation of concerns, by adapting a set of models (for analysis, display, trace, sensors, publication) contributes as well to its adaptability.

The decision support takes a complementary role to the monitoring support. Its main objectives are on the one hand to propose solutions to problems identified either by the monitoring support or by the process manager. On the other hand decision support provides the appropriate techniques to analyze and compare alternative solutions.

The techniques for fulfilling the first objective depend on the goal of process evolution. This means, it provides different techniques for both modifying a process model and modifying a process instance. Propositions for process model modifications are mainly determined using a database which consists of earlier experiences. The decisions of the process manager with respect to modifications of the process model are stored and are reused in similar situations.

Modifications of a process instance are proposed by decision support using the same algorithm which is also used for analyzing a process instance. The algorithm, which has been described in this paper, produces various sub-results. Decision support generates appropriate solutions on the basis of those sub-results. In addition, these sub-results can also be used for optimizing a process instance.

The other main objective of decision support is to compare and analyze process instances with respect to their risks. Often, the risk inherent in a modification is not obvious, especially concerning distributed and long-lived processes. Our algorithm computes, for possible anticipated situations in the life of the process instance, the probability of occurrence together with the total costs and the throughput time. This information is further elaborated by the analysis algorithm to probability distributions. Two alternative solutions can be compared by elaborating their probability distributions and determining risk measures, which also take into account the preferences of the process manager, on the basis of these distributions.

The propositions presented here were developed in the framework of the PIE LTR ESPRIT IV project, throughout its first completed phase (ESPRIT 24840) as well as the second ongoing phase (ESPRIT 34840, http://www.cs.man.ac.uk/ipg/pie/pie-e.html).

References

1. Allen, A.O.: Probability, Statistics, and Queueing Theory. Academic Press, New York San Francisco London (1978)
2. Alloui, I., Cimpan, S., Oquendo, F., Verjus, H.: Tuning a Fuzzy Control System for Software Intensive Processes via Simulations. Proceedings of the IASTED International Conference on Modeling and Simulation, Philadelphia PA, USA, May 5-8 (1999)
3. Alloui, I., Cimpan, S., Oquendo, F., Verjus, H.: A Fuzzy Sets based Mechanism Allowing the Tuning of a Software Intensive Processes Control System via Multiple Simulations. Proceedings of the AMSE International Conference on Modelling and Simulation MS'99, Santiago de Compostela, May 17-19 (1999)
4. Arrow, K.J.: Social Choice and Individual Values. Wiley, New York (1963)
5. Basili, V.R., Caldiera, G., Rombach, H.D.: The Goal Question Metric Approach. Encyclopedia of Software Engineering, Wiley (1994)
6. Bouchon-Meunier, B.: La logique Floue et ses applications. Addison Wesley France, ISBN: 2-87908-073-8, Paris, France (1995)
7. Bradac, M., Perry, D.P., Votta, L.G.: Prototyping a Process Monitoring Experiment. IEEE Transactions on Software Engineering, vol. 20, no. 10 (1994)
8. Cimpan, S., Alloui, I. Oquendo, F.: Process Monitoring Formalism. Technical Report D3.01, PIE LTR ESPRIT Project 34840 (1999)
9. Cimpan, S., Oquendo, F.: On the Application of Fuzzy Sets Theory on the Monitoring of Software-Intensive Processes. Proceedings of the Eight International Fuzzy Systems Association World Congress IFSA'99, Taipei, Taiwan (1999)
10. Cimpan, S., Oquendo, F.: Fuzzy Indicators for Monitoring Software Processes. Proceedings of the 6th European Workshop on Software Process Technology EWSPT'98, Springer Verlag, London, UK (1998)
11. Cook, J., Wolf, A.L.: Toward Metrics for Process Validation. 3rd International Conference on the Software Process, Reston, Virginia, USA (1994)
12. Cook, J.E., Wolf, A.L.: Software Process Validation: Quantitatively Measuring the Correspondence of a Process to a Model. ACM Transactions on Software Engineering and Methodology 8 (2) (1999) 147-176
13. Cunin, P.Y., The PIE project: An Introduction, accepted for EWSPT'7 (2000)
14. Cunin, P.Y., Dami, S., Auffret J.J.: Refinement of the PIE Workpackages. Technical Report D1.00, PIE LTR ESPRIT Project 34840 (1999)
15. Feiler, P.H., Humphrey, W.S.: Software Process Development and Enactment: Concepts and Definitions. Proceedings of the Second International Conference on the Software Process, February 25-26, Berlin, Germany (1993), 28-40
16. Fenton, N.E.: Software Mesurement : A Necessary Scientifiec Basis. IEEE Transactions on Software Engineering, vol. 20, no. 3, pp. 199-206, mars (1994)

17. Fishburn, P.C., Foundations of Risk Management: Risk as a Probable Loss. Management Science **30** (1984) 396-406
18. Greenwood, M., Robertson, I. and Warboys, B.: A Support Framework for Dynamic Organizations, accepted for EWSPT'7 (2000)
19. Guth, V., Oberweis, A.: Delta-Analysis of Petri Net based Models for Business Processes. In: Kovács, E. , Kovács, Z., Csertö, B., Pépei, L. (eds): Proceedings of the 3rd International Conference on Applied Informatics (Eger-Noszvaj, Hungary, August 24-28) (1997) 23-32
20. Hapner, M., Burridge, R., Sharma, R.: Java Message Service™. Sun Microsystems, Java Software, Version 1.0.1, October (1998)
21. Humphrey, W.S.: Characterising the Software Process: A maturity framework. IEEE Software, 5(2) (1988) 73-79
22. Iida, H., Mimura, K., Inoue, K., Torii, K.: Hakoniwa: Monitor and Navigation System for Cooperative Development Based on Activity Sequence Model. Proceedings of 2nd International Conference on Software Process, Los Alamitos, California, IEEE CS Press (1993)
23. Jorion, P.: Value at Risk: A New Benchmark for Measuring Derivatives Risk. Irwin Professional Publishing, Chicago (1997)
24. Lonchamp, J.: A Structured Conceptual and Terminological Framework for Software Process Engineering. Proceedings of the Second International Conference on the Software Process, February 25-26, Berlin, Germany (1993), 41-53
25. Luce, R.D., Several Possible Measures of Risk. Theory and Decision **12** (1980) 217-228
26. Moskowitz, H., Bunn, D.: Decision and Risk Analysis. European Journal of Operational Research **28** (1987) 247-160
27. von Neumann, J., Morgenstern, O.: Theory of Games and Economic Behaviour. Princeton University Press, Princeton (1947)
28. PIE Consortium: Process Instance Evolution. Technical Report *Annex 1*, PIE LTR ESPRIT Project 34840 (1998)
29. Pratt, J., Risk Aversion in the Small and in the Large. Econometrica **32** (1964) 122-136
30. Ramsey, F.P.: Truth and Probability, The Foundations of Mathematics and Other Logical Essays. Harcourt Brace, New York (1931)
31. Selby, R.W, Porter, A.A., Schmidt, D.C., Berney, J.: Metric-Driven Analysis and Feedback Systems for Enabling Empirically Guided Software Development. Proceedings 13th International Conference on Software Engineering. Los Alamitos, California. IEEE CS Press(1991).
32. Zadeh, L.A.: Fuzzy Sets. Information and Control, Vol. 8 (1965)
33. Zadeh, L.A.: Quantitative Fuzzy Semantics. Information Sciences, Vol. 3 (1971)

Support for Software Federations: The PIE[1] Platform

G. Cugola[1], P.Y. Cunin[2], S. Dami[2], J. Estublier[2],
A. Fuggetta[1], F. Pacull[3], M. Rivière[3], H. Verjus[2,4]

[1] Politecnico di Milano, Italy.
Cugola@elet.polimi.it, Alfonso.Fuggetta@polimi.it

[2]LSR laboratory, Grenoble University, France.
{Pierre-Yves.Cunin, Samir.Dami, Jacky.Estublier}@imag.fr

[3]Xerox Research Centre Europe, Grenoble France.
{Francois.Pacull, Michel.Riviere}@xrce.xerox.com

[4]LLP/CESALP laboratory, Savoie University, Annecy France.
verjus@esia.univ-savoie.fr

1 Introduction

Research about software processes modelling and support, even during the last decade, has suffered from a lack of practical credibility. Most of the solutions proposed have not gained wide acceptance by the software industry and, moreover, some fundamental issues like evolution have not yet found any reasonable solution. For these reasons, it was a clear decision in the PIE project to build a platform providing the requisite features for evolution support, and also addressing many of the aspects that have so far impeded wide acceptance of process support.

Therefore, a major objective of the PIE platform is to facilitate the implementation, in a company, of a complete process support system. This includes the tools, systems and techniques that process participants (developers, managers) are familiar with, as well as PIE specific components. The tools that process participants are used to are likely to be Commercial Off The Shelf (COTS). The motivation to build such a Process Support System (PSS) endeavors to interoperate a number of components, including COTS systems, such that they collectively perform an expected service. We call this set of components a *federation*.

We define a *federation* as an application built mainly from COTS tools, which implies that they are (mainly) autonomous, and they are not modifiable. The Apel[2] foundation is a federation manager, specialized in process support.

The goal of the PIE federation (as well as most federations) is not only to provide collectively a (complex) service, but also to preserve the independence and autonomy of its components, to be open to dynamic change in composition and distribution

---

[1] PIE: Process Instance Evolution. Esprit Project 34840. UJF Grenoble, Victoria U. Manchester, Dortmund U., Savoie U., Politecnico di Milano, Xerox Grenoble, Teamware, Dassault Systèmes.

[2] Apel is the process support system from which the PIE platform is built.

(new/changed/ removed/moved components), as well as in changes and enhancements of the behaviour and characteristics of the whole federation.

Until now, most work addressing interoperability within a federation has focussed on basic interactions between distributed components. We believe that federations must rise above this level; we need new concepts for federation interoperability and new approaches for the definition, control and evolution of software federations.

In section 2, we will explore the concept of federation and the interoperability paradigms that can be used. In section 3, we show how these paradigms can be defined and controlled. Section 4 presents the PIE Middleware to which a large part of federation control has been delegated. Conclusions are reported in section 5.

2   Federations paradigms

Today, many COTS tools are available like workflow tools, GroupWare tools, configuration management tools, change management tools, document management tools, but also more general ones like text editors, spreadsheets, databases and web browsers, etc. Building a distributed software application [10] often consists of building a federation where most components are COTS and only a few are application specific. Such components are autonomous and manage their own resources or internal processes. It is interesting to note that the design and architecture of software systems is evolving under the pressure of a number of factors:

- Distribution requires components to communicate through explicit means,
- Maintainability requires minimal change to the source code of components,
- Evolutivity and mobility require that components are kept independent and autonomous.
- Cost requires buying instead of building.

The number of COTS tools is rapidly increasing, their functionality is more comprehensive and their price is dropping. Software products are evolving from being monolithic and proprietary toward federations. It is of strategic importance to find a practical way to build federations. Different strategies [13] can be used to define a federation out of a number of COTS.

2.1   Control-based paradigm. The "dictatorship".

The basic idea is to abstract (i.e. encapsulate) the *services* provided by each component in order to hide their heterogeneity (formalism, platform etc.). The services (API) have to be (re)defined in a common formalism (IDL), in such a way that one tool can call another, whatever their respective internal formalisms and communication technology. This is a Corba-like philosophy.

To program a federation, a modeller will have to write a specific piece of code, the *supervisor*, which calls the right components at the right time with the right parameters. This approach is the usual way to build an application from software components. Components have local models and local states inaccessible from the outside. They provide and call services and have neither independence nor autonomy (see Fig. 1). However, each component may still interact on their own with users or other federations, so they keep some independence and autonomy outside the federation.

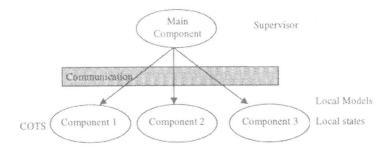

Fig. 1. The dictatorship paradigm

Let us use a metaphor with a human society to illustrate process federation architectures. Each society agent (COTS) is a human or a business with its own model and goal, and it is capable of providing some services in an autonomous way.

The control-based paradigm belongs to a fully centralized society. The goal and the rules of the society are clearly defined and enforced by a centralized government (the supervisor). The place and role of each human/company is defined and controlled by the government. This is a dictatorial society in which agents are supposed neither to know to which goal they should contribute, nor to take any initiative to contribute to change the state of the society. This may be found to be undesirable for a human society, but is perfectly acceptable for a software federation.

2.2 The Common Universe approach.

COTS tools are usually large and designed to fit a number of client's needs without it being possible for clients to change or to extend the source code. For that reason most COTS provide clients not only with an API, but also with a specific formalism, usually different from the source code language, designed to easily adapt the COTS tool behavior to each client's specific use. For example, a database provides schemas, spreadsheets provide computation sheets, planners provide planning modellers, PSSs provide process modellers and so on. We call the "program" written in this formalism the *behaviour model* of the component[3]. See Fig 2.

COTS tools, being designed to be autonomous, directly interact with the external world (users and/or common computer resources like network, database, operating system or file system). These features and devices being common to all COTS tools, we call them the *Common Universe* (CU). The fact that a component has direct interaction with the common universe has profound consequences on its design: it has to behave in an unpredictable context. COTS designers usually try to identify a number of "abnormal" behaviours, and to identify convenient responses to them, in a

---

[3] Usually, it is not possible to adapt the behavior of not COTS components. In this case, the component source code is its own behaviour model (but at a lower abstraction level).

fixed or customizable (i.e. programmable) way. This kind of behaviour can be said to be the *Common Universe model* of the tool[4].

Each COTS contains:

- Behaviour model. Description of what the component does (its specific customization).
- Interface. External description of the services that the component provides (API).
- Common Universe model. Description of component action/reaction to CU evolution.
- Current state (persistent or not).

For software applications, the common universe always contains the computer itself (files, network, modems, processors, databases, screens, etc.). However, applications can include (and potentially share) many other real world knowledge (users, mechanical artifacts, activities, etc.) or they can share abstractions (language concepts like variables, "objects" and so on). All this, when reified, constitutes the common universe.

If different components in the federation have a similar application domain, it is likely that their local states contain the same knowledge. However, it is unlikely to be represented in the same way, or to be modeled using the same concepts. This is particularly true in process federations where each component deals with different facets of the same process. For example, the fact "activity *FixBug* is under way", is known by different components and interpreted in different ways: the SCM tool builds a workspace for the activity, the workflow tool adds an activity in an agenda, the planner starts the tasks and allocates resources, and so on. Further, a tool can use the concept of task, another one of activity, a third one of workspace, and their knowledge overlaps but is not identical; their have only partial views; none has a complete knowledge. Still this knowledge is part of the CU.

Many aspects of the CU model appear as atomic from the federation point of view but involve different components. For example, creating an activity in the CU, (which is an atomic operation) may involve MSProject (for planning), Lotus Notes (for notification), Adele (for workspace creation) and a monitoring tool (for the team leader control board). There is a need to coordinate, in a fine-grained way, the actions of all the components.

The CU provides a sound basis on which the federation components can synchronize their work, because they can all observe the CU, and update their local state accordingly, or change the CU according to changes performed in their local state during execution. In the above example, the creation of a common activity changes the CU; this is noted by the components, each one reacting in its own way: updating planning (MSProject), creating a workspace (Adele) and so on.

The CU approach, consisting in bringing as much as possible into a single common formalism and data repository, borrows similarities from database federations, but there are at least two major differences. In a database federation, the goal is to find a common schema from which the data stored in the different databases can be

---

[4] For standard software components, the CU model is missing; for usual COTS, it is simple. PSSs are unique in that their "raison d'être" is to deal with CU changes; the PSS behaviour model is its CU model.

accessed. In our approach, the local store of components is never accessed through the common model. The goal of the common universe model is to define the behavior of the federation as a whole, whether or not this overlaps with the component process and/or persistent data. In case of overlap, it is up to each component to make its local data consistent. It is up to the component to decide what consistent means. The other major difference is that the purpose is not the static definition, but the dynamic behavior, i.e. the process. Really there is not much similarity between these two approaches.

2.3 The simple CU approach. The "anarchy"

The simple implementation of such an approach is presented by the ProcessWall [3]. There is no CU model; the architecture is based only on the effective presence of the CU, on which each component synchronizes its activity during execution (see Fig. 2).

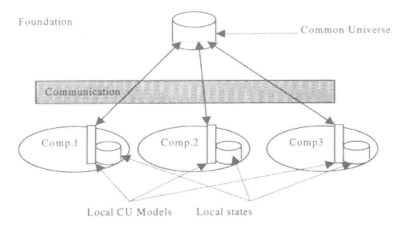

Fig. 2. The anarchy paradigm

In our society metaphor, the CU-based paradigm corresponds to an ultra-liberal society, where each human/organization observes the state of the society (CU) and decides to "collaborate" freely to its evolution. Groups of humans can handle work in common by observing the actions of the others (cooperation between overlapping PSSs). No federation process (the goal i.e. the desired future) is defined, no rules (correct behaviours and laws) are enforced. It is an anarchic society; which can work only if each component (human) behaves "correctly", which is unlikely in a human society, but not in a computer federation.

2.4 The controlled CU approach. From "dictatorship" to "anarchy".

In the control-based approach 2.1, components do not know in what they are participating, but there is formal knowledge of exactly what will be executed and how (it is the supervisor's source code). In the simple CU approach 2.3, each component knows to what it contributes, but there is no plan for future actions.

The first approach provides the goal and control desirable in a federation, but introduces severe limitations (partitioning) and lack of flexibility. The simple CU approach provides the desirable flexibility and generality, but at the cost of losing global control (goal and rule enforcement). There are, however, intermediate positions between dictatorship and anarchy.

If a CU is shared by components, its behaviour is an abstraction of the "composition" of all components' CU behaviours. If the federation CU model is formally defined and executed, it avoids anarchy, and it allows modellers and managers to understand, customize, and optimize the federation process. The federation CU model expresses (part of) the federation goal. If this federation CU model is executable (and executed) and if each one of the federation's components is able to execute its part, the goal of the federation becomes explicit and enforceable. It is semantic interoperability [2][1].

The CU model contains the *functional* aspects of the CU behavior (the *what*), not the *operational* ones (the *how*). We also define an *operational model*, whose purpose is to focus on defining *how* aspects mentioned in the CU model should or must be handled. Instead of relying on implicit and asynchronous invocation, this model prescribes the reaction to CU changes, and explicitly indicates the consistency required for a given reaction. The operational model contains information related with the consistency control of the CU model implementation much as the ordering of component invocations for the same CU change, transaction control and so on. To do so, the interpreter of that model has to know of the federation components and their services, and has the capability to explicitly invoke these services. It relies on an explicit and synchronous invocation paradigm. See figure 3.

In our metaphor, the society has a global society development plan (CU model) and has a government (the interpreters of the CU and operational models). If using only the CU model, the government executes the plan, which means it simply asks the society to do the work (e.g. build a highway). Agents, collectively, are supposed to be aware of what has to be done and to do it as they like. This society has both a goal (CU model) and a government, even if the latter has very little power and initiative. It is unlikely to work in human society.

If using the operational model, the government not only can ask for something to be done but can also decides who will do it and how it will be done (the operational model interpreter directly calls the components that can do the job). The government can thus decide which aspects of the development plan are to be under complete control (like the army), or partially controlled (like health services), or completely free (most normal trade). This society can cover the complete spectrum from dictatorial (the operational model controls everything; it is the supervisor), to anarchy (neither operational model nor CU model).

3 PIE architecture

The PIE architecture implements the last federation paradigm (2.4). The foundation has to provide a repository for the CU, a CU model (and its interpreter) and an operational model (and its interpreter). The operational model interpreter relies on a *dedicated middleware* responsible for providing basic communication facilities (messages and method calls), but also to provide specific control services.

The components of the federation (see Fig. 3) are of two kinds:

- Components which provide the functionalities of the PIE system. These components are the standard ones developed within the project: pro-active monitoring support, change and decision support [14] and evolution strategy support [15].
- Components which are COTS tools or proprietary components specific to an application and fulfilling the application users requirements.

In PIE, it is the operational manager who is in charge of translating the operational model into a number of rules and laws applied to the communications (thick double arrow). The PIE Middleware will be in charge of supporting and interpreting these rules, and realizing the communication. The PIE Middleware is different from usual middlewares (such as CORBA [4], [5] or Java Message Service [7], etc.) in that existing middlewares provide a communication mechanism but do not ensure or enforce any system property. We consider that federation control requires the close control of a number of communication properties like roles played by components in the federation context, rights and duties associated to these roles, substitution of components, mobility of components and so on.

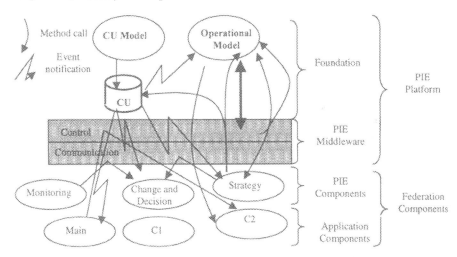

Fig. 3. Architecture of a controlled federation

This architecture arises from the following considerations:

- Most federation control can be translated into communication control.
- Most of the communication controls are services of very wide applicability.
- The set of communication services can be easily and dynamically extended and changed.

These considerations explain why we decided to delegate a large part of the federation control to a generic communication layer: the PIE Middleware. It basically relies on a "standard" message-passing system ('communication' in Fig. 3), almost JMS compliant, and on a control layer for the support of federation control.

The services that must be provided by the PIE Middleware control layer should include:

- Simple communication control: Inhibit messages, Redirect messages, Change message content, Replace a message by a method call (or vice versa), Duplicate, broadcast a method call, Reject a method call, and so on.

- Advanced services: Enforce reactions ordering, Enforce transactional like capabilities, Handle messages with multiple replies, method broadcast, Provide advanced delivery properties and so on.

Both layers are described in the following section.

4 PIE Middleware

To satisfy the requirements identified in the previous section, the PIE Middleware has to provide a rich set of services. It has to include 1) basic asynchronous, message-based communication services and 2) synchronous, service-request-based communication services. In addition, more advanced services have to include support for atomic delivery of a set of messages, for distributed transactions, and, more in general, for controlling a federation of COTS. These services must be integrated in a unified API to minimize the effort needed to use the middleware and to avoid duplication, redundancy, and inconsistency among different services.

To pursue this ambitious goal the *communication* and *data model* of the PIE Middleware have to be carefully designed to offer the common basis for implementing the required services.

Among the set of services provided by the PIE Middleware, we can distinguish four areas:

- basic message-based communication services,
- basic service-request-based communication services,
- services to change the middleware behaviour dynamically,
- and enhanced services, such as atomic delivery of messages and transactions.

For compatibility with current standards, the basic communication layer is compliant with JMS (for message services) and RMI (for method calls). Any tool using these standards can be used as is in a PIE federation.

The set of services, which allows the behaviour of the PIE Middleware to be changed at run-time, is a key feature of the PIE Middleware that is crucial to support run-time changes of the architecture of the PIE federation.

4.1 Communication layer

Communication and data models constitute the basis of any middleware. The first describes the underlying model of communication adopted by the middleware, while the second describes the properties of the information exchanged by the clients of the middleware (i.e., the components of the resulting architecture) through the set of services provided.

Different middlewares adopt different communication and data models. As an example CORBA [4] [5] and RMI [6] adopt a model based on service requests, with a complex type system, while message-oriented middlewares [7] [11] adopt a model based on message passing with much simpler type systems (often messages are untyped). To allow high level interaction between components (e.g. [12]) the PIE Middleware offers both models of communication, each with an appropriate data model, very simple (untyped) for message-based communications and richer (Java types) for service-requests.

The communication model

As mentioned above, the PIE Middleware offers both message-based and service-request-based communication services, giving its users the chance to choose an appropriate communication model. These two communication models have been integrated by translating service requests into messages in a way that is transparent to the programmer. By doing so, the clients of the PIE Middleware (i.e., the *PIE clients*) can adopt any of the two models of communication, while internally both messages and service requests are managed in the same manner.

As for message-based communication, the PIE Middleware implements both push and pull communication models. In a push approach the PIE Middleware pushes messages to their recipients. According to the semantics of JMS, when they connect to the middleware (or when they subscribe to a class of messages), clients have to provide a method to be invoked to process incoming messages (i.e., a *callback*). Conversely, the pull model assumes that it is the recipient that "pulls" messages from the PIE Middleware.

As for service requests, the PIE Middleware is totally compatible with RMI. This means that both RMI clients and servers can use the PIE Middleware without any modification. More specifically, service requests are managed as standard RMI communications (i.e., they are sent directly from the client to the server) as soon as the PIE Middleware is not required to intercept them to offer richer services. When this happens, the PIE Middleware becomes an intermediary for service requests. This shift, from direct client-server connection to the mediated one is made transparently to both the clients and the servers.

The data model

The adopted communication model has strong relationships with the chosen data model. The PIE Middleware adopts a very simple data model for message-based communications and a richer model for service requests. This choice was motivated by the need for keeping message-based communication as simple and lightweight as possible, and to enhance scalability and interoperability among heterogeneous PIE clients that want to exchange messages. Conversely, service requests adopt a complex data model to allow PIE clients acting as servers to export a complex and expressive interface.

In the context of message-based services, the PIE Middleware introduces the concept of a *PIEMessage*. As mentioned above, in order to support scalability and heterogeneity, the PIE Middleware does not rely on any kind of common type system, i.e., PIEMessages are untyped. Each PIE client can send a PIEMessage that includes any set of user-defined fields. The interpretation of messages is made at the application level and the PIE Middleware does not perform any kind of type checking on the behalf of the application.

The content of a PIEMessage, is composed of three parts: a *set of recipients*, a set of *named fields* (composed of a set of *system fields*, which are always present, and a set of *user-defined fields*), and a *payload*.

- Each PIEMessage recipient can be a (list of) *topic* and/or a (list of) *component identifier*. Topics are used to implement *multicast* communication in a publish/subscribe style. Each topic has a name, which is a string composed of a dot-separated list of identifiers. Component identifiers are used to implement point-to-point communication. Each PIE client has an associated identifier. By using these identifiers, PIEMessages can be addressed to specific PIE clients.
- Each field has a name and a value. Both names and values are strings. The PIE Middleware distinguishes between a set of system fields, which are always present, and a set of user-defined fields. PIE clients can create PIEMessages having any number of user-defined fields. Fields can be used to perform content-based subscription when the publish/subscribe communication style is adopted.
- The payload is a special field, an array of bytes containing application-specific data that cannot be used to perform content-based subscription.

A message identifier (contained into the *messageId* system field) uniquely identifies each message.

While message-based services adopt a quite simple data model, a complex data model characterizes service requests. Each PIE client can export a set of public methods that compose the interface of the client. Each method is characterized by a *name*, a *set of typed parameters*, and by the *type of the return value*. Any valid (serializable) Java types can be used for parameters and for the return value. As mentioned, the PIE Middleware service requests are totally compatible with RMI. This is true also for the data model adopted. As a consequence the interested reader may refer to the RMI specification [6] for further details.

Basic message-based communication services

To use the services of the PIE Middleware, PIE clients have to open a *PIESession* to the PIE Middleware[5]. More specifically, from the point of view of the PIE Middleware, a PIE client is, by definition, any executing unit that has at most one session opened.

---

[5] Observe that the PIE middleware does not have any concept of "connection" similar to the one provided by JMS. It is responsibility of the PIE middleware to share connections as much as possible to improve scalability.

A PIESession can be in one of three states: *closed, opened,* or *suspended.* When created for the first time a PIESession is in the closed state. A closed session can be opened by specifying the address of the *PIE dispatching server* the client wants to connect to. To support migration of PIE clients, the PIE Middleware allows PIESessions to be suspended and reopened from a different location and/or to a different PIE dispatcher.

Each PIESession is uniquely identified by a middleware, provided identifier that can be used both as a proxy to issue service requests to the PIE client that opened it (see next section), and as a recipient of messages that have to be addressed to the same PIE client. In the remainder we will use the term "identifier" of a PIE client C to indicate the identifier of the PIESession opened by C.

The PIE Middleware provides a *name service* to let a PIE client export its identifier to other clients. In particular, the PIE name service adopts the standard JNDI interface [8], thus allowing a PIE client to export its identifier under a symbolic name chosen by the client itself. Other PIE clients may query the PIE Middleware for the identifier of the PIE client having a known symbolic name. Observe that, to simplify client programming, symbolic names can be directly used to address PIEMessages to specific clients.

A PIE client connected to the PIE Middleware through a PIESession is able to browse the list of available topics; create a new Message, send a Message to a specific set of recipients (using topics or component identifiers), subscribe to an existing topic, receive Messages and reply to messages. PIE Middleware *administrators* can also create and remove topics.

Basic service-request-based communication services
In addition to the message-based services described in the previous section, PIE clients can take benefit of advanced services based on the service-request paradigm. In particular, PIE clients can export some of their methods to other clients, allowing them to invoke such "services" in a transparent manner. As already mentioned, the PIE Middleware adopts the standard RMI facility to implement such services. This means that any standard RMI/JNDI component can act both as a client and as a server in an RMI communication supported by the PIE Middleware.

The value added by the PIE Middleware to the standard RMI facility is the ability of providing one or more handlers (see 4.2) [9] capable of changing the way service requests issued by RMI clients are dispatched and served by RMI servers. As an example, it is possible to write a middleware handler capable of intercepting a service request issued to a PIE client in order to translate them as a pair <message, reply> issued to a different client. As another example it is possible to implement a middleware handler capable of supporting transparent management of a replicated set of RMI servers. This handler would intercept any call issued to a PIE client C translating it in a call to one of a set of PIE clients <C1, ..., CN> acting as a set of replicated servers.

4.2   The Control Layer

Process enactment in a widely distributed environment, composed of several COTS components, and subject to process instance change is complex. It sets strong requirements to the middleware in charge of supporting the communication among components. The dynamics of the application and the complexity of the communication patterns that need to be put in place, makes it very hard to anticipate the communication services required.

To overcome this problem the PIE Middleware adopts two complementary approaches. First, as described in the first part of this document, it supports different communication patterns ranging from asynchronous multicast message to simple method calls. Second, it offers a set of services to change the middleware behaviour at run-time and to add new communication services dynamically.

This last feature is obtained by means of *PIE handlers*, special kind of plug-in modules that can be added to a PIE dispatching server at run-time to change its behaviour or to add new services.

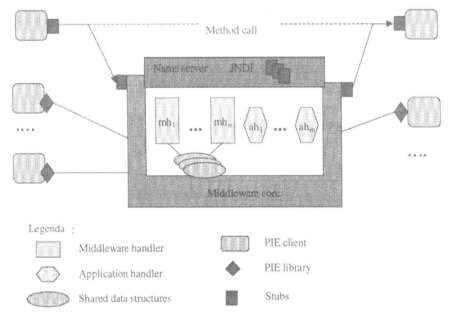

Fig. 4. The logical architecture of the PIE Middleware

From a logical point-of-view, the PIE Middleware is composed of a *core*, a *set of handlers*, and a *set of shared data structures* (i.e., shared among different middleware handlers). PIE clients interact with the PIE Middleware by taking advantage of a library, which implements the PIE Middleware API (see Fig. 4). The role of the PIE Middleware core is to manage activation of handlers. It encapsulates also the JNDI [8] name service used to export PIE client identifiers.

Middleware behaviour: handlers
Handlers implement all the user functionalities provided by the middleware. In particular, a (small set of) middleware handlers is provided with the system to implement the functionalities described in the previous sections. Middleware vendors can add new middleware handlers to extend the set of functionalities provided by the system.

A unique name, a message selector, a priority, and a body characterize each PIE handler. The message selector is used to specify the set of PIEMessages the handler applies to. The priority is used to choose the ordering in which message handlers have to be applied. Handlers with the same message selector must have a different priority. The body describes the actions that have to be made when a PIEMessage that matches the message selector is sent to the PIE Middleware for dispatching.

The PIE Middleware distinguishes between two classes of handlers: *application handlers* and *middleware handlers*.

- *Application handlers* are application specific, stateless plug-ins whose body can specify a limited set of operations to change the PIEMessages content: basically the set of recipients of the message and its fields. They are supposed to be defined by clients using a very limited and controlled language.
- *Middleware handlers* are generic plug-ins used to extend the middleware functionalities by providing additional features. Like application handlers they can access and change the set of recipients of messages and their fields. Moreover, they can access and change the message payload. Most important, they can hold an internal state and can access shared data to cooperate with other middleware handlers. They are supposed to be defined by middleware vendors using a complete programming language.

To understand how PIE handlers work, we have to describe how the PIE Middleware logically operates. When a PIE client invokes a service of the PIE Middleware an internal PIEMessage M is inserted it in the "delivery queue" of the PIE Middleware.

For each message in this "delivery queue" the PIE Middleware looks for the highest priority handler whose message selector matches M. Let be H such handler, whose body is then executed.

The body of H can either discard the message, or it modifies the message M and/or generates new messages. A modified message keeps its original identification while generated messages have their own identification. The modified initial message and the possible generated ones are inserted in the 'delivery queue' and can thus be processed at their turn.

A standard middleware handler with the lowest priority is in charge of replacing any topics that are in the set of recipients and to convert them in a list of component identifiers.

The following policy is followed:

- A handler is used only once on a message (same message identifier).
- If several handlers match a message M with the same priority, one of them is picked up in a non-deterministic way.
- If at the end of the process (no more handlers may be applied including the standard middleware handler, see below) all messages that contain topics are discarded.

Usual middlewares like JMS are implemented in the PIE Middleware as the core plus the standard handler. Unlike usual middlewares, any additional service can be added by simply adding handlers implementing the service.

The needs for federation control, as explained above, are such that a number of handlers, other than the standard handler, are predefined.

Enhanced services

The PIE Middleware supports several kinds of " higher level services", for instance:

Grouped delivery. A client can start a grouped delivery operation to send a set of messages as a single atomic operation. This ensures two basic properties at the level of the messages delivery. First, the 'all or nothing' property ensures that either all the messages are eventually delivered, or none of them. Second, the messages external to the group are either delivered before or after the group of messages.

Atomic delivery. This is a special case of grouped delivery to ensure that the groups of messages are delivered at the same logical instant. This means that if two clients send two grouped messages to common recipients, they receive the two groups of messages in the same order.

Method calls. The method call we consider in the PIE Middleware follows the classical RMI scheme. However, in the frame of the PIE Middleware we provide the possibility of intercepting an invocation from a client to a server in order to modify, thanks to a set of handlers, the initial behaviour. It allows the adaptation of a method call to a modified interface, or to redirect the method call to the new location of the client.

Method handlers can also be used to manage a set of clients as if it were single.

The above concerns message/method delivery, but PIE clients may want to have more guarantees about the real processing of the message. For that purpose we introduce the *transactional processing* of messages and method calls. Even if it is technically possible to realize real ACID transactions, the real problem is that the server's behaviour is not controlled, and that the semantics is not always clear, in particular regarding the actions to do when a transaction is aborted. Is the component able to roll back? If it cannot, how critical are the consequences? Basically we consider a classical two-phase commit protocol where the message/method is delivered in the first phase. The replies of the first phase inform the middleware handler of the possibility to process the message or not. If all the involved recipients reply favorably, a commit message is sent, otherwise an abort message is sent.

The behaviour of the two phases is left to the responsibility of the servers that can either consider a partial, optimistic or pessimistic approach. In the partial approach, servers may only partially (or not at all) roll back the transaction. In the optimistic approach, processing the message/method is done in the first phase and rollback is necessary in case of reception of an abort message. The pessimistic approach consists of verifying that the message/method can be processed, possibly locking some resources and effectively processing it when the commit message is received.

Here we can clearly see the difference between the protocol that is imposed by the middleware (e.g. the two phase-commit) and the behaviour of the servers that can in theory implement what they want for the two phases according to their own semantic and the semantics attached to the message.

Let us exemplify how the PIE middleware is used to support federation building and control.

Usually, most methods declared in CU classes are executed by a given component. This is realized by putting a handler that redirects these method calls to the responsible component and simultaneously emits the corresponding notification. On the extreme, the CU can be totally virtual, all calls to the CU being directed toward the right components, in a completely transparent way; allowing to build realistic and efficient distributed federations. Component mobility is solved that way; components rights are also dynamically checked by handlers.

Event "activity *FixBug* starts" (see example in **Erreur! Source du renvoi introuvable.**) is simply captured by a handler which deletes it and transactionaly calls the SCM tool to build a workspace for the activity, the workflow tool to add an activity in an agenda, the planner to start the tasks and allocates resources, and so on.

5 Conclusions

A number of factors deeply influence the way modern applications are to be designed and built. Among the most obvious, we could mention distribution and that applications are being built from large existing pieces of software, mostly often coming from third parties and COTS tools. Thus new applications must be designed as a federation of distributed and autonomous components.

Our work in process support is a special case of this evolution. We think it contributes to federations in three respects. First we have shown that new paradigms have to be used for the design and control of federations. Second, we have shown these new paradigms have to rely on the existence of a common universe, and that process technology is the "natural way" to deal with CU definition and control. Third, federations, being distributed, have to rely on a middleware. We have shown that many of the features needed for federation control can and should be part of the middleware services.

Regarding federation, we believe our work contrasts with contemporary approaches. In these federation approaches, components are linked together to constitute the application. The fact that we have explicitly introduced the universe, common to different components, and that we used process technology to model and control it, is a major change. The separation of operational and CU models is another major improvement over the classic approaches. We believe our approach could become a general approach for building federations.

Regarding middleware, we believe this work also contrasts with earlier work. In normal middlewares, layers are added on top of a basic communication layer (e.g. CORBA services on top of an ORB). The classic approach does not provide any control over the communication, and services can be used only explicitly. Our requirements are to control the communication, to provide advanced services and to change dynamically the middleware behaviour, transparently from the client's point of view. Instead of layers, controls and services are plugged into the core middleware. Due to its generality, extensibility, flexibility and (supposed) efficiency, we consider our approach could contribute to an alternative approach to the building of middleware.

We believe that the solutions proposed are going farther than software process federation. Indeed, we have tried in this work, as well as in this paper, to address the issues, and to design solutions potentially usable for many software federations. We hope the experiments under way will show the validity of our claims.

References

[1] J. Estublier and N.S. Barghouti. *Interoperability and Distribution of Process-Sensitive Systems.* Software Engineering for Parallel and Distributed Systems (PDSE'98). Kyoto April 19-25, 1998.

[2] S. Heiler. *Semantic Interoperability.* ACM Computing Surveys, 27(2):271-273, June, 1995.

[3] D. Heimbigner. *"The ProcessWall: a Process State Server Approach to Process Programming".* ACM-SDE, December 1992.

[4] Object Management Group, *"CORBA services: Common Object Services Specification"*, July 1997.

[5] Object Management Group, *"The Common Object Request Broker: Architecture and Specifications (revision 2.0)"*. OMG, Framinghm, MA, July 1995.

[6] Sun Microsystems, *"Java Remote Method Invocation Specification"*, February 10, 1997.

[7] Sun Microsystems, *"Java Message Service"*, Version 1.0.5, October 5, 1998.

[8] Sun Microsystems, *"Java Naming and Directory Interface"*, Version 1.2, July 14, 1999.

[9] D. Garlan, *"Low-cost adaptable tool integration policies for integrated environments"*, in Proceedings of SDE90.

[10] G. Cugola, E. Di Nitto, A. Fuggetta, *"Exploiting an event-based infrastructure to develop complex distributed systems"*, in Proceedings of ICSE'20, April 1998

[11] OVUM, *"OVUM Evaluates: Middleware"*, OVUM Ltd, 1996

[12] J.M. Andreoli, D. Arregui, F. Pacull, M. Riviere, J.Y. Vion-Dury, J. Willamowski, *"CLF/Mekano: A Framework for Building Virtual-Enterprise Applications"*, in Proceedings of International Enterprise Distributed Object Computing, 1999, (to appear)

[13] J. Estublier, H. Verjus, *"Definition of the Behaviour Paradigms of a Heterogeneous Federation of Evolving Process Components"*, PIE2 Deliverable D2.01, 1999

[14] I. Alloui, S. Beydeda, S. Cîmpan, V. Gruhn, F. Oquendo and C. Schneider, *"Advanced Services for process Evolution: Monitoring and Decision Support"*, EWSPT7, Salzburg, Austria, February 2000

[15] M. Greenwood, I. Robertson and B. Warboys, *"A Support Framework for Dynamic Organizations"*, EWSPT7, Salzburg, Austria, February 2000

Keynote on "Thirty Years in Software Process"

M. M. (Manny) Lehman,
Imperial College, London, UK

Abstract

The results of a 1968 study of IBM's programming process triggered little interest in IBM, but initiated my later software process studies. The IBM study lead to four main results: recognition of the software process as a feedback system, system evolution encompassed both development and maintenance, recognition of the disciplined nature of the evolution process, and formulation of three laws of software evolution. The laws reflected forces outside the direct technical process of software development and evolution, and must therefore be accepted as laws.

Subsequent studies of several non-IBM, systems largely confirmed the observations. These studies also led to: development of the Software Process Evolution program classification scheme, phenomenological models of the software process, five more laws, a series of International Software Process Workshop, a Principle of Software Uncertainty and, above all, deeper understanding of the process of software evolution. The studies in 1969-84 were summarised in the book "Program Evolution – Processes of Software Change" by Lehman and Belady.

In the 80s and early 90s, research interest in the software process was confined to a small community, focusing on process models and their formal representation and enactment. Since then, a growing interest is primarlily due to an increased concern for business process improvement, the search for disciplined methods of software process improvement, and emerging awareness of the relationship between the two. Development and successful marketing of models and procedures such as CMM and SPICE played a major role in this growth. It did not, however, generate a wider understanding of the process or how it could be improved based on that understanding.

Major process improvement is difficult, since the software process is a feedback system – cf. the 1971 observation and the recent *FEAST hypothesis*. Following three FEAST workshops at Imperial College, the UK EPSRC supported the FEAST/1 and FEAST/2 projects in 1996 and 1999 (http://www-dse.doc.ic.ac.uk/-mml/feast/). Findings in several systems have supported the FEAST hypothesis and provided confirmation of six of the eight laws of software evolution. The FEAST work also suggested that outer loops of the total process – including influences from management, marketing and user sources – dominated system evolution trends.

The long-term implications of this insight and continuing studies include practical guidelines for software evolution planning and management. They also provide basis for an initial, formal Theory of Software Process and Evolution. Such a theory will focus future process studies and guide practical application of advanced software technology.

Transcribing Process Model Standards into Meta-Processes

Carla Blanck Purper

Universität Bremen, FB3 Mathematik/Informatik, Postfach 33 04 40,
D-28334 Bremen, Germany
Cpurper@informatik.uni-bremen.de
http://www.informatik.uni-bremen.de/~uniform/gdpa

Abstract. Standards on process models are commonly delivered by means of static documents, usually paper based which are difficult to handle and to become skilled at. It is a difficult task to abstract the process model from the informally written standard and then to tailor it into a particular project. As the standard process model and the customized enactable process for a real-world project are stored in different frameworks, an automatic standard compliance, on-line retrieval of the original content of the official regulations etc. are not feasible. One proposal to bridge this gap is the construction of meta-processes. This paper introduces a schema for formalizing the meta-process for process standards, illustrates the application to four different standards and describes its implementation in the web-based learning environment of GDPA[1].

1 Introduction

Software process standards such as GD 250, also known as the V-Model [GD250], IEEE1220 [IEEE1220], ISO 12204 [ISO 12204] describe generic process models that should be tailored to the needs of a specific project. Usually, these models are informally described and delivered by means of static, paper-based documents, which are unwieldy and strenuous to learn. Few of them are optionally available as *postscript* (or PDF, RTF, Word documents), *help-based* documents or *web-based* documents.

In a typical use, the person responsible in constructing a project process compliant to a standard "reads" the contents of the standard and mentally maps the regulations into the intended process model. During and/or after constructing the process model, he (or another person) performs manual checks against the standard mandatory prac-

---

[1] GDPA is one tool of the UniForM Workbench [K+99] which is a project developed by a partnership between academia (Universität Bremen and Universität Oldenburg) and industry (Elpro LET GmbH), sponsored by the German ministry of education and research (BMBF - Bundesministerium für Bildung und Forschung, 1996-1998). The UniForM Workbench is a generic framework, instantiated with specific tools for formal methods to handle communication, distributed systems and real-time requirements. UniForM focuses on the combination of formal methods [KSW96,TW97], development by transformation [L+99], integrated tool support [Kar98,99] and incorporation of process standards [Purp99a ,b].

tices. These practices may concern the constraints to hold for the process itself or for the artifacts (documents, software or hardware components, systems etc.) which are produced by the enactment of the process. The fact that the standard model is not on the same platform and architecture as the project model leads to a significant consumption of resources to harmonize them. This problem is strongly increased when the process of the real-world project evolves and this is not reflected in the process model.

Meta-process concepts [Warb99] have been employed to deal with these problems. This paper outlines the properties of meta-processes for process-standards. First, it introduces a schema for formalizing the *standards meta-process*, illustrates the application to four different standards and describes the implementation in a web-based learning environment.

2 Standard Meta-Process

The following definitions used in this paper are due to [Warb99]. A *real-world production process* (*P*), which assigns human resources, methods, tools etc. to the activities needed to produce a software product, is modeled in a *process model* (*PM*). Frequently, when *P* evolves to cope with the dynamics of system development, its evolution is not reflected in the original *PM*. As a consequence, *PM* and *P* may no longer be in accordance. Nevertheless it is possible to define a process in order to assure that *P* and *PM* remain consistent. This process is called the *meta-process*.

In this context, a *real-world standard for software process* (*SP*) which defines activities, artifacts and practices that are needed to produce software, is modeled in a *standard process model* (*SPM*). Based on the *SPM*, the process participant defines the *PM* for a particular project. The project *PM* must obey the constraints of the practices defined in *SPM*. Whenever the project *PM* evolves, the affected constraints of *SPM* must be reviewed. This process is called the *standard meta-process*. Figure 1 illustrates the flow among the process models and meta-processes for both project and standard.

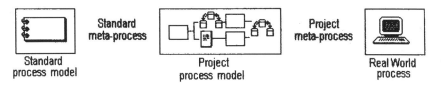

Figure 1: *Overview of the standard meta process.*

3 E-R Model for Standard Meta-Processes

In order to define the meta-process for different standards it is necessary to specify a common repository where the process models could be stored. The E-R model of the repository should support:

- the diversities among the process models of the standards,
- the formalization of the rules extracted from the standards
- an experience library based on the experience factory [Basi93].

For the definition of the E-R model illustrated in Figure 2, six standards were analyzed: GD250 [GD250], ISO 12207 [ISO12207], ISO 9000-3 [ISO 9000-3], IEEE 1220 [IEEE1220], IEEE 1074 [IEEE1074], ESA PSS-05 [PSS05] and AQAP-150 [AQAP150]. This is a simplified model and does not reflect the internal details. For instance, the data-flows only represent the main flow. The model distinguishes between the *standard, standard rules* and *experience library*. The *standard* contains information of the process model that has mostly been extracted straightforwardly from the standard and constitutes a sort of information center for the standard. The *standard rules* entail the constraints for the standard compliance which are the formalization of the rules taken from the regulations written informally in the standard. The standard rules are usually drawn by hand from the original standards. The *experience library* includes information that is independent from standards and provides support, advise and previous experiences for enacting the activities expressed in the standard. The next sections depict each element of the E-R model presented in Figure 2 and outline the forms for collecting information from the standards.

Standard. For the purpose of this paper only four from the six analyzed standards are considered: GD 250 [GD250] also known as the V-Model, ESA PSS-05, ISO 12207 and IEEE 1074.

Delivery forms. Typically, software process standards are delivered by means of static documents, usually paper-based. Few of them are optionally available as:
(a) Postscript, PDF, RTF, Word documents
(b) Help-based documents. Usually, these are generated from word-processor formats.
(c) Web-based documents. Frequently, these are automatically converted from word-processor formats into HTML documents for direct display via Web-browsers. The hyper-links are usually limited to references within the same document.
(d) Data files to be directly imported by other databases.

GD 250 V-Model	ESA-PSS05	ISO 12207	IEEE 1074
(a),(b),(c),(d)	(a), (b)	Paper, (a)	Paper, (a)

Table 2: *Delivery forms*

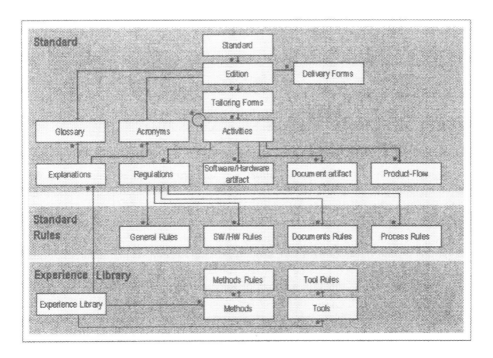

Figure 2: *The repository model*

Edition. Most of the analyzed standards call their released versions as "editions". In order to serve as an effective instrument for continuous improvement, process standards should be dynamic. Probably in the near future, the period for delivering new versions of process standards will diminish and it will be necessary to implement substantial version control. The following table identifies the version actually used for the research described in this paper.

GD 250 V-Model	ESA-PSS05	ISO 12207	IEEE 1074
09/1997 (2nd edition)	02/1991 (2nd edition)	1995 (E) 1st edition	04/1995 - 2nd edition
First edition 1992	First edition 1987		First edition 1991

Table 3: *Standards Editions*

Tailoring forms. Tailoring forms contain the templates for tailoring the process model according to pre-classified characteristics of the project, development environment, etc. The tailoring forms are the only element that could not be modeled. Each standard offers its own method for describing and performing the tailoring. Tailoring forms are stored in the repository as text.

GD 250 V-Model	ESA-PSS05	ISO 12207	IEEE 1074
Ad-hoc	Ad-hoc	Ad-hoc	Ad-hoc

Table 4: *Tailoring Forms*

Activities. Although the standards organize and classify the activities in a different manner, almost all of them can be modeled in three levels. The table below identifies the given titles and the quantity, and illustrates one example for each level. For instance the GD 250 has 5 *sub-models* ordered into 42 *activities* which, in turn, are composed of 128 *sub-activities*. The letter "D" used in the following tables means that the information can be directly collected from the standard, and "I", indirectly, resp.

Level	GD 250 V-Model	ESA-PSS05	ISO 12207	IEEE 1074
Level A				
Title	D: "Sub-models"	D: "Standards"	D: "Lifecycles"	D: "Processes"
#	5	2	3	6
E.g.	SD - System Development	Product Standard	Primary Lifecycle	Software Lifecycles Process
Level B				
Title	D: "Activities"	D: "Phases"	D: "Processes"	D: "Processes"
#	42	10	17	17
E.g.	SD1 - System Requirement Anal.	UR - User Requirements	Acquisition Process	Software Lifecycle Model Process
Level C				
Title	D: "Sub-Activities"	D: "Activities"	D: "Activities"	D: "Activities"
#	128	47	74	65
E.g.	SD1.1 Recording of Actual Status and Analysis	3.2.1 Capture of user Requirements	5.1.1 Initiation	2.3 Identify Candidate Software Lifecycle models

Table 5: *Standards classifications for activities*

Regulations. Despite the fact that regulations are the core of controlling compliance with the standard, most standards have their regulations mixed up with explanations and recommendations. The task of splitting them in order to fit into the E-R model is quite laborious. Table 6 identifies for each standard from where the regulations should be taken, the minimal quantity of regulations, and one example of the original regulation before extracting the practice. The regulations are formulated in [Emme99] as "practices" and the explanations and recommendations as "rationale".

GD 250 V-Model	ESA-PSS05	ISO 12207	IEEE 1074
I: "Handling" + I: "Explanation"	I: "Mandatory Practices"	I: "Tasks"	I: "Description"
170	199	232	65
An overall horizon must be specified for the system functionality within the scope of this activity. This is realized by means of a preliminary system description which is the background for all further refinements and additions of the User Requirements	UR01 The definition of the user requirements shall be the responsibility of the user	5.1.1.1 The acquirer begins the acquisition process by describing a concept or a need to acquire, develop, or enhance a system, software product or software service.	2.3.1 In this activity, the set of Available SLCMs and applicable Constraints shall be considered and Candidate SLCMs identified. A new model may be constructed by combining elements of others SLCMs.

Table 6: Standards regulations

Rules. The rules are the formalization of the informal and unstructured *regulations* written in the standards. Here are four categories of rules:

Document rules
These are the most frequent ones. Typically they entail phrases like "the document ... shall describe the ...."

Process rules
These might be constraints on the order of the activities, on roles that must perform the activity, on hardware or software resources, on schedules or on the budget, e.g. "the software unit test must be performed by a person outside the development team and completed before the system test".

Software/Hardware rules
These make explicit reference to attributes or qualities that the software or hardware shall have, e.g. "the user-interface must ...."

General rules
These are rules that are defined in a broad spectrum and cannot be allocated to any of the above categories, e.g. "the supplier shall ensure that this policy is understood.."

Furthermore, the following information must be retrieved for each rule:
- The activity that contains the rule
- The artifact being checked for compliance
- The properties of the rule:

1. *Obligation:*

   The sort of rule obligations are taken from the PS-005 classification:

   1.1. *Mandatory*: Usually defined by "shall", "must", "have to be", "is to be", "is". These rules must be followed without exception.

   1.2. *Recommended*: Usually defined by "should". Generate a warning when not followed.

   1.3. *Guidelines*: Usually defined by "may" or "could".

2. *Automation:*

   This classification is only used as an additional help. So far, there is no automation provided.

   2.1. *Automatic*: The name of the software tool to be activated and the parameters to be checked must be defined.

   2.2. *Semi-automatic.*

   2.3. *Manual checklist.*

3. *System Type*:

   This classification is not much used in the system yet. It is designed with the intention to hold in other standards.

The extraction of the rules from the informal definition described in the standards is a burdensome task. The "rules" are essential for defining a rank for the standard compliance.

Explanations (Rationale). The explanations have to be separated from the regulations in the original text but the link between an explanation and its rationale must be preserved.

Artifact Flow. The artifact-flow is essential to construct the process model. It can be straightforwardly extracted from GD 250, ESA-PSS05 and IEEE 1074. The process model can be illustrated in a matrix form as in Table 8 or in a graphical form with the graph visualization tool daVinci [FW94].

GD 250 V-Model	ESA-PSS05	ISO 12207	IEEE 1074
D: "Product Flow"	D: "Inputs to the Phase" D: "Outputs from the Phase"	I: "Activities" I: "Tasks"	D: "Input Information" D: "Output Information"
160	47	74	65

***Table** 7: Artifact Flow*

The ISO 12207 is a particular standard because it sets the practices to construct a software life cycle. Although it claims not to be a lifecycle it is possible the define the "meta-process" of this standard which is a process itself. For example it is possible to reconstruct the following artifact flow from the text of the activity 5.3.7.2 "The developer shall test each software unit and database ensuring that it satisfies the requirements. The test results shall be documented":

From		Artifact	To	
Activity	State		Activity	State
5.3.7.1*	Not tested	SW unit	5.3.7.5*	Tested
5.3.7.1*	Not tested	Database	5.3.7.5*	Tested
5.3.4.2*	Approved	Requirements Document	-	-
-	-	Test Results Document	5.3.7.5*	Submitted

* Information was extracted indirectly from the description of other activities.

Table 8: *Artifact flow for the ISO 12207 - 5.3.7.2*

Artifacts. Three sorts of artifacts can be produced by enacting the activities defined in the standards: documents, software/hardware products and process lifecycles (IEEE 1074). Although the last two artifacts are mentioned in the standards, they are not easily extracted from the content or the regulations. For example, to select the practices that shall be conducted for a software/hardware unit the user has to review all of them. Table 9 identifies the form for collecting the information about the artifacts and the number of them.

Table 9: *Documents*

The ISO 12207 is not intended to prescribe the name, format, or explicit content of the documentation to be produced. It may require development of documents of similar class or type. However, it does not imply that such documents be developed or packaged separately or combined in some fashion

The IEEE 1074 is not projected to be a software lifecycle model (SLCM). Rather, it describes the practices in order to select and adapt an SLCM. In this context, the Input Information matrices and Output Information matrices provides information on what should be documented but do not specify how.

Glossary and acronyms are indirect explanations and rationale for the regulations.

GD 250 V-Model	ESA-PSS05	ISO 12207	IEEE 1074
D: "Appendix A: Definitions"	D: "Appendix A: Glossary-List of Terms"	D: "Section 3 "Definitions"	D: "1.3.1 Definitions"
109	37 + reference to other standards	37	31 + reference to other standards

Table 10: Glossary

GD 250 V-Model	ESA-PSS05	ISO 12207	IEEE 1074
D: "Appendix B1: List of Abbreviations"	D: "Appendix A: Glossary-List of Acronyms"	none	D: "1.3.2 Acronyms"
64	43	0	11

Table 11: Acronyms

Experience Library. The experience library is not contained in the standards. Rather, it is a collection of "experiences" well-organized in order to provide various kinds of assistance for the process participants. In GDPA the experience library includes:

- The e-mails sent to the GD 250 mailing list (ca. 400)
- The publications which are a substantial reference to the standard (ca. 800)
- Projects and products which apply or automate the standard (ca. 200)
- General directories and catalogues (ca. 2000)
- Other ad-hoc information

Methods and Methods Rules. Methods, methodologies or techniques that help to enact the activities defined in the model. In GDPA, the standard GD251 "Methods Allocations" [GD251] was the basis for the data collection. Circa 140 methods were identified. The repository of methods is independent of the standard being applied.

Tools and Tool Rules. Tools implement one or a set of methods, methodologies or techniques that may be used to enact activities. In GDPA only the functional requirements for software tools are considered and not the tools themselves. These requirements are taken from the standard GD 252: "Functional Tool Requirements" [GD252]. The repository of tools is independent of the standard being applied.

LIFECYCLE PROCESS MODEL "V-MODEL"
SD - System Development
SD 1.1: Recording of Actual Status and Analysis

SE1.1 - Ist-Aufnahme/-Analyse durchführen

▸ Contents
- Product Flow
- Handling
- Explanation
- Recommendation
- Roles
- Methods
- Tools Requirements
- External Norms
- Pre-Tailoring forms
- Links to the V-Model Mailinglist

▸ Product Flow

From			Product		to		Methods	Tool Req	Ext. Norms
Activity/State	Chapter		Title		Activity	State			
External	-	All	External Specifications (customer)						
-	-	2	User Requirements, Actual Status and Current Analysis		SD1.2 SD1.3 SD1.4 SD1.5 SD1.5	being proc	COM DFM ER FCTD UCM	SSD06 SSD08 SSD22 SSD25 SSD29	ISO IEC 12207/ Acquis. Proc. - Initiation

*Chapter are extra columns from the original printed version of GD 250

▸ Handling

The recording of actual status and analysis concentrates on the user-level part. Within the scope of this activity, information about the actual state has to be obtained, analyzed, and documented.

▸ Explanation

This is where an organizational analysis can be realized. The following aspects must be considered in an organizational analysis:
- Preparation of organizational analysis (definition of objectives/performance of user-level tasks and analysis depth, generation of corresponding documents for workshops or questionnaires for interviews);
- Integrating business processes (main and partial business processes have to be separated, interfaces between processes must be defined, business processes must be mapped to an actual state model);
- analysis of business processes (actual state model must be evaluated by including the persons in charge of business processes, weak points, e. g. redundancies, delays and the corresponding causes have to be found out. In a very complex business processes a simulation of the actual state model may be helpful for the evaluation.);
- evaluation of analysis results (suggestions for improvements must be collected and prioritized, possibilities for IT support, etc., are to be found out).

▸ Recommendation

An organizational analysis should be taken into particular consideration when the handling of user-level tasks cannot or no longer be guaranteed without effective IT support. While doing so, the possible interactions between organizational development and realization of the corresponding IT support must be absolutely observed since setting up an optimal structure and process organization also are one of the most influential factors for the IT support of the user (e. g. required equipment of workplaces with computers, peripherals, software, network and communications facilities) and since technological improvements in the field of IT may have a direct impact on the possibilities for the organizational structure (e. g. when using process control and archivation systems).

------- The following part is an extension of the original printed version of GD 250 -------

▸ Roles

Role	Participation
Project Leader	cooperating
CM Manager	advising
CM Representative	responsible

▸ Methods

Product	Methods Allocation	Use
Chapter 2 User Requirements Actual Status and Current Analysis	COM - Class/Object Modeling [2]	Generate
	DFM - Data Flow Modeling	Generate
	ER - E/R Modeling [1]	Generate
	FCTD - Functional Decomposition	Generate
	UCM - Use Case Modeling [2]	Generate

Notes:
[1] Method ER is to be applied for information systems.
[2] The methods have to be applied in object-oriented developments.

▸ Tools Requirements

Product	Functional Tools Requirements
Chapter 2 User Requirements Actual Status and Current Analysis	SSD06 - Supporting Function Specification
	SSD08 - Supporting Information Structuring
	SSD22 - Supporting Class/Object Modeling
	SSD25 - Supporting Process Diagrams
	SSD29 - Supporting Use Case Modeling

▸ External Norms

Norm	Process	Chapter	Obs
ISO IEC 12207/Acquisition Process	Initiation	(s. Part 1 - ISO 3.2.1)	

▸ Pre-Tailoring forms

Pre-tailoring Forms	SD Products	Implementing Conditions
Small Administrative IT Projects		
Medium Administrative IT Projects		
Large Administrative IT Projects		
Small/Medium Technical-Scientific IT Projects		
Large Technical-Scientific IT Projects		
Selection, Procurement and Adjustment of Off-the-Shelf Products		

Matrix Entries:
- ■ Always required
- ▨ Always required under given circumstances
- ☐ Not required
- ℀ Description of data or database only

▸ Links to the V-Model Mailinglist

Mail 0304 - Re: Anwenderforderung zur Datenhaltung auf Ebene der SE 1.2
Mail 0301 - Re: Anwenderforderung zur Datenhaltung auf Ebene der SE 1.2

4 The Web-Based Environment

Once the information is adequately stored in the repository it is possible to construct templates to generate html files. The previous page presents the information provided for the activity sd1.1 from GD 250 (V-Model) in the Web-based environment of GDPA [Purpc99]. Table 12 maps the contents of the E-R from figure 2.

E-R element	Web-based environment
Standard	First Line
Edition	Not shown
Delivery Forms	Not shown
Tailoring Forms	"Pre-Tailoring forms"
Glossary	Hyperlinks - underlined terms as "business process"
Acronyms	Not shown
Activities	The index of activities is shown in the 2nd and 3rd lines
Regulations	Indirect in "Handling" and "Explanation"
Explanations	Indirect in " Explanation" and "Recommendation"
Artifact Flow	"Product Flow"
Software/Hardware artifacts	Not shown
Document artifacts	The chapter and title are shown in the product flow
General rules	Not shown
SW/HW rules	Not shown
Document rules	Not shown
Process rules	Not shown
Experience Library	"Links to the V-Model mailinglist" + "External norms"
Methods	"Methods"
Methods rules	Not shown
Tools	Not shown
Tools rules	"Tool Requirements"

Table 12: *Mapping E-R to the page displayed in the web-based environment*

5 Conclusions and Future Work

The meta-process for process standards described in this paper underwent a long and gradual evolution from a former draft schema three years ago. When the first public delivery of the standard GD 250 (V-Model) in the Web-based environment of GDPA took place, numerous users asked for the contents of the standard in structured "flat-files" in order to upload them to their databases. Our very first schema consisted in 3 "comma separated" text files and one MS document containing the instructions.

The idea to formalize process standards into a meta-process was strongly influenced by the chapter "meta-process" in [Warb99]. This work was concentrated in the transcription of process standards into meta-process and not in the mechanisms of controlling the instantiation of the meta-models into real-world process. This is a extremely important work which we haven't study yet. Therefore, all the standards which have been transcribed into meta-process are only displayed in web-pages and it is not possible to enact them.

The separation between "regulations" (practices) and "explanations" (rationale) was suggested in [Emme99].

Although the detailed version of the E-R model (which is not presented in this paper) is quite extensive it is not sufficient to support all the exceptions from the standards. The unique and rare conditions are simply stored in a text field.

Meanwhile only the artifact-flows might be represented in graphs with the graphical visualization tool daVinci [FW 94]. More effort should be directed to the representation of the reference model in some graphical process modeling language.

At the moment of writing this paper, only the information about GD250 is completely stored in the repository for the standard but the definitions of the rules are still not complete. Since the introduction of the "experience library" in GDPA, the usage increased drastically. Though we have not implemented any periodic mechanism to control the number of users and sort of uses of GDPA yet, a host of mails from more than 200 different companies were received since its beginning. We are working on the adaptation of the "experience library" to an experience factory [Basi93]. Currently we are adapting the trial standard for the LTSA (Learning Technology Systems Architecture) [LTSA] from for the "standards meta-process" introduced in this paper.

Formalizing the standards "regulations" into the well-defined structured "rules" permitted us to identify the similarities among the standards and provided a common framework to merge their viewpoints. Actually it was not an intended aim, but it offers a propitious environment to study how to harmonize the different standards. The automatic check of standard compliance against the "rules" haven't been implemented yet. A promising work in managing standard compliance focused on documents rules is defined in [Emme99].

If process standards were delivered by means of meta-processes, a lot of effort could be rationalized and many of the standard regulations could possibly be checked automatically.

Acknowledgements

I would like to thank the numerous users of GDPA who sent their suggestions/claims. Special thanks for the reviewers for all the valued remarks. Many indebtedness to Prof. Bernd Krieg-Brückner from Bremen University for the fruitful, harmonious, almost 4 years support and for the long hours reviewing this work. My acknowledgments to Prof. A. Finkelstein for the incentive to and observations on this paper.

References

[AQAP150] NATO AQAP-150. NATO "Quality Assurance Requirements for Software Development". March 1993.

[Basi93] V. Basili. "The experience factory and ist relationship to other improvement paradigms". In Sommerville and M. Paul (eds): 4th ESEC, LCNS 717, Springer-Verlag, 1993, 68-83.

[Emme99] W. Emmerich, A. Finkelstein, C. Montangero, S.Antonelli, S. Armenise and R. Stevens. "Managing Standards Compliance". To appear in IEEE Transactions on Software Engineering. 1999.

[FW94] Fröhlich, M., Werner, M.: The interactive Graph-Visualization System daVinci – A User Interface for Applications. Informatik Bericht Nr. 5/94, Universität Bremen, 1994. updated doc.: http://www.tzi.de/~daVinci

[GD250] General Directive 250. Development Standard for IT Systems of the Federal Republic of Germany. Process Lifecycle. June 1997.

[GD251] General Directive 251. Development Standard for IT Systems of the Federal Republic of Germany. Methods Allocation. June 1997.

[GD252] General Directive 252. Development Standard for IT Systems of the Federal Republic of Germany. Functional Tool Requirements. June 1997.

[IEEE] IEEE - Institute of Electrical Engineering. http://computer.org/, http://standards.ieee.org/catalog/olis/.

[IEEE1074] IEEE-STD 1074-1995. "IEEE Standard for Developing Software Lifecycle Processes".

[IEEE1220] IEEE-STD 1220-1994. "Trial Use Standard for Application Management of the Systems Engineering Process".

[ISO9001-3] ISO 9001-3 Quality Management and Quality Assurance Standards - Part 3: Guidelines for the application of ISO 9001 to the development, supply and maintenance of software.

[ISO12207] ISO/IEC 12207 Information Technology - Software life cycle processes. First edition, 1995-08-01. http://www.iso.ch/cate/d21208.html

[Kar98] E.W. Karlsen: The UniForM Workbench, a Higher-Order Tool Integration Framework. In: D. Hutter, W. Stephan, P. Traverso, M. Ullmann (eds.): Applied Formal Methods – FM-Trends 98. International Workshop on Current Trends in Applied Formal Methods. LNCS 1641. Springer (1999) 266-280.

[Kar99] E. Karlsen. Tool Integration in a Functional Setting. Ph.D. thesis. Bremen University, 1999.[KSW96] Kolyang, Santen, T., Wolff, B.: A Structure Preserving Encoding of Z in Isabelle/HOL. In Proc. Int'l Conf. on Theorem Proving in Higher Order Logic. LNCS 1125. Springer (1996). http://www.tzi.de/~kol/HOL-Z

[K+99] Krieg-Brückner, B., Peleska, J., Olderog, E.-R., Baer, A.: The UniForM Workbench, a Universal Development Environment for Formal Methods. In: J.M. Wing, J. Woodcock, and J. Davies (eds.): FM'99, Formal Methods. Proceedings, Vol. II. Lecture Notes in Computer Science 1709. Springer (1999) 1186-1205.

[LTSA] LTSA- Learning Technology Systems Architecture. Version 4.0, 1998-05-21. Review Copy. http://www.edutool.com/ltsa/ [L+99] C. Lüth, H. Tej, Kolyang, B. Krieg-Brückner: TAS and IsaWin: Tools for Transformational Program Development and Theorem Proving. In J.-P. Finance (ed.): Fundamental Approaches to Software Engineering (FASE'99, at ETAPS'99). LNCS 1577. Springer (1999) 239-243.

[Purp99a] C. B. Purper "Process Web-Center as a learning environment for software process standards". 2nd Asia-Pacific Web-Conference, Hong-Kong, Sept, 1999 (to appear).

[Purp99b]   C. B. Purper "A Process Web-Center". 2nd Workshop on Software Engineering over the Internet" at ICSE. Los Angeles, USA. May 17, 1999.

[Purp99c]   C. B. Purper. "An Environment to support flexibility in process standards". *Proc. SITT"99*. Aachen, 15-17 Sept, 1999 (to be published).

[PSS05]   ESA PSS-05-0 Issue 2. February 1991, Software Engineering Standards.

[TW97]   H. Tej, B. Wolff: A Corrected Failure-Divergence Model for CSP in Isabelle / HOL. *Formal Methods Europe, FME'97*. LNCS 1313, Springer (1997) 318-337.

[Warb99]   B. Warboys, Ed.. "Meta-Process". In: J.-C. Derniame, A. Kaba and D. Wastell (eds): Software Process: Principles, Methodology, Technology. Lecture Notes in Computer Science 1500. Springer Verlag. 1998.

A CMM-Based Evaluation of the V-Model 97

Viktor Schuppan[1] and Winfried Rußwurm[2]

[1] Institut für Informatik, Technische Universität München, 80290 München, Germany
Viktor.Schuppan@gmx.de
[2] Siemens AG, ZT SE 3, 81730 München, Germany
winfried.russwurm@mchp.siemens.de

Abstract. The V-Model 97 is a widely used process model in Germany and Europe. It is the development standard for IT-Systems of the Federal Republic of Germany and the basis of Austria's and Switzerland's corresponding standards. Software process assessment and improvement efforts world-wide are based on the Capability Maturity Model (CMM) for Software. We present a detailed evaluation of the V-Model 97 based on the key practices of the CMM. For each key process area of the CMM we identify the strengths and weaknesses of the V-Model 97. While project-related issues are covered well by the V-Model 97, organizational aspects leave room for improvement. The algorithm specified by the CMM Appraisal Framework sees the V-Model 97 at level 1 whereas a BOOTSTRAP-based algorithm results in a more appropriate rating of level 2.

1 Motivation

During the last 15 years different groups published – official or de-facto – standard software process models. More and more commercial software development organizations use one of these process models as the foundation of their development process. Increasingly, these organizations are faced with the need to assess and improve their development processes. Here, too, a number of standards exist. To select the appropriate standard process model, to prepare for a standardized process assessment, and to improve their development process organizations need to know the strengths and weaknesses of their process and the expected performance in an assessment. The maintainers of a standardized process model can also use this information as input for further versions of the standard.

In Germany and Europe the V-Model 97 (V-Model[1]) is a widely used process model. It is the current version of the development standard for IT-Systems of the Federal Republic of Germany. Its use is compulsory in IT-projects with the German federal administration. The Capability Maturity Model for Software (CMM), developed by the Software Engineering Institute (SEI), is the root of

---

[1] In this paper, "V-Model" is used to refer to the V-Model 97 and "CMM" is used to refer to the Capability Maturity Model for Software Version 2.0 Draft C.

most efforts for software process assessment and improvement. Many of the organizations working with the V-Model have started software process assessment and improvement efforts or are awaiting them. An evaluation of the V-Model process based on the CMM, the world's de-facto standard for software process assessments and improvements, can generate valuable input for both, users and maintainers of the V-Model.

The term "evaluation" is used instead of "assessment" throughout this paper. An assessment as defined in [1] appraises the state of the software process in an organization and is usually based on questionnaires and interviews. This evaluation determines the state of a software process as described in a set of documents without considering an organizational implementation. It is based on a mapping between the elements of a process model (the V-Model) and a reference model (the CMM). However, the purpose of both, assessment and evaluation, is the same: to identify strengths and weaknesses of a process and to generate input for improvement.

In this paper, we present a detailed evaluation of the V-Model. The evaluation is based on the practices of the CMM. We briefly describe the relevant characteristics of the V-Model and the CMM in Sect. 2. Next, in Sect. 3 we explain the approach taken for the evaluation. General aspects of the V-Model and the CMM, that are not covered by that approach, are compared in Sect. 4. Then, in Sect. 5 the strengths and weaknesses of the V-Model are identified and compliance of the V-Model with the CMM is evaluated for key process areas, key practices common to key process areas, and maturity levels. The results are validated with the CMM-based assessment procedure of Siemens AG. Finally, the results are discussed in Sect. 6 and a conclusion is drawn in Sect. 7.

The evaluation [2] was carried out in a cooperation with the Institut für Informatik (Dept. of Computer Science) at Technische Universität München and the corporate technology division of Siemens AG, Munich.

2 Background

In this section we give an introduction to the V-Model 97, the Capability Maturity Model for Software, and Siemens Process Assessments. Due to space considerations the introduction can only be brief. For additional information please refer to the literature given in the references.

2.1 The V-Model 97

The V-Model 97 [3] is the second released version of the standard for carrying out IT-projects with the German federal government authorities. Austria's IT-BVM [4] and Switzerland's HERMES [5] standards are based on the V-Model as well. Mappings to other standards (ISO 9000 family [6][7], ISO 12207 [8], MIL-STD-498 [9]) are provided. The V-Model covers software development and optional software/hardware co-development. The V-Model is available in German and English versions from the official web site of the V-Model [10].

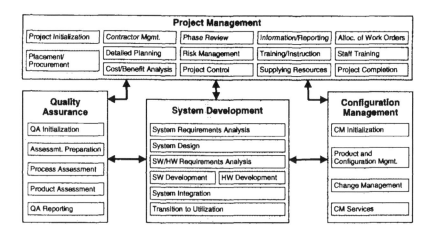

Fig. 1. Submodels and selected activities of the V-Model

The standard consists of three parts. The first part describes the *activities* to be performed and the *products* resulting from these activities. A *collection of manuals* provides information on selecting an appropriate life cycle model, process tailoring, assignment of roles, etc. The second part describes the *methods* to be used to perform the activities. *Functional tool requirements* are contained in the third part.

Activities and products are arranged in four *submodels*. Development is performed according to the submodel *system development*. Both, *quality assurance* and *configuration management* activities are grouped into submodels of their own. *Project management*-related activities and products are contained in the fourth submodel. Figure 1 shows the submodels and selected activities of the V-Model.

2.2 The Capability Maturity Model for Software

The Capability Maturity Model for Software [1] is a well-known reference model for assessing and improving the software development process. Its first version was developed by Watts Humphrey at the SEI in 1987. The latest version available is version 2.0 draft C [11]. Work on version 2.0 has been stopped to integrate several capability maturity models into a coherent framework, the Capability Maturity Model Integration (CMMI). Draft 0.2 [12] was released in August 1999. Nevertheless, CMM version 2.0 draft C is being widely used for software process assessments and improvements. Therefore, that draft was used as the basis of this evaluation.

In the CMM, five *maturity levels* characterize the *process capability* of an organization. With the exception of the first (the lowest) maturity level, a number of *key process areas* describe what is expected at a certain level. Some key process areas are concerned with organizational issues, others are relevant for individual projects. Each key process area contains several *goals*. How these goals can be reached is explained in *key practices*. The key practices are grouped into five *common features*. While some key practices are unique to the relevant key process area, others are common to most or all of the key process areas. The unique practices guide the implementation of activities to reach the goals of a key process area. The common practices are concerned with their lasting institutionalization.

2.3 Siemens Process Assessments

The importance of processes in software development was recognized early within Siemens AG. As a result a company-wide "Software Initiative" [13] was founded and Siemens corporate technology division started assessing and helping to improve the software development processes within the business units at Siemens AG. For this purpose, a standardized assessment procedure, a questionnaire, and an associated set of templates for the resulting documents were developed. Siemens Process Assessments [14] are based on the CMM and the BOOTSTRAP algorithm [15]. The focus of Siemens Process Assessments is the identification of improvement measures.

Siemens AG adapted the source models to suit its needs. For this purpose, additional questions were introduced regarding, for example, hardware development or patents. The questions are grouped into 15 process areas. Each question is assigned to a maturity level from two to five. The questions are answered and evaluated using the four-point scale and rating algorithm of the BOOTSTRAP approach.

While there is no one-to-one relationship between process areas of the Siemens Process Assessment and key process areas of the CMM, the assignment of questions to maturity levels is the same. Questions that go beyond the CMM are clearly marked.

3 Approach

The scope of this evaluation is the process as it is described in the original documentation of the V-Model [3]. Organizational implementations of the V-Model are not rated.

In most process assessments the compliance of the assessed process with some kind of reference model is investigated. Often, process assessments are based on questionnaires. These questionnaires are used as a guideline to cover the important aspects of the underlying reference model and enable an experienced assessor to come up with a qualified judgement on the strengths, weaknesses, and the maturity of the process in the assessed organization. However, there is a danger that the structure and some details of the reference model are hidden by the questionnaire. To grasp all details and retain the structure of the CMM, its key practices, and, if applicable, their sub-practices are selected as the basis for the evaluation in Sect. 5.

However, some aspects of the V-Model cannot be covered by an evaluation based on the key practices of the CMM. These are more general aspects like, for example, origin or life cycle-independence. These are compared on a qualitative basis in Sect. 4 rather than evaluated quantitatively.

In the evaluation, for each key practice or sub-practice the corresponding elements of the V-Model (i. e., activities, products, manuals, methods, and functional tool requirements) are documented. On this basis, the compliance of the V-Model with each key practice or sub-practice is rated. The original questionnaire used for assessments at the SEI employs a two-point rating scale. While two-point scales seem to have advantages in interrater agreement [16], four-point scales allow for a more detailed judgement. In assessments for selecting a contractor, interrater agreement is an important criterion. However, the focus of this assessment is on the identification of strengths and weaknesses of the V-Model. For this purpose a four-point scale seems more appropriate. Therefore, the four-point scale of the BOOTSTRAP algorithm (weak or absent $\hat{=}$ 0 %, basic or fair $\hat{=}$ 33 %, significant or strong $\hat{=}$ 67 %, extensive or complete $\hat{=}$ 100 %) is used in the rating process. Aggregated ratings are calculated as the average of the individual ratings to avoid artificial weightings.

The key practices in the CMM can be divided into two groups: those unique to a certain key process area and those common to a number of key process areas. The key practices in the "activities to perform" common feature are – with the exception of the first key practice – unique to the relevant key process area. All other key practices are common to all, the organizational or the project-related key process areas. This is used to structure the ratings of the key practices. The ratings of key practices unique to a key process area are grouped by key process area (i. e., one group per key process area). The ratings of key practices common to all key process areas are grouped by key practice (i. e., one group per key practice). This way, commonality between key process areas can be exploited in the assessment whereas their specific characteristics are preserved.

4 Comparing general aspects of the V-Model and the CMM

In this section general aspects of the V-Model and the CMM are compared qualitatively that cannot be covered by the quantitative evaluation in Sect. 5.

4.1 Origin, Approach, and Scope of Application

The first versions of both the V-Model and the CMM were created to attack time, budget, and quality problems in large military software projects. The approach taken is different. The V-Model is a prescriptive process model – contractors of the German federal administration generally have to follow that model. The CMM on the other hand is to be used as a guide for assessing government contractors. There is no binding minimum maturity level for contractors, the results of the assessment are one of several selection criteria [17].

Much supporting material is available for software process assessment and improvement with the CMM. Although the V-Model was not designed for that purpose and does not provide any support, user surveys indicate that it is being used for continuous process improvement [18].

The focus of the V-Model is an individual project. Only few organizational aspects are covered by the V-Model. The CMM focuses on project issues at level 2 but at level 3 and above organizational aspects are at least equally important.

The V-Model is an integrated process model for developing hardware/software systems. The CMM covers only software-related aspects. Other capability maturity models exist for systems development (see [19]) but are less comprehensive for software issues.

Safety and security play an important role in the V-Model. The CMM does not provide any support for these aspects. Specialized capability maturity models were created for developing security systems [20] but are separate and not in conjunction with the CMM.

4.2 Features

In the V-Model, submodels can be exchanged in part or as a whole with so-called *operative modules* described in the collection of manuals. In a reengineering project the system development submodel would probably be replaced by a submodel for reengineering. In the CMM, the exchange of key process areas might compromise the validity of the maturity level rating resulting from an assessment [21].

The descriptions of the activities and products in the V-Model are generic, i.e. they are described once but implemented as often as they are performed or produced. In the CMM key practices which are to be performed in several key process areas are described separately in each key process area. Templates are used for these descriptions. The current draft 0.2 of the CMMI makes use of generic activities.

Both models are life cycle-independent. The V-Model favors incremental development. The collection of manuals also contains information on other life cycles.

Neither the V-Model nor the CMM imply a specific organizational structure. The CMM suggests some organizational units, for example a software engineering process group.

The CMM and the V-Model define a number of roles performing the software engineering process. Only in rare cases does the CMM specify which role should perform a specific task. The concept of the V-Model is more elaborate. A separate manual assigns roles to all activities. Participation of a role can be responsible, cooperating or advising.

The CMM gives some advice on the content of work products. The V-Model specifies all products resulting from the activities including their structure and contents.

5 Results of the Evaluation

In this section the assumptions and the results of the quantitative evaluation of the V-Model are described. General aspects of both models are compared in Sect. 4.

5.1 Assumptions

External support for the V-Model is available in many ways. A change control board for the V-Model is institutionalized by the German federal authorities. A web site provides an introduction, an electronic version and a list of frequently asked questions (FAQ) on the V-Model. A mailing list answers questions not covered by the FAQ. Training and consulting is offered by various vendors. The V-Model even has a user group, called ANSSTAND e. V. [22], which, for example, organizes annual meetings to share experiences among V-Model users. But because the V-Model has no activities performing or roles responsible for process management this support is not guaranteed to take effect in an organization. Therefore, these activities are not taken into account in this evaluation.

Descriptions of activities and products in the V-Model are generic. Planning, for example, is described once but done for all activities performed in the V-Model. To avoid rating of institutionalization of activities that are not implemented properly, upper limits are defined for the ratings of common key practices. If the average rating of the unique key practices of a certain key process area is below 50 %, the common key practices are rated at most strong (67 %). If the rating of the unique key practices is less than 25 %, the rating is limited to basic (33 %).

5.2 Strengths and Weaknesses at Key Process Areas

This section lists the key findings of the evaluation grouped by key process areas. A general statement indicates strength or weakness of the V-Model with respect to a key process area. Key practices that deviate significantly in their rating from that of the key process area are stated. The detailed results can be found in [2].

Most key practices of the *requirements management* key process area are covered well by the V-Model. Weaknesses in the V-Model are reviews of requirements and of the effects of changes to the requirements by those affected.

A good correspondence between V-Model and CMM can be seen in *software project planning*. Coordination of planning, metrics, and estimates of computer resources are the only weak points in the V-Model.

Coverage of the key practices of *software project control* is split. Whereas project progress is reviewed and risks are monitored, there is no tracking of size estimates in the V-Model. Furthermore, the weaknesses of the previous key process area continue here.

In *software acquisition management*, the CMM is more detailed than the V-Model. The coverage is the weakest at level 2. There are no reviews of technical or management issues with the supplier nor periodic evaluations of the supplier's performance in the V-Model.

A separate submodel results in good coverage of *software quality assurance* in the V-Model. The products and methods of the V-Model go beyond the CMM. However, no regulations for resolving deviations in the performance of activities exist in the V-Model. In addition, deviations detected during product or process assurance activities that cannot be resolved locally are not escalated.

For *software configuration management* there is a separate submodel in the V-Model as well. Apart from software configuration management audits, the V-Model shows no weaknesses here. The rating is second-best of all key process areas.

Organization process focus is weak in the V-Model. There are no software process assessment or improvement activities nor an organizational learning process. Only the deployment of software process assets is covered to some extent.

Some of the sub-practices in the *organization process definition* key process area are concerned with activities for creating and managing a process model. The V-Model is the result of such activities but that process itself is not covered in the V-Model. Therefore, only those sub-practices for which the coverage can be determined by inspecting the result of the process can be fulfilled by the V-Model. The key practices regarding the organization's process model, software life cycles, and process tailoring are moderately covered. A software measurement database and a library with software process related documentation are mentioned in the functional tool requirements of the V-Model but no detailed regulations are found.

In the V-Model there is only one activity related to the *organization training program* key process area. Training is provided as needed by the project team but training requirements for roles do not exist. Additional, more advanced criteria of the CMM are not fulfilled.

The key practices regarding the project's software process and project risks in the *integrated software management* key process area are covered well by the V-Model. In contrast, coordination of the project with the rest of the organization is weak, as is management of training project staff.

Software product engineering is performed in the system development submodel (with some complements in the quality assurance and configuration management submodels). CMM and V-Model match well in the early phases. Later, both models have some weaknesses. The V-Model gives no details on user documentation and product support is only mentioned briefly while the CMM does not state integration as a separate task.

V-Model and CMM have different views on *project interface coordination*. The scope of the V-Model is the project as a whole whereas the CMM sees itself as the software part of a larger project. Therefore, the CMM emphasizes coordination and communication aspects where the V-Model provides little guidance. This leads to a weak coverage in this key process area.

Peer reviews are among the most important quality assurance methods in the V-Model. The result is the best rating of all key process areas.

Although the V-Model provides some support for reuse the CMM goes far beyond that in the *organization software asset commonality* key process area. Reuse of components is considered in the system architecture in the V-Model's system engineering submodel. However, there are neither activities for evaluation of the components on their potential for reuse nor for feedback on the use of common software assets.

In the V-Model, basic metrics on effort, schedule, cost, errors, and changes are collected. But no advanced metrics are derived and no quantitative models of process performance are built. Accordingly, the rating of the *organization process performance* key process area is relatively poor.

In this key process area the CMM expects the use of the data and models of the previous key process area for *statistical process management.* The weaknesses of the previous key process area continue here. Process management is performed only as a comparison between planned and actual figures. Historical data or quantitative models are not used. The rating of this key process area is slightly better than that of the previous one.

Defect prevention is performed regularly in the quality assurance submodel of the V-Model. But because the translation of suggestions into practice is not required by the V-Model, the analyses might have no effect. Furthermore, the effects of measures are not tracked.

Neither *organization process & technology innovation* nor *organization improvement deployment* are covered by the V-Model.

Figure 2 illustrates the average ratings of the V-Model for the unique key practices of each key process area.

5.3   Strengths and Weaknesses at Common Key Practices

This section lists the key findings of the evaluation grouped by common key practices. Again, a general statement indicates strength or weakness of the V-Model; key process areas that deviate significantly in their rating are stated. For details please refer to [2].

In general, no *policies* are given in the V-Model as are required by the CMM for each key process area. Only in rare cases can products fulfill some of the relevant criteria.

Sponsorship only applies to organizational key process areas. The V-Model does not contain any corresponding regulations.

Activities which are prescribed by the V-Model are also *planned.* Therefore, this key practice is usually covered as far as the coverage of the specific key practices of the relevant key process area allows for (cf. Sect. 5.1).

Funding, people, and tools are provided for the activities in the V-Model. As a result, the requirements of the *resources* key practice are fulfilled as far as possible.

The same applies for the assignment of *responsibilities.* The V-Model has a separate manual detailing the assignment of roles to activities. Project members are assigned to their roles during project planning.

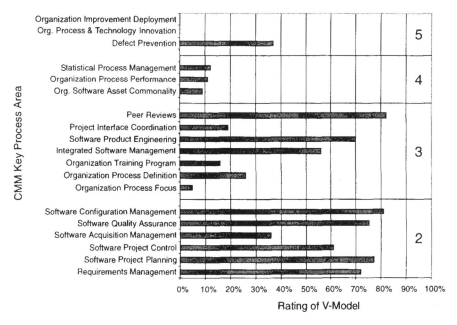

Fig. 2. Average ratings of the V-Model for the unique key practices grouped by key process areas

Training is provided as needed by the project members. No required training is defined.

A *perform* key practice emphasizes the practical implementation of each key process area. As stated in Sect. 3, this key practice is not rated.

Basic metrics to gain *insight* into the process performance are collected and analyzed with simple tools in the V-Model. However, because of its well-designed structure the V-Model is ideally suited for the introduction of additional metrics and analysis methods.

How *process assurance* is done is assessed in the software quality assurance key process area. What activities are subject to process assurance is stated in this key practice. In the V-Model, process assurance is mandatory only in rare cases. The requirements of the CMM are not fulfilled here, but this could be changed easily.

A further key practice states what products should undergo *product assurance*. While for products of the system engineering submodel quality assurance is obligatory, it is optional for most other products in the V-Model. Therefore, the rating here is not as good as it could be.

Senior management reviews and *project manager reviews* are held in the V-Model. The project is assessed technically and economically. Not covered are conflicts and issues escalated and appropriate corrective action.

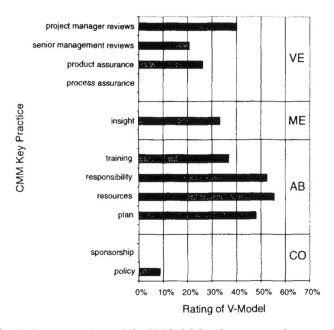

Fig. 3. Average ratings of the V-Model for the common key practices

Figure 3 illustrates the average ratings of the V-Model for the key practices common to several key process areas. The perform key practice is not rated and, therefore, not shown in the figure.

5.4 Aggregation into Ratings for Maturity Levels

By aggregation of the ratings of all key process areas in each maturity level we can obtain ratings for the maturity levels of the CMM. At level 2, 62 % of the criteria of the CMM are fulfilled by the V-Model. At level 3 the rating is 32 %. Level 4 is weakest at 10 % with level 5 being slightly better at 12 %. The ratings of the V-Model for the maturity levels are shown in Fig. 4.

The algorithm for calculating the overall maturity level of a process specified by the SEI in the CMM Appraisal Framework (CAF) [23] is rather strict. To reach a certain maturity level, the goals of the key process areas at that and all lower levels must be satisfied. As the V-Model shows weaknesses at level 2 (for example, in the software acquisition management key process area) it is rated a level 1 process by this algorithm.

5.5 Validating the Results with the Siemens Process Assessment

For the validation of the results obtained by rating the key practices of the CMM, all questions of the questionnaire used for Siemens Process Assessments which relate directly to the CMM are answered for the V-Model. Additional

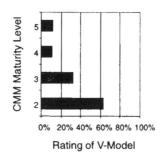

Fig. 4. Ratings of the V-Model for the maturity levels

questions specific for the Siemens approach (regarding, for example, hardware development or patents) are not rated and thus do not influence the results. The questions were rated and evaluated using the four-point scale and rating algorithm of the BOOTSTRAP approach.

As stated in Sect. 2.3 there is no one-to-one relationship between process areas of Siemens Process Assessments and key process areas of the CMM. Therefore, the ratings of the process areas are not given here. However, the assignment of questions to maturity levels is the same as in the CMM. Here, a comparison makes sense.

The results are encouraging. In general, the same strengths and weaknesses are identified in the V-Model. Moreover, the aggregated ratings of the maturity levels correlate well with those stated in Sect. 5.4. At level 2 the rating is 68 %. At level 3 it goes down to 38 %. Level 4 is weakest again at 8 % and level 5 is at 11 %.

The BOOTSTRAP-based algorithm used for Siemens Process Assessments gives an overall maturity level of 2 for the V-Model.

6 Discussion

The V-Model was created as a development standard for individual projects. Separate submodels for system development, quality assurance, configuration management, and project management are provided.

Accordingly, here are the strengths of the V-Model. In the CMM key process areas requirements management, software project planning, software project control, software quality assurance, software configuration management, integrated software management, and software product engineering the V-Model can achieve ratings above 50 %, often above 70 %. Reviews are rated best at more than 80 %.

Among the project-related key process areas at levels 2 and 3 of the CMM, only software acquisition management and project interface coordination are weak.

Organizational aspects are hardly covered by the V-Model. The reason is that the V-Model was designed to be included in contracts for projects and not as a process model for an organization.

Having said this, external support for some organizational issues is available (see Sect. 5.1). If the V-Model included a role and activities for process management in an organization, the external support would be guaranteed to take effect in the organization and ratings in the organization process focus and organizational process definition key process areas would improve.

Other organizational issues like training, reuse or quantitative modeling of processes require more effort for improvement in the organization.

The focus on projects is reflected in the ratings of maturity levels as well. Level 2 of the CMM contains project-related key process areas only. The V-Model can fulfill more than 60 % of the requirements. At level 3 focus shifts to a coherent standard process for the organization with the projects tailoring that standard process according to their needs. Here, the V-Model is rated only slightly above 30 % but with good potential for improvement. Statistical process control is the main theme at level 4 of the CMM. While the V-Model does not use metrics extensively its structure is well suited for that purpose. Quantitatively controlled process improvement which is the level 5 focus of the CMM is not covered at all by the V-Model. The non-zero rating of level 5 results only from the defect prevention key process area.

The algorithm of the CAF rates the V-Model a level 1 process. The CMM characterizes a level 1 process as being "ad-hoc" and "chaotic" with few processes defined and project success depending on individual project members [1].

Carrying out a project according to the V-Model should ensure a smooth running with repeatable success. At DaimlerChrysler Aerospace, Defense and Civil Systems division, an integrated development process based on the V-Model was introduced in cooperation with Siemens corporate technology division. All four piloting projects were in time and below budget. A positive return on investment is expected in the second year of the improvement project [24].

However, it is not guaranteed by the V-Model as is that this success is taken to the organizational level. This is the typical characteristic of a level 2 process.

Therefore, the level 2 rating calculated by the BOOTSTRAP-based algorithm of the Siemens Process Assessment seems to be more adequate than that of the CMM Appraisal Framework.

This confirms earlier results [25] of a less detailed evaluation of the V-Model 92 with a questionnaire based on version 1 of the CMM.

7 Conclusion

The V-Model provides a strong basis for carrying out software development projects but leaves much room for improvement in organizational aspects. Although CMM and V-Model have different cultural backgrounds, there are no regulations in the V-Model contrary to the CMM.

Siemens AG plans to specify modifications to the V-Model based on these results. These modifications could be included in organizational implementations of the V-Model or might even find their way into a future version of the standard V-Model. This would be one step further on the way to making the V-Model a CMM-compliant process.

8 Acknowledgements

The first author's research was sponsored by Siemens AG. He wishes to thank the department members of ZT SE 3 for their support.

References

1. Paulk, M., Weber, C., Curtis, B., Chrissis, M. (eds.): The Capability Maturity Model: Guidelines for Improving the Software Process. Addison-Wesley Publishing Company, Reading, Massachusetts, 1995
2. Schuppan, V.: Das V-Modell 97 als Softwareentwicklungsprozeß aus der Sicht des Capability Maturity Models (CMM) für Software. Master's thesis. Institut für Informatik, Technische Universität München, Munich, August 16, 1999
3. Bundesministerium des Inneren, Koordinierungs- und Beratungsstelle der Bundesregierung für Informationstechnik in der Bundesverwaltung (ed.): Entwicklungsstandard für IT-Systeme des Bundes. Bonn, June 1997
4. Freitter, Michael: Bundesvorgehensmodell IT-BVM Vorgehensmodell für die Entwicklung von IT-Systemen des Bundes Version 1.0. Available in Internet: URL: http://www.bv-modell.at/set_info.htm [as of September 15, 1999]
5. Bundesamt für Informatik: HERMES Führung und Abwicklung von Informatikprojekten Ausgabe 1995. Bern, 1995
6. International Organization for Standardization: International Standard ISO 9001 Quality systems – Model for quality assurance in design, development, production, installation and servicing. ISO Copyright Office, Geneve, 1994
7. International Organization for Standardization: International Standard ISO 9000-3 Quality management and quality assurance standards – *Part 3:* Guidelines for the application of ISO 9001:1994 to the development, supply, installation and maintenance of computer software. ISO Copyright Office, Geneve, 1994
8. International Organization for Standardization; International Electrotechnical Commission: International Standard ISO/IEC 12207 Information technology – Software life cycle processes. ISO/IEC Copyright Office, Geneve, 1995
9. Department of Defense: Military Standard: Software Development and Documentation MIL-STD-498. US Department of Defense, 5 December 1994
10. IABG: Das V-Modell. In Internet: URL: http://www.v-modell.iabg.de/ [as of September 15, 1999]
11. Software Engineering Institute: Draft C of the Software Capability Maturity Model (SW-CMM) v2.0. Software Engineering Institute, Carnegie Mellon University, Pittsburgh, Pennsylvania, October 22, 1997. Available in Internet: URL: http://www.sei.cmu.edu/cmm/draft-c/c.html [as of September 15, 1999]
12. Software Engineering Institute: Capability Maturity Model – Integrated – Systems/Software Engineering CMMI-SE/SW Staged Representation Version 0.2. Software Engineering Institute, Carnegie Mellon University, Pittsburgh, Pennsylvania, August 31, 1999

13. Gonauser, M., Paulisch, F., Völker, A.: Siemens' Experience with People / Process / Technology: Lessons Learned. In: Proceedings of The third annual Software Engineering Process Group Conference 1998 (European SEPG '98), London, United Kingdom, June 8–11, 1998.

14. Mehner, T., Messer, T., Paul, P., Paulisch, F., Schless, P., Völker, A.: Siemens Process Assessment and Improvement Approaches: Experiences and Benefits. In: Proceedings of The Twenty-Second Annual International Computer Software & Applications Conference (Compsac 98), Vienna, Austria, August 19–21, 1998. IEEE Computer Society, Los Alamitos, California, 1998

15. Haase, V., Messnarz, R., Cachia, R.: Software Process Improvement by Measurement BOOTSTRAP/ESPRIT Project 5441. In: Mittermeir, R. (ed.): Shifting Paradigms in Software Engineering, Proceedings of the 7th Joint Conference of the Austrian Computer Society (OCG) and the John von Neumann Society for Computing Sciences (NJSZT), Klagenfurt, Austria, 1992, pp. 32–41. Springer Verlag, Wien, 1992

16. El Emam, K., Briand, L., Smith, B.: Assessor Agreement in Rating SPICE Processes. European Software Institute, July 1, 1996

17. Newberry, G.: The Relationship Between the SEI's CMM Levels and Source Selection. In: CrossTalk 9 (1996) 5

18. Steinmann, C.: Verwendung des V-Modells (387). Mail to the V-Model mailing list, July 26, 1999. Archived in Internet: URL: http://www.v-modell.iabg.de/maillst.htm [as of September 15, 1999]

19. Bate, R., Kuhn, D., Wells, C. et al.: A Systems Engineering Capability Maturity Model, Version 1.1. CMU/SEI-95-MM-003. Software Engineering Institute, Carnegie Mellon University, Pittsburgh, Pennsylvania, 1995

20. Members of the SSE-CMM project team: Systems Security Engineering Capability Maturity Model SSE-CMM Model Description Document, Version 2.0, April 1, 1999. Available in Internet: URL: http://www.sse-cmm.org/SSEdocs/TheModel/SSECMMv2Final.pdf [as of September 15, 1999]

21. Paulk, M.: Questions and Answers on the CMM Issue #1, April 5, 1994. Available in Internet: URL: http://www.sei.cmu.edu/activities/cmm/docs/q-and-a.1.html [as of September 15, 1999]

22. ANSSTAND: ANSSTAND e. V. Homepage. In Internet: URL: http://www.ansstand.de/ [as of September 15, 1999]

23. Masters, S., Bothwell, C.: CMM Appraisal Framework, Version 1.0. Technical Report, CMU/SEI-95-TR-001. Software Engineering Institute, Carnegie Mellon University, Pittsburgh, Pennsylvania, 1995

24. Rußwurm, W., Kranz, W.: An Integrated System Development Process for Software, Hardware, and Logistics: Definition, Implementation, and Experiences. In: Proceedings of The European Conference on Software Process Improvement (SPI 99), Barcelona, Spain, November 30–December 3, 1999

25. Ehlting, J.: Konformität des V-Modells der Bundesbehörden mit den Prinzipien des Total Quality Management Konzeptes in der Softwareentwicklung unter Einbeziehung des CMM. Master's thesis. Universität zu Köln, Cologne, 1994

Overcoming Inadequacies in Process Modelling: The Need for Decisioning Be a First-Class Citizen

F. Oquendo[1], K.N. Papamichail[2] and I. Robertson[2]

[1]School of Engineering, University of Savoie at Annecy, France
oquendo@esia.univ-savoie.fr
[2]Department of Computer Science, University of Manchester, Manchester, M13 9PL, U.K.
{nadia, ir}@cs.man.ac.uk

Abstract. Process modelling is a way of analysing, describing and enacting the behaviour of processes. A behaviour that process modelling fails to address is that of decision making. Despite the importance of organisational decisions, process modelling languages do not provide any semantics for expressing decision-making aspects such as the identification of alternatives and the handling of uncertainty. This paper proposes an approach, drawing on ideas from decision analysis, to enhance process modelling in the support of decision making. A decision-analysis process model is used to demonstrate the applicability of the approach.

1 Introduction

Process modelling is a way of capturing and studying the behaviour of software processes for analysis and enaction. It is based on concepts such as goals, activities, agents, control flow and data flow [1][2]. For example, agents in an organisation assume roles, interact with software tools or other agents and carry out activities to fulfil their goals.

The adoption of software process technologies (SPT) has been disappointing, and as yet no clear reason has emerged as to why this should be [3]. One possibility is that enactment systems may not, as yet, provide complete support for process participants. An early definition of enactment referred to 'symbiosis between human being and computer' [4]. Current enactment systems are far from this ideal, and this is reflected in a contemporary definition of enactment as 'the act of interpreting and executing an enactable process' [5].

There are a number of behaviours (known as tacit behaviours [6]), which occur on an organisational basis and on an individual basis, that are not well supported by SPT - learning is one, decision making another. This paper will focus on the latter. In the context of software engineering, decisions range from individual decisions on a bug-fix strategy, to decisions relating to the evolution of software systems. Even though decision making, or simply decisioning can be viewed as being as important as activities, the process-modelling community has largely overlooked them.

Contemporary process modelling languages (PMLs) do little to support decision making. Alternative activities need to be hard coded with the model definition and no mechanisms for the automatic generation of appropriate options are available. This is very restrictive in dynamic environments where alternatives can be identified only during process model enaction. Another limitation of process modelling is its assumption that organisational activities have deterministic consequences, when in fact activities may lead to different or uncertain outcomes and this should be taken into account when deciding among two or more alternatives.

Process modelling currently supports only a few aspects of decisioning and uncertainty. The solution, now proposed, is to employ 'decision analysis' to enhance the capabilities of process modelling. Decision analysis [7] is the discipline of assisting decision makers in solving complex decision problems. It can be used to extend the semantics of a process modelling language to support decisioning. Decisioning could therefore be represented as a first-class citizen of the modelling language, to be used wherever process participants individually or collectively have to make decisions in the course of their work.

2   Decision Analysis

Decision analysis is the discipline of evaluating alternatives in light of uncertainty, value preferences and risk preferences [8][9]. One of the main advantages of decision analysis is its ability to replace complex problems with simpler ones. It provides insight into the decision problem at hand by helping the decision makers identify the best alternatives.

The need for taking a decision arises when there are at least two alternative solutions to a problem. Various alternatives can lead to different outcomes or consequences. Real-life decisions usually involve uncertainty about what the outcome of each alternative will be.

Decision making can be decomposed into the following phases (but note that the dependency between them is not simply temporal) [10][11]:

- Formulate a decision model for the decision problem. This involves the identification of alternatives and the expression of objectives.
- Appraise the decision model. This stage allows the decision makers to gain insight into the decision problem by interpreting the decision model or the results of the decision analysis.
- Evaluate the decision model. This requires the computation of the outcomes and the evaluation of the alternatives based on the preferences of the decision makers and the inherent uncertainties of the decision problem.
- Refine the decision model. A feedback or refinement path is provided to give the opportunity to the decision makers to refine their preferences.

3 Position

In process modelling, 'activities' are generally taken to be units of work that have definable start states and end states, inputs and outputs. They are usually capable of being supported by a straightforward user interface - a form for completion, a word processor for editing a document, a tool for implementing a design in software, etc. PML designers have generally excluded behaviours that do not conform to this template.

A behaviour that often arises in both the individual and co-operative work undertaken in software development is decisioning. By glossing over the essence of the decision-making behaviour, process modellers are failing to address one of the core issues that cause difficulties in organisations: the problem of having to make the best decisions, often in inadequate time frames and with inadequate information. And in failing to address such an issue, the modelling activity is relegated to dealing with relatively simple processes that are sequential, uncontroversial, and are undertaken by clerical staff. High-level and possibly higher-value processes are not seen as candidates for support.

There is a need to address this problem. We propose that decisioning needs to be represented as a first-class citizen in our modelling formalisms and enactment systems. By this we mean that we should be able to support the way of taking a decision about x in context y just as simply as we can represent the activity of doing x in process y.

Our position is that doing and decisioning are normally interleaved. The reason is simple: there is no point in hard-coding choices because the nature of organisational processes is such that in many cases it is not possible to foresee all possible outcomes. Events can occur while executing early activities that make the hard-coded choices for later activities inadequate or unacceptable.

Because there is no concept of decisioning in current PMLs, process models contain ad hoc choice activities, which are hard coded using conditional control flow constructs. In other words, between activities that actually accomplish process steps there are crude activities whose only function is to support selection among alternative possible outcomes that have to be hard coded.

Our idea is to let the process engine interleave doing and decisioning. Of course this framework will provide support for straightforward low-level decisions (such as those provided by current PMLs) as well as for more high-level and complex decisions (currently lacking in process technology).

The concept of decisioning thereby becomes a first-class citizen of the process modelling formalism, as is the concept of doing (activity) in contemporary PMLs.

As an example of this notion, consider a simple process model with some defined pattern of activities and in the course of enaction. On encountering an activity whose outputs will influence the pattern of subsequent activities, the system will 'escape' to a different level containing an instantiated model of the decision-making behaviours. This model is then enacted, and the outputs will define the pattern of subsequent activities in the original model, and also implement them at the original level. Enaction then passes back to that level, and the original process continues using its new definition to conclusion.

4 Proposal

This notion has been encapsulated in a new architecture represented in Fig. 1, known as 'Decisioning for Decision Support in Processes' (D2P). Influenced by earlier work on the meta-process [12], this represents the separation of concerns between the enacting operational process (the process that achieves the organisational goals) and the (also enactable) decisioning behaviour that is intended to support decision-making activity. Under normal conditions, the enacting process is executing at the Doing level. When a problem arises, the Decisioning model is instantiated at a higher level and the execution at the Doing level halts. After the new pattern of subsequent activities is implemented at the Doing level, Decisioning is terminated and execution passes back to the Doing level.

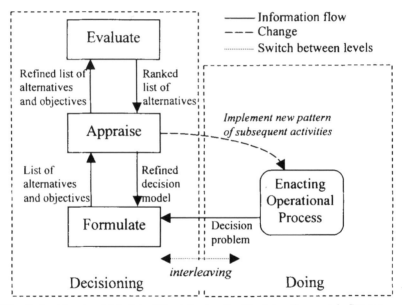

Fig. 1. Architectural Model of Decisioning for Decision Support in Processes

The Decisioning behaviour supports the phases identified in section 2. In Formulate, the decision model is formulated and a list of alternatives and objectives is passed to Appraise. Appraise refines the list and sends it to Evaluate. Evaluate has access to a library of methods for the ranking of the alternatives. A suitable method is selected based on the constraints and requirements of the decision problem at hand. The alternatives are ranked - taking into account the objectives and their importance - and sent back to Appraise. In Appraise there are two options: either the decision maker is happy with the ranking of the alternatives and is able to choose one, or the decision maker is not satisfied with the evaluation process and wants to reformulate the decision model. In the former case, Appraise implements the activities associated with the most preferred alternative and in the latter, a refined decision model is passed as feedback to Formulate for re-formulation. The phase of 'refining the decision model' is supported through this feedback loop between Appraise and Formulate.

In order to validate the D2P it is intended to define an experiment, which will involve the modelling of an operational process from industry and implementation of D2P. The implementation language at both levels will be the same i.e. Process Model Language [2] and the models will be supported by ProcessWeb [13], which is a process support system.

The operational process will be selected from an industry-based case study, known as 'Hood and Headlights'. It is typical of the 'lack of fit' problem that often arises in the design of assemblages. This example relates to the motor industry and deals with the resolution of a problem where an integration test reveals a conflict between the shape of a motor car hood design and the design for the headlights.

When the conflict is revealed, a separate process is initiated in the organisation that identifies existing and possibly new alternative processes for solving the problem. These alternatives have to be evaluated with respect to impact and risk. The evaluated alternatives are appraised and a proposal for a process to reconcile the difference is made. This process is initiated, and, when its execution is completed, the conflict will have been reconciled.

The integration activity will be modelled as part of the body design process (the operational process), and supported by an instance of the body design process model which is the Enacting Organisational process referred to in Fig. 1. When the conflict is revealed, the D2P will be instantiated, suitably parameterised for the problem and its context. The D2P will be enacted, eventually returning a process model fragment (providing a new pattern of subsequent activities) to be implemented (i.e. compiled into the instance of the Enacting Operational Process Model).

It is intended that this approach will be evaluated by a panel of industry experts in the Process Instance Evolution (PIE)[1] project. Many of the concerns of software process modelling are shared by the wider business community [14] and it is anticipated that the results will be of value in both domains.

5   Conclusions

There has been little debate about what we mean by the term 'support', but lack of acceptance of SPT in the wider community suggests that the facilities provided for certain common organisational behaviours such as decisioning are inadequate. Decisioning has to be integrated in some way into the modelling formalism and into the enactment system so that non-technical professionals (such as managers) will be able to use them and, by so doing, to have their work quality and performance improved. Of course it may be that other concepts may need to be supported by enactment systems if the goal of widespread and effective support of software processes is to be attained.

---

[1] Esprit Long Term Research Project 34840, http://www.cs.man.ac.uk/ipg/pie/pie-e.html

6 References

[1] Alloui, I., Cimpan, S., Oquendo, F. and Verjus, H.: Alliance: An Agent-Based CASE Environment for Enterprise Process Modelling, Enactment and Quantitative Control. Proc. 1st International Conference on Enterprise Information Systems (ICEIS'99), Setubal, Portugal (1999)

[2] Bruynooghe, R.F., Greenwood, R.M., Robertson, I., Sa, J., Warboys, B.C.: PADM: Towards a Total Process Modelling System. In Finklestein, A., Kramer, J. and Nuseibeh, B. (eds.): Software Process Modelling and Technology. Research Studies Press Ltd., Taunton, UK (1994)

[3] Software Process Automation: Interviews, Survey and Workshop Results. Technical Report CMU/SEI-97-TR-006 (1997)

[4] Armenise, P., Bandinelli, S., Ghezzi, C., Morzenty, A.: Software Process Representation Languages: Survey and Assessment. Proc 4th International Conference on Software Engineering and Knowledge Engineering, Capri (1992)

[5] Derniame, J.-C., Kaba B.A., Wastell D. (eds.): Software Process Principles, Methodology, and Technology. Lecture Notes in Computer Science, Vol. 1500. Springer Verlag, Berlin Heidelberg New York (1999)

[6] Sachs P.: Transforming Work. Comms ACM 38 (9) (1995)

[7] von Winterfeldt, D. and Edwards, W.: Decision Analysis and Behavioral Research. Cambridge University Press, New York (1986)

[8] Keeney, R.L. and Raiffa, H.: Decisions with Multiple Objectives: Preferences and Value Tradeoffs. Willey, New York (1976)

[9] Watson, S.R. and Buede, D.M.: Decision Synthesis - The Principles and Practice of Decision Analysis. Cambridge University Press (1987)

[10] Holtzman, S.: Intelligent Decision Systems. Addison-Wesley, Reading (1989)

[11] French, S.: The Process of Decision Analysis. Lecture Notes, Management Business School (1999)

[12] Warboys, B.C. (ed): Meta-Process. in [5] 53-93

[13] Greenwood, R.M. and Warboys, B.C.: ProcessWeb – Process Support for the World Wide Web. in C. Montangero. Proc 5th European Workshop on Software Process Technology, Lecture Notes in Computer Science, Vol. 1149. Springer Verlag, Berlin Heidelberg New York (1996)

[14] Gruhn, V. and Wolf, S.: Software Process Improvement by Business Process Orientation. Software Process - Improvement and Practice 1 (1995) 49-56

Process metrics for requirements analysis

Vincenzo Ambriola and Vincenzo Gervasi

Dipartimento di Informatica, Università di Pisa
{ambriola,gervasi}@di.unipi.it

Abstract. In this paper we propose a class of process metrics based on the continuous monitoring of product attributes. Two such metrics are defined for the requirements analysis process, namely *stability* (i.e., how smoothly the process of introducing information in a requirements document flows) and *efficiency* (i.e., which part of the effort of the analysts is spent in reworks). These measures can be used for the timely identification of risky trends in a requirements analysis process.
The paper also gives some results from an experiment on the collection and use of the measures we introduced.

Keywords: Requirements, process metrics, quantitative process evaluation.

1 Introduction

In recent years significant advancements have been made in the field of process modeling and on process-supporting technologies. However, the issue of measuring attributes of the software process has often received less attention. Classic work in this area has been mainly focused on the testing activity [4]. Test-like processes have a *reductive* nature: the goal of the process is to minimize some well-understood attribute of the product. For example, the testing process tends to the identification and removal of defects, while reducing the injection of new defects. A well-understood theory supports reasoning on such process (e.g., by using prey-predator models).

Design-like processes are different in that they exhibit an *accumulative* nature: their goal is to "grow" a product, increasing some of its attributes in the process. However, there is no optimal value for those attributes, again in contrast with the case of reductive processes. A typical example of accumulative process is the requirements elicitation and analysis activity.

It is well known [3] that requirements analysis is one of the most critical parts in the software development process: the late correction of errors in the requirements can cost orders of magnitude more than the correction of coding errors, due to the rework involved. It is thus not surprising that, from a managerial point of view, there is a strong need for some *control* on the requirements process.

Controlling a process means observing it, to obtain an understanding of the current situation; monitoring it, to follow its evolution; and providing guidance, to drive the process to the effective and efficient achievement of its proposed goals. The requirements process can be characterized as the progressive refinement of a document describing a (software-intensive) system. Consequently, it can be observed — and possibly measured — along three dimensions:

- the *document* dimension, pertaining to intrinsic attributes of the requirements document (e.g., size, structure, lexicon);
- the *system* dimension, related to the attributes of the system described in the requirements (e.g., number of components, functional score);
- the *process* dimension, that focuses on the activities involved in the production of the document (e.g., months/man spent, frequency and distribution of changes, mean time between releases).

In this paper we concentrate on those process attributes that can be measured by tracing the evolution of document and system attributes during the process. A simple example of this kind of attributes is the sampling of the document size at regular intervals during the writing process. Such a measure can be used, for example, to estimate the size of the document at some future date, or to verify if new information is being added to the document (increasing size), or rather if the information already present is being polished and structured (stable size).

2 Stability and efficiency analysis

We consider two attributes of the requirements process that are particularly interesting for the correct management of the process itself, namely *stability* (i.e., how "smooth" the analysis activity is) and *efficiency* (i.e., which part of the effort is spent on reworks). We propose a quantitative characterization of these two attributes, and then report on our experiences on their use in a case study.

2.1 Stability

While the requirements process can be ideally modelled as the progressive accumulation of information about the system to design, in practice it often has an *impulsive* behaviour. Experience shows that analysts tend to proceed in alternating phases of writing (adding new requirements) and polishing (correcting errors, restructuring descriptions). Stability is a measure of how smoothly these two phases are integrated. It is maximal for the ideal process in which information grows linearly with time, and gets worse for highly impulsive processes.

To measure stability, we first consider some measure $F(t)$ of the amount of information contained in the requirements[1] at time t. The differential measure $\delta F(t) = F(t) - F(t-1)$, defined for $t > 0$, indicates, for each instant t, the difference in information content with respect to the previous version of the

---

[1] See Section 3 for examples of such measures.

requirements. A frequency analysis (Fourier transform) of $\delta F(t)$ provides the information about the distribution and magnitude of the impulsive phenomena in the analysis activity. We can identify four classes of processes with respect to stability, according to the principal frequency components of $\delta F(t)$:

I. *low peaks on high frequencies.* Small, continuous changes; the activity is strongly incremental in nature.

II. *low peaks on low frequencies.* Small, infrequent changes; the activity proceeds by relatively minor, well spaced impulses.

III. *high peaks on low frequencies.* The activity proceeds by substantial jumps apart each from the other; the development activity is thus strongly impulsive.

IV. *high peaks on high frequencies.* Frequent modifications of relevant magnitude; the process is characterized by continuous and important upheavals.

Under the hypothesis that stable processes lead to products of predictable quality, we can expect that processes of class I (incremental) produce better requirement documents, while processes of class IV (catastrophic) end up producing documents of dubious quality[2]. Processes of class II (sleepy) and III (impulsive) can be expected to produce results of intermediate quality.

This hypothesis can be validated by independent evaluation of the results of processes of the various classes, as described in Section 3 (see also [1]).

2.2 Efficiency

The measure $F(t)$ introduced above can also be used to measure the efficiency of the analysis process. In an ideal accumulative process, every effort made by the analyst corresponds to a certain amount of information that is added to the requirements. In reality, requirements are seldom complete and correct at the first try, and a certain amount of rework is unavoidable. We can approximate the effort spent by the analyst in modifying a document by measuring the difference in information content between two successive revisions. It is worthwhile to notice that our process is *not* conservative: a certain effort is required both to increment *and* to decrement $F(t)$ (in both cases, a certain conceptual and text editing work has to be performed). In other words, there is no such thing as a "potential of information content", analogous to the potential found in conservative fields in physics.

---

[2] We use the term *dubious* here to mean that in some particular case the quality of the requirements could indeed be reasonable, but there is no way to predict the outcome beforehand: it depends almost entirely on the very last "revolution" in the document.

Formally, we can estimate the total effort spent by the analysts between revisions a and b[3] by

$$W(a, b, F) = \sum_{t=a+1}^{b} |\delta F(t)|$$

whereas the effective change in information content between a and b is simply

$$E(a, b, F) = F(b) - F(a)$$

The efficiency of the process is the ratio between the global increase in information content and the effort spent, i.e.

$$\varepsilon(a, b, F) = \frac{E(a, b, F)}{W(a, b, F)}$$

By definition, $0 \leq \varepsilon(a, b, F) \leq 1$. When the efficiency is 0, $F(a) = F(b)$ so no information was added between revisions a and b, regardless of any modification made in intermediate revisions. When the efficiency is 1, all the effort was spent in adding information content, i.e., $F(t)$ is monotonically non-decreasing in the interval $[a, b]$.

Notice that $\varepsilon(a, b, F)$ is only a measure of the efficiency of the *accumulative* component of the requirement process, and not a measure of the quality of the work made by the analysts. Indeed, a significant rework can well decrease the information content of a document while increasing its overall quality (according to some criteria). In this case, a low $\varepsilon(a, b, F)$ would indicate that the accumulative component that preceded the rework was not efficient, since the document needed a rework later, and thus part of the initial effort was lost.

It is also worthwhile to notice that this efficiency measure can only be computed *post hoc*, since there is no way to know if part of the information accumulated in the requirements up to a certain revision t_r will be removed or reworked in later revisions (thus decreasing efficiency) or will stay in place until the end of the requirements analysis activity (thus increasing efficiency). This observation leads to the conclusion that $\varepsilon(a, b, F)$ does not lend itself to a predictive use of the efficiency model; it can be used, however, to estimate the expected efficiency of further iterations of the requirements process in similar conditions — i.e., for the next project by the same team.

3 Experimental validation

To test the usefulness of the two measures we are proposing here, an experiment was set up by collecting a number of system measures on the requirements produced by 16 teams working in parallel on the same project in an academic environment. Each team was given approximately four months to do a complete

---

[3] We consider only those intervals $[a, b]$ in which some work has been done, i.e. $W(a, b, F) > 0$.

requirements analysis for a distributed weather monitoring system, followed by a design phase and by the implementation of a prototype of the system. In particular, requirements analysis was conducted with the support of our requirements engineering environment CIRCE [2, 5].

We selected four "information content" measures to use as $F(t)$, namely functional score F_f (measured in feature points [6]), behavioural complexity F_b (measured by counting decision points), static complexity F_s (measured by counting the number of entities, relationships and attributes) and document size F_d (measured by counting the number of atomic requirements). The measures were automatically computed by CIRCE's metrication modules from the documents written by the analysts. Tool support was fundamental at this stage, to guarantee repeatability of the measures and to reduce the manual effort involved in collecting the measures to almost zero.

We discovered significant evidence that the stability measure had a high predictive value: teams with unstable requirements processes invariably had to do a big amount of rework on the requirements in later stages of the development process. The efficiency measure, lacking predictive value, could only be empirically validated by interviewing the teams about their perception of how their work was spent.

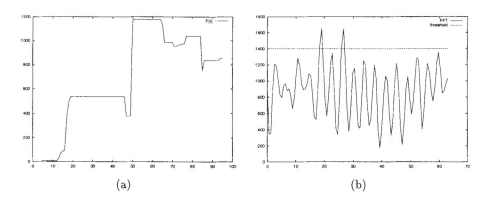

(a) (b)

Fig. 1. Stability measure: (a) functional score, (b) impulse analysis.

As an example, Figure 1(a) shows the $F_f(t)$ function (functional score of the system described by the requirements) over a three-months period for one of the teams participating in our experiment. It can be easily observed how impulsive periods of accumulation of information (e.g., around days 17–20 and 50–52) are followed by stable periods of analysis and rethinking (around days 21–47 and 51–65) and then by periods of refinement and possibly of rework (around days 48–50 and 66–68). The frequency analysis of $\delta F_f(t)$ is shown in Figure 1(b). Notice how the first two principal components (with periods around 7 days, due to the weekly rhythm of work, and around 4–5 days, originating from rework activity that can be observed on days 13–17, 47–51, 71–76 — each period being 4 or 5 days long) let us quantitatively classify this particular instance as a type III process, i.e. with substantial but well-spaced reworks.

Given this information, a project manager could well insist that sudden upheavals like those shown in Figure 1 should be avoided, and take appropriate actions to set up a more stable process instead.

4 Conclusion

Requirements writing has often been associated with high risks due to the difficulty of controlling the requirements process. The continuous sampling of product attributes provides an effective means of obtaining process metrics that can be used to control the requirements activity.

The availability of a supporting environment is an enabling factor that can drive the collection and use of metrics of this kind. Differently from traditional cases, which are based on counting process events (e.g., the number of bug reports coming back from beta testers) and on measuring times between events, our technique of projecting product attributes along the time axis requires some form of automatic support to be applicable without placing an excessive burden on the participants in the process.

Once such an automatic support is in place, however, continuous monitoring of product attributes offers marked advantages. In particular, the two measures of the accumulative component that we proposed make it possible for a project manager to identify risky or inefficient behaviour of the analysis team and to take corrective actions to ensure the timely delivery of stable requirements.

References

1. V. Ambriola, R. Di Meglio, V. Gervasi, and B. Mercurio. Applying a metric framework to the software process: an experiment. In B. C. Warboys, editor, *Proceedings of the Third European Workshop on Software Process Technology*, pages 207–226. Lecture Notes in Computer Science Nr. 772, Springer–Verlag, Feb. 1994.
2. V. Ambriola and V. Gervasi. Processing natural language requirements. In *Proceedings of ASE 1997*, pages 36–45. IEEE Press, 1997.
3. B. W. Boehm. Verifying and validating software requirements and design specifications. *IEEE Software*, 1(1):75–88, Jan. 1984.
4. N. Fenton and S. L. Pfleeger. *Software Metrics - A Rigorous and Practical Approach*. International Thomson Computer Press, London, 2 edition, 1996.
5. V. Gervasi and B. Nuseibeh. Lightweigth validation of natural language requirements. In *Proceedings of the Fourth IEEE International Conference on Requirements Engineering*, June 2000. (to be published).
6. C. Jones. *Applied Software Measurement: Assuring Productivity and Quality*. McGraw-Hill, New York, N.Y., 1991.

Software Process Technology and Software Organisations

M. Letizia Jaccheri, Reidar Conradi and Bård H. Dyrnes

Norwegian University of Science and Technology, Trondheim, Norway
letizia@idi.ntnu.no, tel: +47-73-593469 fax: +47-73-594466

Abstract. SPT which have been developed by our research community is barely used in software organisations. This paper tries to discuss the relation between software SPT and software organisations: it first describes some examples of applications to the software industry. Then it tells about an ongoing case in which we are trying to capture SPT requirements from one software organisation which is operating with its own process representation and associated tools.

1 Introduction

"So far, we have substantially failed to demonstrate that SPT is useful". [CFJ98]. This assertion will be discussed in this paper. In this work we concentrate on the subset of SPT which consists of methods and guidelines, languages and formalisms and tools to support elicitation and description of software processes. We do not focus on process enaction. We will discuss evaluation and validation experiences of languages and tools to support the description and elicitation of software processes.

Software organisations are not using SPT to support their processes. Software organisations are rather using ad hoc technical solutions to represent their software processes. These solutions include informal diagrammatic languages to express data flow among activities and connections between tasks and roles. Some organisations rely on the intra-net to represent and communicate processes.

There are several published cases, which conclude that, the examined SPT is useful [ADH94] [BFL+95] [EB94] [KH89] [BRB95] [TSK+95] [JBD99] [Ang98] [Høy97]. The common factor of these cases is that one or more researchers use some sort of SPT to support a problem that is derived from the industrial world, and they discuss the bane and benefit of such application. But still there is no evidence that industry has been convinced to adopt SPT on the basis of such cases. These papers and the process modelling community in general base the research work on the assumption that an explicit process representation is the starting point for process understanding, improvement, and communication. This is also the view shared by some improvement frameworks such as CMM.

On the other hand, some researchers from other research communities, such as the computer supported co-operative work one (CSCW), argue that creative work with strong co-operation aspects, such as software development, does not benefit from static descriptions [Sac95]. They also argue that such work descriptions, when present in organisations, are not followed. These assumptions are always based on empirical studies. The process modelling community has made some efforts to capture requirements for SPT from the observation of software organisations and projects [RKHS94]. However the main part of the research work has concentrated on development of SPT, and eventually application of such technology to the real world for evaluation. Our work in the last years also falls mainly in this last category. It is only recently that we are trying to revert to SPT requirement capture, without focusing on the technology we have developed.

This paper is structured as following: Section 2 is about five SPT validation trails that we have been performing in the last years. It also discusses the main weaknesses of our approaches. Section 3 tells about an ongoing work in which we are observing the process definition activities in a company and we try to capture the requirements toward SPT. Section 4 provides references to related work. Some conclusions are given in section 5.

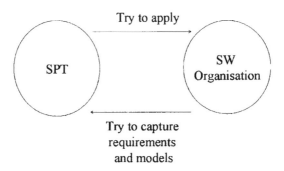

Fig. 1. On the Relationship between SPT and Software Organisations

2   Applying SPT to software organisations

Here we will give a summary of a series of attempts we have done in the last years to validate SPT. If we look at figure 1, all these cases try, in some ways, to apply SPT to organisations and to learn from these applications.

The investigative methods used in the trials can all be considered some kinds of case studies [Sta94]. Trial 1, 2, 3 and 5 were instrumental case studies since the cases were examined to provide insight into software process modelling issues. The cases played a supportive role for improving our understanding of the phenomena under investigation. Trial 4 was a collective case study, since data was collected from several organisations/cases which merely played a supportive role. The trials are all discussed according to summary, goal, and an evaluation section.

2.1 Trial 1 Iveco

Summary In 1993, when the E^3 project was started, we decided to concentrate on software process description (understanding and static analysis) and not on execution. We started by using object-oriented techniques (Coad-Yourdon) to model the software process described in a quality manual we had obtained from Iveco (a division of Fiat). From this first modelling phase we deduced the requirements for the E^3 system. After the first modelling phase, we had one meeting with the process owners. During the meeting we communicated to them the problems (mainly inconsistencies) we had found in the original description and we showed a Smalltalk simulation of the model. They seemed to like our approach, but they did not commit to use our model instead of the original description.

During the years, we have been using the Iveco process as a reference for internal benchmark [TB97] for subsequent implementations of the E^3 system. The study is documented in [JBD99]. The requirements from this case were: multiple representation levels, inheritance, process specific constructs, inspection and analysis, associations, and formal syntax and semantics.

Goal Our goal was to validate our initial idea that process descriptions are important per se although they are not executable. Moreover, we wanted to capture requirements on SPT from the interaction with the software organisation.

Evaluation The strengths of this case were: We validated that process descriptions are important, which was our initial idea. We succeeded to capture some requirements from the organisation.

The limitations of this case are:

1. The interaction with the real world is mainly based on the sharing of a document (the quality manual), rather than human interaction with the process owners.
2. As a consequence of the point above, the requirements stem mainly from a modeller point-of-view and not from the process owner one.

2.2 Trial 2 Software Engineering Education

Summary Starting from 1994, the E^3 system has been used for four years (1994-97) in a software engineering course being taught at Politecnico di Torino to describe the software process prescribed for all the student project activities [JL96] [JL97].

Goal Our main goal was educational, i.e., we want the students to learn how to read, understand, and work according to a defined software process model. The research goal was that of evaluating the suitability of E^3 description for process understanding.

Evaluation We achieved both goals, since the students had gained a thorough understanding of working with processes and E^3 were considered well-suited for description.

The limitations of this study (from the research point of view) are:

1. Students were 5th year computer science students who are well acquainted with modelling techniques. This is not always the case for process users and especially process owners (e.g. managers).

2. No modification of the model was required. In that way students never tested the evolutionary capabilities of the E^3 supporting tool, but only the legibility of E^3 PML models.

2.3 Trial 3 Olivetti

Summary One process modeller worked in strict collaboration with the process owners at a Department of Olivetti [FJ99]. The modelling phase triggered changes in the original process descriptions. The process owners seriously considered adopting E^3, but a subsequent reorganisation of the Quality Department caused that this never happened.

Goal We had two goals: first, to evaluate the second implementation of the E^3 system in general and the partitioning mechanisms in particular; second, to evaluate the suitability of the E^3 system for modelling of general manufacturing processes.

Evaluation This case study had a set of positive results. First, the E^3 research team gained insight in the activities related to process description and maintenance at Olivetti. Second, the process owners admitted their need for an automatic tool that could help in process description management. We found out that it is often the case that two or more processes from different departments have to be merged together and this merging process often lead to inconsistent models. Third, we took into consideration the requirements of the process owners and not only those of the modellers as in 2.1. The crucial limitation is that the modeller belongs to the E^3 research team, is very acquainted with the system and manages to overcome the system limitations. In this way, almost no "problems" of the system came out from the case.

2.4 Trial 4 Modelling in SPIQ

Summary This work was done in the context of the SPIQ [1] project [Ang98]. The SPIQ industrial partners formal "house" PML (NOVIT, Storebrand, Tandberg Data, Telenor FoU, Telenor 4Tel, and Ericsson) have a rather informal PML and a home-made corresponding tool. These software organisations all have models of their software processes.

---

[1] SPIQ is a Norwegian project on Software Process Improvement. 1997-1999. SPIQ means Software Process Improvement for better Quality.

A master student received three process description fragments from three different software companies and modelled them by using the PML E^3 and IDEF0. He also developed a Goal Question Metric model [BCR94] to evaluate the two PMLs.

Goal The goals were to develop evaluation criteria for a PML and to evaluate the extended IDEF0 and E^3 PMLs.

The goals were:

1. Gain experience from modelling real world software processes as a process modeller.
2. Develop evaluation criteria for PML as a process modeller.
3. Evaluate extended IDEF0 and E3 as PML used by process modeller.

Evaluation The results were: concerning understandability, E^3 was considered more appropriate than IDEF0, which respectively was considered more appropriate than the original process description. The same pattern was identified for ease of creating new models and suitability for the organisation. However, neither of the three process owners were convinced to adopt a formal PML and its corresponding tool.

The advantages of this case with respect to the other ones are: the modeller does not belong to the E^3 research team and has very little contact with the team itself. Also, a goal-oriented metric is defined and measurement are collected from several cases. The limitations are in that the same person designed the metrics, modelled the processes, and collected the measurement data.

2.5 Trial 5 Software Process Improvement Education

Summary This work has been performed in the context of a bigger case in which 40 students (organised in 10 groups) from a software quality and software process improvement course interacted with a major Norwegian [2] telecom company, named company A. During the case the students came in contact with three actors: the quality manager, the manager of the process group, and a project leader. Among other tasks [Jac99], the students were asked by the manager of the process group to model a process fragment, and to report about the encountered problems. Five groups modelled with E^3 and 5 modelled with IDEF0.

Goal The research goals are: First, to improve our understanding of the relationship between software process models and software process improvement; second to get an evaluation of E^3 and IDEF0 by overcoming the limitation of the previous case (Trial 4 Modelling in SPIQ) in which the modeller and the researcher coincides.

Evaluation The advantages of this instrumental case study with respect to the previous ones are: The modellers do not belong to the E^3 research team and do not have direct contact with the team itself. They are not part of

---

[2] The department we interacted with, has more than 500 employers and this is classified as big in Norway.

the evaluation (research) team, nor are they interested in giving a positive evaluation of SPT in general or of E^3 and IDEF0 in particular.

The evaluation shows that the overall research goal can be considered successful. Both the E^3 and IDEF0 languages are considered more appropriate for comprehensibility and model evolution/change than the original description. However, the students reported problems in interpreting the original process description, and said that both E^3 and IDEF0 were easy to understand. They also reported problems with the tools.

The reported problems with E^3-pdraw are:

- It is difficult to learn how to choose the right associations.
- The tool crashed several times.
- The tool does not provide on-line textual description of the buttons it provides.
- The information regarding associations are not updated automatically as the user creates new associations.
- The tool is poor concerning basic facilities such as cut and paste and printing.

Concerning the IDEF0 supporting tool (AIOWIN), only two groups out of five used it, the other three groups decided to use the general purpose drawing tool Visio. This may mean that E^3-pdraw is easier to learn and use, since all the groups which were supposed to use it, decided to use it.

The two groups reported about the following problems:

- the AIOWIN version which was available only allowed the creation of 15 activities.
- the decomposition of activities into sub-activities was not intuitive. Moreover the strict decomposition rules in IDEF0 were not considered appropriate for modelling the original process description.
- Difficulties differentiating between inputs and control flows in the IDEF0 models were also reported.

The reaction of the process owner resembles the ones discussed in trial 1 Iveco (section 2.1) and trial 2 Olivetti (section 2.3). He is positive to the new descriptions, but he does not mention the possibility of adopting a formal PMLs and the associated tools.

3 Eliciting SPT requirements from Software Organisations

All trials in section 2 try to apply existing SPT technology to software organisations and to learn from this application. From these trials we have deduced requirements towards process technology and we have get feedback about own languages and tools. The common results of these trials is that the proposed technology has not been adopted by the organisations. This is not necessarily a negative feedback for the technology under evaluation, as this can be due to organisational reasons.

From our trials we have also learned that organisations have spent much work in defining their processes, and have their own languages and sometimes tools to describe their processes.

In this section we describe and discuss our experience with requirement capture. This case has been performed in the same context as the one in trial 5 Software Process Improvement Education (section 2.5). It is an instrumental case which is still ongoing. If we look at figure 1, we want to start from the software organisation and try to capture its possible requirements toward SPT.

Description We have invited three actors (the quality manager, the process group leader, and a project leader) from company A to give a 2 hours presentation each.

The three actors should answer four questions discussed and agreed with the teacher. The questions are:

- Q1: Describe a software system, also by help of quality attributes.
- Q2: Which processes exist around this system?
- Q3: Which are the improvement initiatives around these processes?
- Q4: How general is the software system and the respective improvement initiatives in the general context of the company?

Goal The educational goal: students must elicit an example of software process improvement initiatives from a real organisation which belongs to their culture. Each group is asked to write a document and to give a presentation about their understanding of the case. Students are invited to discover consistencies and inconsistencies both among the three actors and between actors, lectures, and text book [Hum97].

The research goal: in addition to the research goal described in 2.5, we want to observe how the company software development processes look like, how they are described, used, changed, customised, and maintained.

Preliminary evaluation The process model development was started in October 96 and its current version 2.1 was revised in February 99. The process group leader gave a short presentation of the process web support and provided us with a limited copy of it.

A brief description of some of the relevant points related to the process are given:

The software development processes and its representation The process covers Requirements analysis, Design, Implementation, Verification & Validation, Course & User Documentation Development, and Product & Documentation Administration. The main purpose of the process is to increase focus on the early phases and Verification & Validation activities, increase precision and speed by repeating the events, reduce the dependency on experts and generally improve control and understanding by visualising the tasks. The process is product, method, language and tool independent. It hence specifies activities, documents, and activity ordering documents are mostly formalised in Adobe FrameMaker.

The process descriptions consist of templates, checklists, review logs, surveys and general project documentation on the Intranet. The Figure 2 gives a flavour about the level of formality exhibited by a process fragment, represented on the company intranet. The descriptions include templates (both html, word, pdf, and framemaker) for 18 document types, including Specification, Market Requirements, Test cases, etc.

Process Usage The process descriptions are available to process users on the company Intranet. Since we have not talked to process users yet, we cannot tell in which degree and how the process is userd by performers.

Change and Adaptation Adaptations to new projects are performed in three steps: modify rules and guidelines, create a new server application using the new rules and guidelines, and distribution on the Intranet. The company has performed four adaptations used in 12 projects.

The project leader talked about an adaptation used in a project which involves the use of an online SDL-manual, templates and guidelines for both UML [JRB99] and MSC (Message Sequence Chart). They used prototyping, which is not described in the original company process.

Model adaptations and changes are not automatically supported. We are observing that it is not easy for the company to change their models and that errors (inconsistencies) are introduced during model change.

Technical support to the process The supporting web based system offers the following functionality:

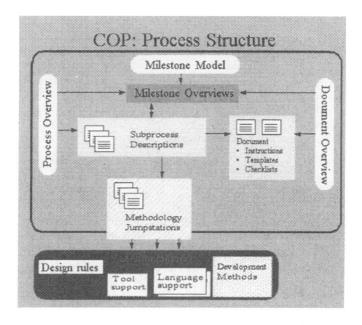

Fig. 2. The structure of the software process as available on the company A Intranet.

- Process Overview
- Document Overview
- Activity Overviews
- Sub-process Descriptions
- Document Instructions with check-lists
- Document templates
- Milestone Descriptions with check-lists
- Review Process with templates
- Baseline and Change handling
- Working Methods
- Methodology Interface
- Links to corresponding processes
- Tool-links
- Introduction Course

The quality manager talks about the process as an item in a more complex business process. She never mentions if the process is used or not. The project manager mentions the process, but she never discusses the advantages or the problems bound to its use. It is not clear which level of visibility that project participants have on the process. This will be investigated as part of a Master thesis by the end of '99.

Company A is now in the process of transforming the process from a waterfall like model to an evolutionary and incremental one. The nature of process descriptions, i.e., Framemaker drawings, makes it difficult to reuse the original process description when making a new one.

4   Related work

Section 4.1 is about trials of technology application to software organisations. These trials are similar to our ones and each one is strongly dependent on the SPT under evaluation. A common factor is that modelling help in discovering inconsistencies.

Section 4.2 compares our ongoing work on requirement elicitation with similar works.

4.1   Applying SPT to software organisations

A survey of previous work shows that much effort have been spent applying SPT to software organisations.

The work of Barghouti et al. [BRB95] is about two case studies that have been performed with the aim of determining the feasibility, utility, and limitations of using a process support tool to model and analyse real processes of organisations. The case studies aim at assessing the utility of formal models and enaction techniques provided by the Marvel 3.1 PSEE. This is similar to our trial 3 Olivetti, except from the enactment issues. There is not evidence that Marvel was adopted by the target organisations.

Kellner and Hansen [KH89] report on a modelling experience whose main goal is the development of a meta-process model for process improvement. The resulting model consists of three sub-models: a functional model, represented by Activity Charts; a behavioural model, represented by Statecharts; a structural model, represented by Module Charts. Textual schemas describe the connections. The Meta-process starts with an information gathering phase with interviews with the people involved in the process. Second, a preliminary process model is developed by use of DFD-diagrams. Third, a set of requirements for software process modelling is developed. Finally, the model is implemented and simulated by use of the Statemate tool, originally conceived for reactive system specification using Statecharts. The results of the case study have two directions: the first is process modelling understanding, the second is a set of recommendations for change to the methods and procedures in the original process. This is similar to our trial 1 Iveco in which we also performed a process simulation.

Process Weaver have been investigated in at least two case studies: the one reported by Aumatre et al. [ADH94] and the one reported by Ett et al. [EB94]. Aumatre et al. [ADH94] report both modelling of the identified process model specifications and validation of the model by enaction in a simulated environment.

The Spade environment has been evaluated [BFL+95] in the context of a case in co-operation with the Business Unit Telecommunication for Defence (BTUD) of ItalTel. The quality manual has been modelled by the SLANG language and the modelling process has lead to the detection of inconsistencies, ambiguities, incompleteness and opportunities for improvement.

Tanaka [TSK+95] reports about an experience of software process improvement at OMRON corporation. One of the goals were to describe and define the current software process correctly and in detail by a Petri net, and estimated the benefits obtained. It was confirmed that, compared to a similar project, approximately 10% of the total effort/KLOC was reduced at test phases as a consequence of better control.

4.2 Eliciting SPT requirements from software organisations

Industry is not likely to publish experience with new tools or methods (e.g. UML or SCM tools). So silence here does not need to indicate that SPT is not used.

Ethnographic studies have been extensively performed in the CSCW community [SK97] and not so much in our SPT community. There are however few exceptions [SR92] . Rodden et al. [RKHS94] [ISS95] report about a series of ethnographic studies. These studies are intended to gain insight into the nature of software development as it actually occurs in practice and to inform the development of effective support for the software development process. Based upon how the organisations performs its everyday work, like "cutting corners" and informal "bending rules", they warn against over prescription, but they advocate the construction of appropriate lightweight mechanisms to support the central features of the process, i.e. communication between software developers. These mechanisms should be augmented with facilities that allow process models to be referred to as a common resource for the work taking place.

5 Conclusions

Our SPT application trials and the ones surveyed in literature show that some form of technical support for modelling, consistency check, and browsing helps in developing understandable models and to remove errors and inconsistencies. Moreover, all the persons from software organisations being in contact with SPT have been positive to it though they did not choose to adopt it. Then, we cannot conclude that SPT is not useful, but rather that we can show some evidence for usefulness. We are not sure about the reasons about why they did not choose SPT. We assume that there is a combination of technical and organisational reasons. The technical reasons may be that the SPT we have tried to introduce is still in the prototypical stage, as shown for example by trial 5 Software Process Improvement Education (2.5).

This consideration opens two directions for process researchers: first re-- engineering of the existing prototypes and further validation of them. The second is less technical and can be performed in collaboration from experts in other fields, e.g., business administration people, sociologist, etc. This is about discovering the reasons why SPT has not been adopted.

Most software organisations also have a software process and they use some form for process representation and management. Company A has a software process and has build a technical support for it. They declare that the main reason for having their own "SPT" is process sharing among users by help of intra-net. The developed SPT does not offer any support for consistency check nor changing. At the same time we are observing that the company is having problems with model change. Also model adaptations are not automatically supported.

From our case at company A, it is still not evident which use of the process (both general and customised) is made at project level. Deeper investigations at project level must and will be done by talking to process users.

From our trials and our case with company A, we came in contact with people who believed in the importance of having a defined process and who actually worked with process descriptions. However, this does not prove that software process descriptions are useful. Deeper investigations at project level together with a deeper study of related field literature (e.g. CSCW) will eventually give SPT researchers better answers to these questions.

References

[ADH94]   J. Aumaitre, M. Dowson, and D. Harjani. Lessons learned from formalizing and implementing a large Process Model. In *[War94]*, pages 227–240. Springer Verlag LNCS 772, February 1994.

[Ang98]   E. Angelvik. Evaluation of Software Process Modeling Languages. Technical report, Norwegian University of Science and Technology, 1998. Master thesis, EPOS TR 346.

[BCR94]   V. R. Basili, G. Caldiera, and H.D. Rombach. The Goal Question Metric Paradigm. In *[Mar94]*, pages 528–532, 1994.

[BFL+95]   S. Bandinelli, A. Fuggetta, L. Lavazza, M. Loi, and G.P. Picco. Modeling and Improving an Industrial Software Process. *IEEE Trans. on Software Engineering*, 21(5):440–454, May 1995.

[BRB95]   N.S. Barghouti, D.S. Rosenblum, and D.G. Belanger. Two Case Studies in Modeling Real, Corporate Processes. *Software Process: Improvement and Practice*, 1(1), 1995.

[CFJ98]   R. Conradi, A. Fuggetta, and M.L. Jaccheri. Six Thesis on Software Process Research. In *6th European Workshop, EWSPT98*, pages 100–104. Springer Verlag 1487, September 1998.

[Der92]   Jean-Claude Derniame, editor. *Proc. Second European Workshop on Software Process Technology (EWSPT'92), Trondheim, Norway. 253 p.* Springer Verlag LNCS 635, September 1992.

[EB94]   W.H. Ett and S.A. Becker. Evaluating the Effectiveness of Process Weaver as a Process Management Tool: A Case Study. In *Proc. of the 3rd Symp. on Assessment of Quality Software Development Tools*, pages 204–223, June 1994.

[FJ99]   A. Fuggetta and M.L. Jaccheri. Dynamic Partitioning of Complex Process Models. Technical report, Norwegian University of Science and Technology, 1999. 8/99, ISSN 0802-6394 To Appear in Information and Software Technology.

[Høy97]   G. M. Høydalsvik. Experiences in Software Process Modelling and Enactment. Technical report, Norwegian University of Science and Technology, 1997. PhD thesis.

[Hum97]   W.S Humphrey. *Managing the software process*. Addison Wesley, 1997.

[ISS95]   S. Viller I. Sommerville, G. Kotonya and P. Sawyer. Process viewpoints. In *Proc. of the European Workshop on Software Process Technology*, pages 2–8, April 1995.

[Jac99]   M.L. Jaccheri. A Software Quality and a Software Process Improvement Course. In *Forum for Advancing Software engineering Education (FASE) Volume 9 Number 05 (112th Issue)*, May 1999.

[JBD99]   M.L. Jaccheri, M. Baldi, and M. Divitini. Evaluating the Requirements for Software Process Modeling Languages and Systems. In *Process support for Distributed Team-based Software Development (PDTSD'99), SCI/ISAS'99 Technical Session On Software Development Methodologies, Orlando, Florida*, pages 570–578, August 1999.

[JL96]   M.L. Jaccheri and P. Lago. Teaching Process Improvement in an Industry Oriented Course. In *Proc. of the British Computer Society Quality SIG Int. Conf. on Software Process Improvement—Research into Education & Training (INSPIRE'96)*, September 1996.

[JL97]   M.L. Jaccheri and P. Lago. Applying Software Process Modeling and Improvement in Academic Setting. In *Proc. of the 10th ACM/IEEE-CS Conf. on Software Engineering Education and Training*, April 1997.

[JRB99]   Ivar Jacobson James Rumbaugh and Grady Booch. *The Unified Modeling Language Reference Manual*. Wiley, 1999.

[KH89]   M.I. Kellner and G.A. Hansen. Software Process Modeling: A Case Study. In *Proc. of the 21st Annual Hawaii Int. Conf. on System Sciences*, January 1989.

[Mar94]   John J. Marciniak, editor. *Encyclopedia of Software Engineering – 2 Volume Set*. John Wiley and Sons, 1994.

[RKHS94]   T. Rodden, V. King, J. Hughes, and I. Sommerville. Process Modelling and Development Practice. In *[War94]*, pages 59–64. Springer Verlag LNCS 772, February 1994.

[Sac95]   P. Sachs. Transforming work: Collaboration, learning, and design. *Comm. of the ACM*, 38(9):36–45, September 1995.

[SK97]   J. Simonsen and F. Kensing. Using Ethnography in Contextual Design. *Comm. of the ACM*, 40(7):82–88, July 1997.

[SR92]   I. Sommerville and T. Rodden. Understanding the Software Process as a Social Process. In *[Der92]*, pages 55–57, September 1992.

[Sta94]   R.E Stake. *Case studies*. Sage, 1994.

[TB97]   K. Gatford T. Bendel, L. Boulter. *The benchmarking workout*. Pitman Publishing, 1997.

[TSK^{+}95] T. Tanaka, K. Sakamoto, S. Kusumoto, K. Matsumoto, and T. Kikuno. Improvement of Software Process by Process Visualization and Benefit Estimation. In *Proc. 17th Int'l Conference on Software Engineering, Seattle, BC*, pages 123–132, April 1995.

[War94]   Brian Warboys, editor. *Proc. Third European Workshop on Software Process Technology (EWSPT'94), Villard-de-Lans, France. 274 p.* Springer Verlag LNCS 772, February 1994.

Modeling Management and Coordination in Development Processes

Dirk Jäger

Aachen University of Technology
Department of Computer Science III
D-52056 Aachen, Germany
jaeger@i3.informatik.rwth-aachen.de

Abstract. Coordination and management efforts are important activities within every development process. Just as the technical tasks, which directly contribute to the product, coordination and management tasks should be explicitly represented in a process model. Both should clearly be separated to allow the process modeler to modify management and coordination strategies independently from technical tasks, which is important if we consider interorganization cooperation in development processes.

Keywords: process modeling, process management, coordination, interorganization cooperation

1 Introduction

A primary goal of process modeling activities is to support the process manager in his efforts to coordinate the tasks a process consists of. Coordination activities are a subset of management activities and include planning and monitoring of technical tasks as well as assigning resources. Though coordination is itself an important task, it is rarely modeled as such. Most approaches are focused on describing how the technical tasks of a process are organized and give no information on how a process is managed. If management tasks are modeled, they often are not clearly separated from technical tasks. Coordination is often viewed as a technical problem rather than a human activity. Most systems offer low-level support for process synchronization and cooperation, e.g. transactions in COO [4] and EPOS [13] or rules for the interaction of autonomous agents in ADEPT [7]. If systems define a higher-level paradigm for cooperation, e.g. summits in Marvel / OZ [2] or the delegation of subnets in FUNSOFT nets [12], the modeler is limited to this paradigm.

The approaches have in common that they automate coordination. While this may work for technical coordination problems, e.g. ensuring consistency of a programs' source code, many real life problems require the intervention of a human actor to achieve coordination. These situations can not be modeled with the mentioned approaches. We need a process modeling language in which we can express a) which coordination activity has to be performed at some point of the process, b) which tasks have to be coordinated, and c) who is the responsible human actor. Deciding if and how coordination can be automated is only the second step an not in the scope of this paper.

Explicitly modeling coordination activities has several benefits. Firstly, the process modeler is forced to identify critical parts of the process where coordination is necessary as well as appropriate coordination mechanisms. Secondly, the process manager can easily identify those parts of the process and the installed coordination mechanisms. Thirdly, the required management effort can be planned in advance. Fourthly, if the cooperation of tasks fails, it can be traced what coordination mechanism had been installed and why this was not sufficient.

2 Coordination, Management and Cooperation

2.1 Basic Definitions

Representing coordination activities in process models requires a set of appropriate modeling elements. Before we can offer those elements, we have to know what different types of coordination mechanisms exist, for what coordination problems they are suitable, and how they are applied.

Coordination can be defined as *the management of dependencies between activities* [9]. Dependencies can be characterized as being either *pooled*, *sequential* or *reciprocal* [11]. In case of a pooled dependency, activities contribute to a whole but can be executed independently. A sequential dependency means, that the activities have to be executed one after another, because one activity needs as its input the documents produced by another activity. In case of a reciprocal dependency, the activities are not partially ordered with regard to the flow of control. Instead, there are cycles and mutual dependencies.

Corresponding to the three types of dependencies, there are three groups of coordination mechanisms by which the respective dependencies can be managed. Pooled dependencies, which cause the fewest problems, are handled by *standards*. Standards are rules which constrain the execution of each single activity in a way that the results of all the activities will finally fit together. Sequential dependencies demand for *planning* as coordination mechanism. Planning basically means to fix the order of execution and the exchange of documents in advance.

The handling of reciprocal dependencies is the most difficult case. It requires the coordination mechanism of *mutual adjustment*. Mutual adjustment may be achieved by personal contacts between developers and may require additional coordination activities like monitoring, or integration activities, which mediate between two mutually dependent activities [3].

2.2 Interorganization Cooperation

Cooperation of different companies does not differ very much from the cooperation of branches of the same company [8]. Thus, we can generalize the problem of two cooperating companies to the problem of cooperation of organizational units. I will refer to this scenario as *interorganization cooperation* and call the cooperating entities *organizations* in the following. In contrast to *local development*

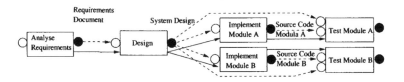

Fig. 1. Sample task net

processes, these *interorganization development processes* require the support by an enhanced process modeling language (PML)[1].

In a development process we can distinguish two kinds of tasks. The *technical tasks* are those tasks producing parts of the final product. Besides, there are *management tasks* which do not exist due to technical requirements but are needed to direct the execution of the development process, e.g. monitoring. These activities can be characterized as coordinating the development process.

Let us now think of a development process which is executed within a single organization and which consists of technical and management tasks. Let us further assume that the same development should take place as a cooperation of several organizations. What tasks would be affected by this transition? A main thesis of this paper is that the transition from a local development process to a development process crossing the boundaries of organizations does not affect the technical tasks but only the management tasks. The technical tasks are driven by the desired product, which remains the same. The management tasks are driven by the organization structure, which changes significantly. Therefore, a PML designed to support interorganization cooperation must include language elements for the explicit modeling of management and coordination aspects of processes. By leaving these aspects more or less implicit, as today's modeling languages do, we are not able to express what really makes the difference between local and interorganization processes.

3 An Extended Approach to Process Modeling

3.1 Dynamic Task Nets

To demonstrate how a PML could be extended with modeling elements for representing coordination and management aspects I will use dynamic task nets as an example, which are a visual language for modeling development processes [5].

Figure 1 shows a sample task net on the instance level. Tasks are shown as boxes. They have *input parameters* (empty circles) and *output parameters* (filled circles). A task's parameters are the documents the task is working on. A task reads its input documents upon activation, works with these documents, and finally produces some output documents. Tasks are connected by control flow relationships, denoted by arrows, which describe the order of execution. Data flow relationships, denoted by dashed arrows, can be viewed as a refinement of control flow relationships. Another important feature of dynamic task nets is the distinction between *complex tasks* and *atomic tasks*. Complex tasks can be refined by a net of subtasks.

3.2 Modeling Coordination: An Example

Figure 2 i) shows a decomposition of the design task of Figure 1. Assuming the design is too complex to be handled by one person alone, a preliminary design is produced based on the requirements. After this, two design tasks, Design A and Design B, produce the final system design. The tasks are assigned to the actors Smith and Jones. Let us further assume that the preliminary design was not able to eliminate all dependencies between the two parts of the system. In this case, the two design tasks (i.e. the actors) have to cooperate. In the dynamic task nets, as they exist now, this is expressed by a cooperation relationship between these tasks. However, this relationship is very unspecific and holds no information regarding the nature of this cooperation and how it is coordinated.

Figure 2 ii) shows a possible extension of the dynamic task net to overcome these drawbacks. By introducing management tasks we can express how the cooperation should work; the coordination is achieved by a design meeting that takes place once a week. The result of every meeting is a protocol which has to be reviewed by the actor Miller. He is responsible for monitoring the progress of the design tasks, based on the meeting results. We can see that he does not participate in the meeting himself, because he is not assigned to this task.

Let us now assume that the same development is to be run as an cooperation of two organizations in which each organization is responsible for one of the design tasks. The geographical distance between the two organizations is too big to have a meeting of the two designers every week, they communicate by e-mail instead. In addition, there is a special integration task for supporting the cooperation. The e-mail exchanged by the actors is forwarded to the integration task. There also are local design meetings every two weeks at each site where the actor responsible for the integration discusses open issues with the designers.

While the technical tasks remained the same, the transition from a local process to an interorganization process has significantly affected the way the process is coordinated.

3.3 Open Issues and Future Research

The presented approach for modeling management and coordination is not fully elaborated yet. Some of the open question are:

- What is the execution semantics of (repeated) management tasks? How is their execution state related to the state of technical tasks?
- How are the documents handled which are produced by the management tasks? Are they subject to configuration and version management?
- How are management tasks refined if the corresponding technical tasks are refined?
- What happens if e.g. a monitoring task notices that the monitored cooperation is going to fail?

The last question leads to an important insight. If within a monitoring task a possible failure of the process is detected, a restructuring of the task net

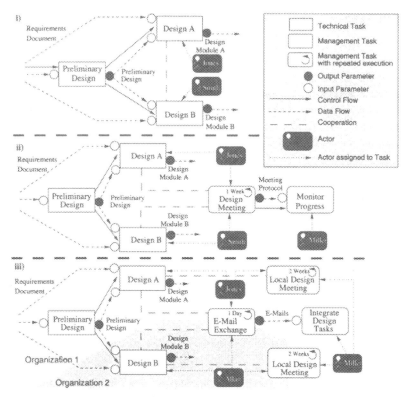

Fig. 2. Management Tasks

may be inevitable, e.g. the distribution of technical tasks among cooperating organizations is altered. Restructuring is coordination by planning. The task of restructuring the net is itself a coordination task and accordingly it should be explicitly represented as such. Modeling it within the net of the technical tasks is probably not desirable, because this would lead to a model that contains rules for its own manipulation. Rather, the observation is that management tasks are on a higher conceptual level than technical tasks. In fact, the net of technical tasks is the product (the input and output parameters) the management tasks are working on. They analyze and alter this product, just as technical tasks analyze and alter the documents they are working on [10]. The management tasks of Figure 2 are only a projection of those task onto the technical level, a convenient view to show the relationships between the two levels.

The overall vision when modeling coordination and management is that it might be possible to identify a catalogue of management patterns. Given a certain constellation of technical tasks, we can then use this catalogue to install the management tasks which are known to be able to handle this situation.

Besides those conceptual problems, the technical problems of implementing the resulting PML must be solved. Our existing process modeling tool [6] must be enhanced by communication interfaces for coupling remote tool instances.

4 Conclusion

I have presented an approach for modeling coordination and management in development processes. The approach is novel in that it takes a human centered view on these aspects. It provides the process modeler with a language in which he can express coordination aspects of real world processes. By including management and coordination tasks, models become more complex and thus more difficult to use. On the other hand, there are situations, e.g. interorganization cooperation, where it is important to include coordination aspects.

References

1. C. Basile, S. Calanna, E. Di Nitto, A. Fuggetta, and M. Gemo. Mechanisms and Policies for Federated PSEEs: Basic Concepts and Open Issues. In Carlo Montagnero, editor, *Proc. of 5th EWSPT*, LNCS 1149, pages 86–91, Nancy, France, October 1996. Springer.
2. Israel Ben-Shaul and Gail E. Kaiser. A Paradigm for Decentralized Process Modeling and its Realization in the Oz Environment. In *Proc. of 16th ICSE*, pages 179–188, Sorrento, Italy, 1994.
3. Jay Galbraith. *Designing Complex Organizations*. Addison-Wesley, Reading, 1973.
4. C. Godart, G. Canals, F. Charoy, P. Molli, and H. Skaf. Designing and Implementing COO. In *Proc. of 18th ICSE*, pages 342–352, Berlin, 1996.
5. Peter Heimann, Gregor Joeris, Carl-Arndt Krapp, and Bernhard Westfechtel. DYNAMITE: Dynamic Task Nets for Software Process Management. In *Proceedings of the 18th ICSE*, pages 331–341, Berlin, March 1996. IEEE Computer Society Press.
6. Dirk Jäger. Generating Tools from Graph-Based Specifications. In Jonathan Gray, Jennifer Harvey, Anna Liu, and Louise Scott, editors, *Proc. First Int. Symph. on Constructing Software Engineering Tools*, pages 97–107, Mawson Lakes, Australia, May 1999. Univ. of South Australia, School of Computer Science.
7. N.R. Jennings, P. Faratin, T.J. Norman, P. O'Brien, and M.E. Wiegand. Agent-Based Business Process Management. *International Journal of Cooperative Information Systems*, 5(2,3):105–130, 1996.
8. Paul R. Lawrence and Jay W. Lorsch. *Organization and Environment*. Division of Research Harvard Business School, Boston, 1967.
9. Thomas W. Malone and Kevin Crowston. The Interdisciplinary Study of Coordination.
10. Manfred Nagl and Bernhard Westfechtel. *A Universal Component for the Administration in Distributed and Integrated Development Environments*. Number 94-8 in Aachener Informatik-Berichte. RWTH Aachen, 1994.
11. James D. Thompson. *Organizations in Action*. McGraw-Hill, New York, 1967.
12. Volker Gruhn und W. Deiters. The FUNSOFT Net Approach to Software Process Management. *International Journal of Software Engineering and Knowledge Engineering*, 4(3):229–256, 1994.
13. Alf Inge Wang, Jens-Otto Larsen, Reidar Conradi, and Bjorn P. Munch. Improving Cooperation Support in the EPOS CM System. In Volker Gruhn, editor, *Proceedings of the 6th EWSPT*, volume 1487 of *LNCS*, pages 75–91, Weybridge, UK, September 1998.

Support for Mobile Software Processes in CAGIS

Alf Inge Wang

Dept. of Computer and Information Science,
Norwegian University of Science and Technology (NTNU),
N-7491 Trondheim, Norway,
Phone: +47 73594485, Fax: +47 73594466,
Email: alfw@idi.ntnu.no
Web: http://www.idi.ntnu.no/~alfw

Abstract. This paper describes a prototype for supporting distributed, mobile software processes. The prototype allows instantiated process models to be distributed in different workspaces, and have mechanisms to allow parts of the process to be moved from one workspace to another. The paper outlines the main concepts, a process modelling language and tools to support distributed, mobile processes. Further, we discuss problems and possible solutions for our prototype, and some experiments are also outlined. This work has been carried out as a part of a project called CAGIS, described in the introduction of the paper.
Keywords: Mobile software process, Process Centred Environment, Workflow tool, Process Modelling Language, Web, XML, CGI, Software agents

1 Introduction

For many years, most process centred environments (PCEs) have made the assumption that one centralised process model is needed to represent the whole software process. Since the introduction of the Internet, more and more organisations work in a distributed way in heterogeneous environments. Distributed organisations must cope with management of people working in different places, on different times, with different tools and on different processes. For most traditional PCEs, it is impossible or at least very hard to model processes with a highly distributed and heterogeneous nature. In addition, when the organisation is divided into smaller, autonomous sub-organisations, it is impossible to use one centralised model to reflect software processes with the scope of the whole organisation. It is unthinkable, that one model, often managed by top-level management, shall represent all autonomous groups. The process model must reflect the organisation and thus be distributed into smaller autonomous parts [9, 12].

In 1986-1996, our research group, managed by Reidar Conradi, worked on a PCE prototype called EPOS [5]. EPOS was an advanced environment for managing software processes as well as software artifacts through various tools. In 1997, a project called *Cooperative Agents in Global Information Space* (CAGIS) [10] was started. One of the main goals of the CAGIS project was to see how heterogeneous, distributed, cooperative work could be supported. The first part of the project identified requirements for how to support software process in a global information space. We soon found that our traditional EPOS environment could not fulfil requirements like openended-ness, distributed processes, heterogeneous tools and dynamic changing and movement of fragments of the process (*process fragments*). All these characteristics can be found in what we call Cooperative Software Engineering (CSE) [16]. EPOS suffered from being too centralised, too static and too closed a system to support CSE. The process models could only be changed in each workspace, and coordination between workspaces was not sufficiently supported. Thus a strict top-down approach changing the process model was enforced. In reality only upper management could evolve the process model.

To put this paper in the right context, we give a short review of an overall architecture, to which this work contributes. In [16], we presented our CAGIS multi-agent architecture for cooperative software engineering (see figure 1). The architecture consists of four components:

1. **Agents**: Agents are set up to achieve a modest goal, with the characteristics of autonomy, interaction, reactivity to environment, as well as pro-activeness. There are three main types of agents: (1) *Work agents* to assist in local software production activities, (2), *Interaction agents* to assist with cooperative work (such as communication, coordination, mediation and negotiation) between workspaces, and (3) *System agents* to give system support to other agents. Interaction agents are mobile agents, while system agents and work agents are stationary.
2. **Workspaces**: A workspace is a temporary container for relevant data in a suitable format, together with the processing tools. It can be private as well as shared.
3. **AgentMeetingPlace (AMP)**: AMPs are where agents meet and interact. AMPs provide agents with support for doing efficient inter-agent communication. An AMP is therefore a "special" workspace for software agents.
4. **Repositories**: Repositories can be global, local or distributed, and are persistent. Workspaces may check in and out information from repositories.

The architecture is implemented in Java, KQML is used for agent communication and IBM Aglets [8] are used to support mobile agents [11]. In figure 1, arrows between agents indicate inter-agent interaction. The arrows related to the *monitor agent*, describe that this agent is logging events in the two workspaces and the AMP, and store event information in the global repository. The *mediation agent* uses this information, retrieved from the global repository, to support the inter-agent negotiation process.

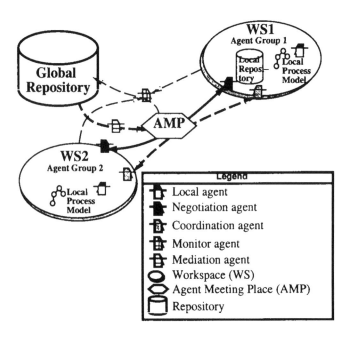

Fig. 1. MAS-based architecture for cooperative software engineering

In the CAGIS CSE architecture, interaction agents perform all collaboration between workspaces. An AMP is the neutral meeting point for agents from different workspaces, and it supports the inter-workspace process. Within a workspace, a simple PCE or a workflow tool can be used to give support for the local process. Since the local process does not involve much coordination between involved actors (interaction agents are taking care of this bit), the local process becomes relatively simple. If a project manager wants to assign a specific job to a project member, interaction agents are used to find available human resources. When the available project member is found, the project manager can use agents to give this person a description of what to do, as well as a local process model (telling him how to do it). This process model will then be moved from the project manager's workspace to the project members workspace.

This paper presents a prototype of a simple PCE/workflow system allowing a process model to be distributed on several workspaces and where parts of the process (process fragments) can be moved between workspaces. Remember that this prototype is not intended used as a stand-alone system, but it is a part of the CAGIS multi-agent architecture for CSE. Our prototype only supports simple and straightforward processes, since the interactive agents in the enclosing CAGIS architecture will take care of the more advanced processes.

The rest of the paper is organised as it follows. Section 2 present related work on distributed PCEs, and mobile workflow. Section 3 presents the main concepts of our approach. Section 4 briefly outlines some preliminary experiences, and discusses problems and possible solution for our prototype. Section 5 concludes the paper.

2 Related work

Within the Software Process community, the research area on how to support distributed and heterogeneous software processes has recently been popular topic. In [13], Tiako outlines how to model federation of Process Sensitive Engineering Environments (PSEEs). In such federation, large development projects can be realized by dividing the whole process in to smaller pieces assigned to distributed teams. The teams work on their own processes using their own PSEEs. Tiako describes a federation process support architecture that aims to support not only the enactment of processes, but also their definition by composition, decomposition and/or federation.

In [2], Ben-Shaul et al. propose the Oz approach to provide a federated PSEE by composing different instances of local PSEEs. Each instance is devoted to support the development process executed by a single organisation. The different PSEEs run autonomously according to their own processes. Interaction of several PSEEs is accomplished through a common activity called *summit*, where one site acts as a coordinator and receives all needed data from other sites. The result is sent back from the coordinator to all involved sites.

In [1], Basile et al. take Oz as a starting point to provide federated PSEEs, and allows several inter-organisation policies to be implemented and combined. A set of basic operations is used to specify any inter-organisational policy (e.g., one operation for searching the physical location of a site, one operation for requesting execution of one service on another site etc.).

In [4], Bhattacharyya and Osterweil address the problem of giving decision support on moving and relocate process fragments to users. When a user wants to go mobile, a request is sent to a relocation request analysis engine (RELOCATE). RELOCATE receives three types of data: Current process, network configuration and user request. The network configuration data is used to compute what the performance will be if the user goes mobile. The process information expresses the process structure (static information) and the process execution state (dynamic information). RELOCATE will produce an answer to the user as well as modified process information. The RELOCATE engine can be given an entire software process and asked to come up with an "efficient" allocation of process fragments to users - in effect, producing a new, modified version of the software process. It can also be asked to deal with problems regarding specific aspects of mobile computing (e.g., use a laptop computer with a low processing speed).

In [18], Yoo and Lee describe a mobile agent platform for workflow systems called X-MAS (proXy acting Mobile Agent Systems). Here, the workflow system using the X-MAS mobile agent platform has a centralised coordinator. The workflow model (process model) is defined centrally in a workflow definition tool. The workflow management engine realizes workflow instances as mobile agents by asking the mobile agent platform to create them. If there are any time-constraints of agents, this information is stored in an agent manager in the agent execution engine. The mobile agents (workflow instances) may move from host to host, and interact with other entities as users, databases, and applications. A worklist handler in each location server enables mobile agents to run applications and interact with humans. When an agent is finished with his job and has come back, the workflow management engine stops the workflow instance of that agent. X-MAS is implemented in Java and Remote Method Invocation (RMI) in Java is used to implement agent mobility.

In [7], Jing et al. address how to adopt workflow systems to support mobile environments. For many companies, the attraction of mobile computing comes from possibly large productivity gains in the out-of-office workplace. There is a need to give process support for this kind of mobile and dynamic environments, and mobility must be supported in workflow management systems. Such systems must deal with mobile resources (equipment as well as human), support for location-independent activities (work at home or anywhere), as well as location-dependent activities (need to go to a specific place, for instance to deal with a customer etc.). Mobile resource management needs to efficiently track resources, status of mobile resources, and the assignment of resources to work activities. This means dealing with problems regarding workflow resources that are not always connected and that they can change status not being connected. Since resources move around, synchronisation of workflow information can also cause some problems.

The first three papers presented in this section (Tiako [13], Ben-shaul [2], and Basile et al. [1]) discuss how to support federation of PSEE. Our paper does not discuss federation in particular, but touches issues such as local autonomy and distribution of process fragments. None of these papers look into how to support mobile software processes. Bhattacharyya and Osterweil [4] however, describe how to analyse the impact of relocation of a process fragment. We only describe the mechanisms to provide mobile process fragments, and does not provide advanced tools for analysing the impact. The two last papers described in this section, discusses mobile workflow from two different perspectives. Yoo and Lee [18] provide mobile workflow by making the process instances mobile agents, while Jing et al. [7] addresses issues for how to adopt workflow systems to support mobile environments. The former is opposite to our approach because we enables mobility of process fragments, and uses stationary process servers to execute distributed process fragments. The latter is more general and touches issues that are discussed in our paper such as mobile resource handling.

3 CAGIS Mobile Software Process Approach

This section describes the main concepts, the process modelling language (PML), how to move process fragments, and the tools to support mobile software processes.

3.1 Main Concepts

It is not so hard to see the similarities between process modelling and software programming. There are also some PMLs that are very similar to general programming languages (for instance the object-oriented text-based PML in ProcessWeb [17]). A running process model (instantiated model) can in this analogy be viewed as a running program. Traditional programs can only execute on the same machine and cannot be changed at runtime[1]. However, if the program is a mobile software agent, it is possible for the program to move between different machines and to change its properties during its lifetime. Our idea is for process models to have mobility as mobile software agents. This means that it is possible for process fragments to move between workspaces during enactment, as well as to evolve process fragment instances.

In our prototype environment, a process model can be distributed as shown in figure 2. The process model consists of several activities that are linked together. The process model is not represented as one centralised model, but is distributed to different workspaces. Within the workspaces, there is local autonomy for the local process models. This means that people working in a workspace can change their own process model. It is the links between activities that tie the process model together (also activities in different workspaces). A link between two activities describes which activity to be executed first (pre-order), and the prelink and postlink tags are used to describe a link in our PML (see section 3.2). To go from one activity to another (related with a link), a user explicitly tells the workflow tool that the first activity is finished by pushing a button in the workflow tool.

The smallest building block in our PML is an activity. All activities are represented as individual model objects, which are linked together in the same way as web pages on the Internet. Another central concept of our prototype environment and PML is *process fragment*. A process fragment is one or more activities that are linked together in a workspace. For example, the four activities in workspace 1 in figure 2, can be a process fragment. But a process fragment can also be any combination of related activities as shown in figure 3. The term process fragment can therefore be used to name the group of activities that are moved between workspaces. Since we use eXtended Markup Language (XML) [14] to wrap the

---

[1] There are programming environments that allow programs to move and change during execution such as SmallTalk- and Java-programs

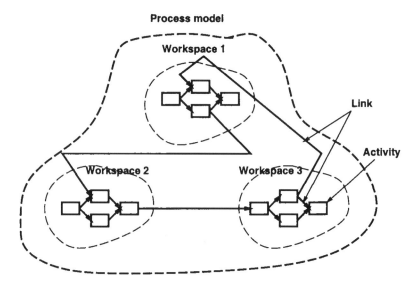

Fig. 2. Composition of a process

process information being moved between workspaces, we have defined the tag
$< processfragment >$ to define the context for linked activities. More about
this in section 3.2.

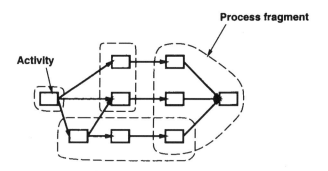

Fig. 3. The concept of process fragment

3.2 The Process Model Language

As mentioned above, an activity is an atomic building block in our PML. A
process (fragment) is modelled as a collection of related activities. To specify
an activity in our PML is similar to creating a small web page. Information is
structured in XML, using $< tags >$ to specify valid syntax. The application

interpreting the PML defines the semantic of the language. In figure 4, the Data Type Definition (DTD) for the PML is described. The DTD describes the elements needed to describe a process fragment and how these elements are structured. Note that '+' is used to describe one or more elements, '*' is used to describe none or more elements, while '?' states that there can be none or one element. *PCDATA* is used to specify the type of data tags, and means that these tags are of type parsed character data (text).

```
<?XML encoding=''UTF-9''?>
<!ELEMENT process (name,
                   (processfragment)+>
<!ELEMENT processfragment (name,
                           (workspace),
                           (activity)+)>
<!ELEMENT activity (name,
                    (workspace),
                    (prelink)*,
                    (postlink)*,
                    (state)?,
                    (due)?,
                    (feedback)?,
                    (description),
                    (code)*)>
<!ELEMENT name (#PCDATA)>
<!ELEMENT workspace (#PCDATA)>
<!ELEMENT prelink (#PCDATA)>
<!ELEMENT postlink (#PCDATA)>
<!ELEMENT state (#PCDATA)>
<!ELEMENT due (#PCDATA)>
<!ELEMENT feedback (#PCDATA)>
<!ELEMENT description (#PCDATA)>
<!ELEMENT code (#PCDATA)>
```

Fig. 4. XML Document Type Declaration of our PML

In our PML (see figure 4) a process consists of one or more process fragments, and a process fragment consists of one or more activities. A process is identified by a $<$ *name* $>$, and a process fragment is identified by a $<$ *name* $>$ and a $<$ *workspace* $>$. Every activity in a process model defines a unique identifier by combining the $<$ *workspace* $>$ defined for the process fragment and the $<$ *name* $>$ of the activity. In order to have a unique identifier in a distributed environment, a URL is used as the workspace path. The $<$ *prelink* $>$ tag defines the preconditions for an activity. This activity cannot start before the activities listed in prelink (listed as unique identifiers) are finished. The $<$ *postlink* $>$ will define what activity(ies) to execute next. The *code* tag is used to specify the HTML code related to the activity. This code may range from a simple descriptive text, to the definition of a complex interaction via a Java applet. An activity can have three different states: *Waiting, Ready,* and *Finish.* The state *Waiting* indicates that the activity is waiting on one or more activities to finish before it can be executed (specified in $<prelink>$). The state *Ready* indicates that the activity is ready to start. When a user is finished working with an activity, (s)he explicitly notifies the workflow tool that the activity is *Finished* by clicking on a button in the agenda tool (see section 3.4). The *feedback* tag is used to specify whether an activity is a part of a feedback loop or not. If an activity is modelled as a feedback activity, it can only have two prelinks, where one of the prelinks represents the feedback loop. A feedback activity is activated **if one** of the prelinks has the state *Finished.* This is different from an activity without feedback, where **all** prelinks must have the state *Finished* before it can be activated.

Figure 5 illustrates an example where the activity *compile* in workspace *Kramer* must wait for activities *code* and *read document* in workspace *Elaine* to finish, and the activity *build* in workspace *George* will be the last activity to be executed.

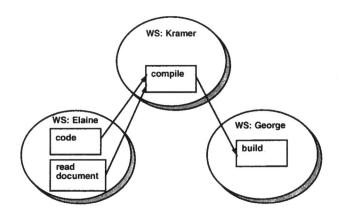

Fig. 5. Example with linked activities in several workspaces

Figure 6 shows how the dependencies between the activities are specified in our PML (XML syntax) for the example shown in figure 5. Since the activity *compile* (in the example above) has more than one $<prelink>$, it cannot be executed before *all* activities specified as $<prelink>$ are finished.

When modelling a process in our PML, it is possible to either write the process model as an XML-document, or it is possible to use a form-based web-tool to create the model. When instantiating the process model, all activities are registered in a process server (see section 3.4) with an initial state, and XML-files defining each activity will be created in the specified workspace. It is not necessary to define the whole process model at once, but you can incrementally add process fragments when desired. The definition of an activity can be modified

```
<Activity>
<Name>compile</Name>
<Workspace>Kramer</Workspace>
<Prelink>Elaine/code</Prelink>
<Prelink>Elaine/read document</Prelink>
<Postlink>George/build</Postlink>
...
</Activity>
```

Fig. 6. An example of use of $<prelink>$ and $<postlink>$ tags

directly by simply editing the XML-file for this activity in its workspace (you can not change the state). For instance to change the activity *code* (in most cases simply HTML describing what to do), will not affect other activities and can be changed directly. However if *prelinks* and *postlinks* are changed, this will affect other activities. Such changes should not be executed, before the effect of the change can be analysed. A simple analysis would be to check that the activities described in the prelinks and postlinks tags are activities registered in the process server. A more advanced analysis would be to go through the whole activity-network to detect live-locks, dead-locks etc.

3.3 Moving Process Fragments

When a process fragment is moved between workspaces at the same process server, the $<workspace>$ tags are changed while the rest of the information are left unchanged. Then the associated XML-files are moved between the workspaces. The state of the activities in the involved process fragment will be unchanged. If a process fragment is moved between two process servers (two sites), this is done as illustrated in figure 7. Let's say that a process fragment in workspace 1 (WS1) at Site 1 is going to be moved to workspace 4 (WS4) at Site 2.

- **Step 1:** Process server 1 will call a CGI-script at Process server 2 with some parameters (e.g.,
  http://www.processserver2.no/movefragment.cgi?parameters). The parameters will contain a reference to the workspace in Site 2 the process fragment is going to be moved to (e.g., *workspace=WS4*), a URL to the XML-file representing the process fragment
  (e.g., *xmlfile=http://www.processserver1.no/WS1/processfragment1.xml*), and possibly a URL to other files related to the process.
- **Step 2:** Process server 2 will send a request for downloading the XML-file and other related files from Process server 1 using the HTTP-protocol.
- **Step 3:** Process server 2 receives the XML file and other related files, and instantiate the process fragment in the process server and WS4, if there are no conflicts.

– **Step 4:** Process server 1 removes the process fragment from WS1 and removes all registered activities in the process fragment from the process server. Note that the state of the activities in the process fragment is also moved from Process server 1 to Process server 2.

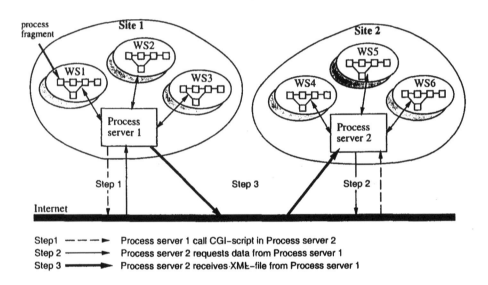

Step1 ─ ─ ─ ►   Process server 1 call CGI–script in Process server 2
Step 2 ──────►   Process server 2 requests data from Process server 1
Step 3 ══════►   Process server 2 receives·XML–file from Process server 1

Fig. 7. Moving process fragments between different process servers

There is also another way of moving process fragments and files between workspaces (also between sites). Our own CAGIS multi-agent architecture for cooperative software engineering described briefly in section 1 can be used for this purpose (see also [16, 11] for details). Coordination agents are used to transport process fragments represented in XML and other related files between workspaces. Other agents can also be used to support the more unpredictable and dynamic aspects of the process, e.g. negotiation about resources. Negotiation agents can also be used to solve arguments when people in a workspace reject process fragments moved from another workspace.

Since our process server has an open interface through CGI, other infrastructures can also be used for moving XML-files between workspaces. BSCW [3] is one example of such a system.

3.4 The Process Support Tools

Our system is programmed entirely in Perl and a web-interface is provided through a CGI. The system consists of four main components:

- **Process server/engine** The process server has three main tasks. *First*, it manages the state information of activities. Through CGI, the state of an activity can be changed. Synchronisation of an activity having several prelinks, is done by checking if all prelinks have the state *Finished* before the activity is activated. The process server also manages information about activity iterations. *Second*, the process server manages registration of new activities as well as unregistration of existing activities (also during enactment). Registration and unregistration of activities are activated through the CGI-interface. *Third*, the process server manages moving process fragments to other process servers. Through CGI, other servers can ask to move process fragments to them. The registration and unregistration of activities described above is used to facilitate movement of process fragments. The process server does not make any decisions for when process fragments are going to be moved or not. These decisions are managed by a GlueServer and specified in a GlueModel [15]. The GlueModel defines rules for how workspaces and sites shall collaborate.
- **Process modeller** A web-client for incrementally writing process models This is a simple web-interface where it is possible to enter the process model, activity by activity, to view, modify and remove existing activities. There is also support for making it easier to model activities that are linked sequentially, by automatically filling in information into the form.
- **Agenda manager** A web-client that provides an agenda to users or groups of users. Through the agenda manager, you can choose what activities to execute next and navigate through the process. Users are separated through the workspace mechanism. A workspace can be for a single user or for a group. The agenda manager also is used to visualise activities.
- **Monitor** This is an administrative tool that makes it possible to monitor the state and the progress of a process. It is also possible to change state information of the process at runtime using this tool.

In figure 8, a screenshot of the three different process tools are shown. In the upper left corner, the **Process modeller** tool is shown, and to the right we can see the window of the **Monitor** tool. The two windows below are both from the **Agenda manager** tool. To the left, the agenda for the workspace *review/author* is shown. To the right, the activity *Edit paper* is shown.

4 Discussion and evaluation

The prototype is yet simple and does not provide much advanced functionality. However we have gained some experiences based on modelling different processes

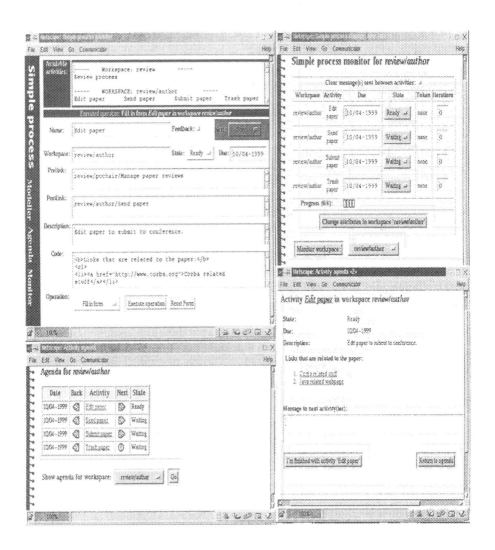

Fig. 8. Screenshots of the Process modeller tool, the Agenda manager tool, and the Monitor tool

and letting user unfamiliar with process modelling try out the prototype. The first we discovered was that our process-modelling tool was very intuitive and easy to use. For an inexperienced user, it was possible to start to model a paper review process after a 5-minute introduction of the basic concepts. We also made the same user to model the same process with a more advanced textual role-based PML [17]. When using the latter PCE, it took several days before the user could do the modelling. In the role-based PML, it was possible to model much more advanced interaction between different roles and the visualisation of activities was more flexible. Our prototype produces simple web-based workflow support, where the activities are shown as web pages defined by the modeller. The few concepts in our PML makes it easier for inexperienced users, but also makes it more limited for advanced users. Since we want inexperienced users to interact, model and change their own processes, we chose the former approach.

One problem in letting process fragments move around is that users connected to workspaces can loose track of process fragments, and it is impossible to know where different process fragments have moved. We propose to solve this problems using software agents. In our multi-agent architecture (see section 1), we have identified monitor agents. Monitor agents are system agents used to monitor events in workspaces and Agent Meeting Places. Shared repositories are used to stored information gathered by the monitor agents. Repository agents are used to retrieve event information, and give answer to users working in workspaces. In this way, it is always possible to know where process fragments are located and what has happened to them by asking agents.

In the current version of our system, there are no restrictions on changing the activity definition (model) in a local workspace. Since an activity is defined by a simple XML-file, we propose to use a configuration management tool (CM-tool) to manage different versions of activities. Any CM-tool can be used since the XML-file is only simple text. The CM-tool can be used to track and manage changes of other files in the workspaces as well. As the system is today, it is up to the user to ensure that the changes result in a valid executable process model. This approach is quite similar to how web pages work on the Internet and it is possible to define dangling links between activities. This gives the users freedom to alter the process as much as they want, but also can generate a lot of problems. We have identified a need for a tool to help the users to the right choices when altering the process model. At least the tool should give a warning that certain changes can cause dangling links between activities. This means that we need a tool for analysing consistency and impact of process model changes.

In this paper we have proposed a framework for allowing a process model to be distributed on several places, and so that parts of the process can be moved around during enactment. In [16], a software development and maintenance process from the software process industry is described. A development department is doing all the coding and changing of code in this company. It is likely to think that a work-order or change-order issued to the development department also contains a process fragment. This means that a process fragment will be moved from the department issuing the work-/change-order to the development department. It is also possible to think of a scenario where a part of a software project cannot be done internally in the company. The process fragment defining this part of the process model can then for instance be moved and executed by an external consultant company. The external consultant company will get a process fragment along with the signed contract for the job. Outsourcing parts of software projects can then be supported in the PCE/workflow tool, even if the job is executed in another environment.

5   Conclusion

Our prototype has formed a basis for supporting mobile software processes within the CAGIS architecture. The integration of the whole architecture is still to be worked on, to see the benefit from supporting mobile software processes. We expect to model and execute real-life CSE processes to gain useful experiences with moving software processes.

In this version of the prototype, there is no checking before adding an activity or a process fragment other than to check that activities already exist. This means that it is possible to instantiate process fragments that don't fit into the already running process model. We are currently working on a tool to check that process fragments fit into the model, before they are instantiated. Future work will try to solve this problem, and see how well real CSE processes can be supported in the CAGIS architecture.

6   Acknowledgement

We want to thank the Information Process Group, Computer science department, University of Manchester giving useful feedback on our work, and giving good introduction to the nice and flexible ProcessWeb environment. We would also like to thank Professor Chunnian Liu from Beijing Polytechnical University for commenting this paper and giving us useful input, and Professor Carlo Montangero and Professor Reidar Conradi for giving useful advises to improve the paper.

References

1. C. Basile, S. Calanna, E. Nitto, A. Fuggetta, and M. Gemo. Mechanisms and Policies for Federated PSEEs: Basic Concepts and Open Issues. In Carlo Montangero, editor, *Proceedings of the 5th European Workshop on Software Process Technology*, volume 1149 of *LNCS*, pages 86–91, Nancy, France, October 1996. Springer-Verlag.
2. Israel Ben-Shaul and Gail E. Kaiser. *A paradigm for decentralized process modeling*. Kluwer Academic Publisher, 1995.

3. Richard Bentley, Thilo Horstman, and Jonathan Trevor. The World Wide Web as enabling technology for CSCW: The case of BSCW. *Computer Supported Cooperative Work: The Journal of Collaborative Computing*, 7:21, 1997.
4. Supratik Bhattacharyya and Leon Osterweil. A Framework for Relocation in Mobile Process-Centered Software Development Environments. Technical report, Department of Computer Science, University of Massachusetts at Amherst, 23 August 1996.
5. Reidar Conradi, Marianne Hagaseth, Jens-Otto Larsen, and Minh Nguyen. EPOS: Object-Oriented and Cooperative Process Modelling. In *[6]*, pages 33–70, 1994.
6. Anthony Finkelstein, Jeff Kramer, and Bashar A. Nuseibeh, editors. *Software Process Modelling and Technology*. Advanced Software Development Series, Research Studies Press/John Wiley & Sons, 1994. ISBN 0-86380-169-2, 362 p.
7. Jin Jing, Karen Huff, Himanshu Sinha, Ben Hurwitz, and Bill Robinson. Workflow and Application Adaptions in Mobile Environments. In *Second IEEE Workshop on Mobile Computer Systems and Applications*, New Orleans, Lousiana, USA, 25-26 February 1999.
8. Danny Lange and Mitsuru Oshima. *Programming and deploying Java mobile agents with Aglets*. Addison-Wesley, 1998.
9. Michael Merz, Boris Liberman, and Winfried Lamersdorf. Using Mobile Agents to Support Interorganizational Workflow-Management. *International Journal on Applied Artificial Intelligence*, 11(6), September 1997.
10. CAGIS project. Cooperative agents in global information space webpage. web: http://www.idi.ntnu.no/~cagis, July 1997.
11. Geir Prestegård, Anders Aas Hanssen, Snorre Brandstadmoen, and Bård Smidsrød Nymoen. DIAS - Distributed Intelligent Agent System. Technical report, Norwegian University of Science and Technology (NTNU), April 1999. Technical Report, Dept. of Computer and Information Science, 387 p.
12. J.W. Shepherdson, S.G. Thompson, and B.R. Odgers. Cross Organisational Workflow Co-ordinated by Software Agents. In *Workshop on Cross-Organisational Workflow Management and Co-ordination*, San Francisco, USA, February 1999.
13. Pierre F. Tiako. Modelling the Federation of Process Sensitive Engineering Environments: Basic Concepts and Perspectives. In Volker Gruhn, editor, *6th European Workshop on Software Process Technologies*, volume 1487 of *Lecture notes in computer science*, pages 132–136, Weybridge, UK, 16-18 September 1998. Springer.
14. Alf Inge Wang. Experience paper: Using XML to implement a workflow tool. In *3rd Annual IASTED International Conference Software Engineering and Applications*, Scottsdale, Arizona, USA, 6-8 October 1999.
15. Alf Inge Wang, Reidar Conradi, and Chunnian Liu. Integrating software process fragments with interacting agents. Submitted to the 22nd International Conference on Software Engineering (ICSE'2000).
16. Alf Inge Wang, Chunnian Liu, and Reidar Conradi. A Multi-Agent Architecture for Cooperative Software Engineering. In *Proc. of The Eleventh International Conference on Software Engineering and Knowledge Engineering (SEKE'99)*, pages 1–22, Kaiserslautern, Germany, 17-19 June 1999.
17. Benjamin Yeomans. Enhancing the world wide web. Technical report, Computer Science dept., University of Manchester, 1996. Supervisor: Prof. Brian Warboys.
18. Jeong-Joon Yoo and Dong-Ik Lee. X-MAS: Mobile Agent Platform for Workflow Systems with Time Constraints. In *The Fourth International Symposium on Autonomous Decenralized Systems*, Tokyo, Japan, 20-23 March 1999.

View-Based Vs Traditional Modeling Approaches: Which Is Better?

Josée Turgeon[1] * and Nazim H. Madhavji[2]

[1] University of New Brunswick, Saint John campus
Saint John, New Brunswick, Canada
[2] McGill University, Montréal, Québec, Canada

Abstract. In this paper, we take a position that models of software processes elicited using a *view-based* approach are generally of higher quality (specially, more complete) than those elicited using traditional, non-view based, modeling approaches. This is validated empirically.

1 Introduction

It is widely recognized that in order to improve software development capability, one should improve software development processes. One of the first steps in process improvement is to have visibility into the existing processes, so as to simplify problem location and analysis of changes an organization needs to make for improvement.

One way to obtain such visibility is to build a descriptive model of the process concerned, by eliciting appropriate process information. This elicitation process encompasses the following key activities: planning, gathering data (from agents involved in the process, observations, documentation, etc.), modeling, analysis, and validation. It is important that the model elicited be correct and complete, because decisions will be made on the basis of such a model.

An important issue for process elicitation is that, often there isn't a single person who knows the complete process. It is thus important to obtain information from multiple sources, to ensure completeness of the model. However, such an approach is not without impediments: different agents may give inconsistent or conflicting information about the same process. Such issue has to be dealt with in the elicitation approach taken.

Our position is that an appropriately supported view-based elicitation approach can lead to more complete models. This is not only because multiple views are used, but also because by focusing on one view at a time, the elicitor can extract more (and relevant) information on a particular view.

In this paper, we explain the reasoning behind our position, and we validate it empirically.

---

* This work was carried out at McGill as part of doctoral research.

2 Related work

Several efforts have been made in eliciting process models from the software industry. In many cases, the elicitation approach used is also described.

Some researchers just present the type of information that can be elicited, and their ordering: Kawalek [6], Galle [4], Aumaitre et.al. [1], and Broeckers et.al. [3]. In other cases, specific elicitation steps are identified (e.g., planning, information gathering, and modeling): Radice et.al. [13], Madhavji et.al. [12], and Bandinelli et.al. [2]. A less formally-defined approach is to perform rounds of interviews and modeling, until the elicited model is satisfactory, such as in the work by Kellner and Hansen [7], or McGowan and Bohner [11]. Although these approaches provide good advice on how to elicit process models, none of them deal with the problem of eliciting a model from different views.

Rombach [14] has proposed to first capture the different views and model them, and then review and modify the models until all conflicts are resolved. This approach has been tried at NASA.

Sommerville [15] has proposed to separately model the views, but not to merge them. Rather, he proposes that only the interfaces between the views should be managed. His position is that the problem of non-conformance cannot be solved by modeling a single model satisfying all agents' needs.

A set of steps for view-based elicitation has been proposed by Verlage [18]: independent modeling of views, detecting similarities between views, detecting inconsistencies between views, and merging views. A similarity analysis function, based on the semantics in the MVP modeling language, helps in identifying the common elements across views. A tentative set of rules can be applied to detect inconsistencies between two views. The choice of the rules to be applied depends on the relationships between the two views (i.e., how much they overlap). The differences in the abstraction hierarchies are not resolved: each hierarchy is kept separately. This research is at an early stage, and full implementation and validation of the approach is still pending.

In an earlier paper [16], we have described an overall elicitation approach and specific techniques. While at the generic level there are parallels between our work and that by Verlage, we have developed specific techniques for supporting the elicitation process. This has been fully implemented in a prototype system called *V-elicit* [17].

3 Advantages of a view-based elicitation approach

First of all, during the planning of elicitation, it is necessary to identify which sources of information should be considered in gathering the process information. A careful planning of the sources required ensures complete or wide coverage of the information to be elicited. In a view-based approach, such an important step cannot be avoided.

The information from different sources should then be gathered and modeled into separate views. By focusing on a single view at a time, the elicitor can spend more effort in understanding the information gathered (from a scope that is easier to manage than when working on the entire process at once), and better identify where additional information is required from this source of information.

For each view, it is necessary to make sure that the information contained is consistent. Such a verification (and necessary modifications) on a view is easier to make than on the entire model, because of the reduced scope of the view. Also, if it becomes necessary to go back to the agents to solve the inconsistency encountered, only a single agent would generally have to be contacted in the case of a view.

After all the views are elicited separately, they should then be merged into a final model. This involves two phases: first the identification of the commonality across the views, and then the resolution of conflicts across views.

The analysis of the commonality across views reinforces the validity of the information gathered, because the same information has been specified by different sources. However, it is too time-consuming to get every piece of information from multiple sources. The key activities only should be validated this way.

Conflicts across views are inevitable. When using a view-based approach, the elicitor can analyze the point of view of each source, and make an enlightened choice. This ensures that all the views are considered in such a decision, not only some views that might be considered as the key ones (such as managers' views), leading to a more accurate model.

The analysis of the final model, to detect quality problems, is still required in a view-based approach. However, it does not require as much effort because many of the quality problems related to single views or conflicts across views have already been resolved.

In summary, a view-based approach necessitates piece-meal elicitation of process information from multiple sources. The analysis and merging of these information fragments then lead to a unified, quality process model.

4 Empirical study

We carried out an empirical study for validating our position that process models developed using a view-based approach are more complete than others developed using traditional approaches. We asked six subjects to model three processes each, using either V-elicit or another process modeling tool (3 tools were compared with V-elicit). We then compared the quality of the models produced across the different tools used.

The metric used to evaluate the completeness of the models is:
  the proportion of the solution model (entities and relationships in the actual process) that are present in the subject's model,

defined as follows:

$$M = A * B$$

where

$$A = \left(\frac{Number\ of\ entities\ modeled}{Number\ of\ entities\ to\ be\ modeled} \right)$$

$$B = \left(\frac{Number\ of\ relationships\ modeled}{Number\ of\ relationships\ to\ be\ modeled\ within\ the\ scope\ modeled} \right)$$

This metric represents the completeness of the model in terms of the scope actually modeled (i.e., the proportion of the solution's entities modeled), and the completeness of the information modeled within this scope (i.e., the relationships that should have been modeled, considering the scope actually modeled). It is necessary to separate the proportions of entities and relationships modeled here (using the scope) in order to avoid the problem of having different measure variations based on the number of links of a missing entity. For example, the proportion could drop more when an entity has many links than when an entity is almost isolated.

Three commercially available tools (referred to as A, B, and C in this paper[3]) were compared against V-elicit. These tools were chosen because they were each using a different notational paradigm (or combination of paradigms). They are also typical of currently available tools in that they do not provide guidance on the elicitation method to be used: the subjects had to use an ad-hoc method, figuring out by themselves how to merge the views.

The subjects were graduate students with prior exposure to process modeling concepts through a graduate course and/or readings on that topic. However, they had different levels of experience in this area. When assigning a tool to each of the students, we made sure that the group using V-elicit and the group using other tools were composed of people with different backgrounds, to ensure that the results would not be affected by this factor. In order to reduce the effect of modeling experience, every subject went through a training period to become familiar with the tools they were going to use in the study.

In order to ensure that the processes to be modeled were not biased in favor of any particular tool, we selected three processes from external (neutral) sources. We also made sure that these processes contain information that is not trivial to model (as typically encountered in real situations), such as management activities and their interaction with development activities. Each of the three processes were described in English, from three different partially-overlapping views.

The first two processes used came from industrial-scale processes, elicited independently by a group of several researchers in another project [10]. One of these processes is a *preliminary analysis phase* of software development, and the other one is a *document review* process. Transcripts of the information captured from the two processes were available to us.

---

[3] The names are withheld for reasons of privacy.

The third process used is the ISPW6 example on how software changes are handled in the development process [8]. We had to reorganize the information provided in this example process by views, from the three agents identified, in order to simulate the environment assumed in a view-based elicitation (i.e., getting information from different sources). No information was added or deleted from the process during such reorganization.

The results of this study are shown in Table 1. The p-value indicated is the result of the statistical analysis using a two-way ANOVA test[4] [5], for the factor "subject" and the block "process".

Tool used	V-elicit			A	B	C	p-value
Subject	#1	#2	#3	#4	#5	#6	
process 1	0.925	0.860	0.698	0.613	0.618	0.562	
process 2	1.000	0.857	1.000	0.612	0.844	0.854	
process 3	0.918	0.838	0.869	0.808	0.667	0.752	
average	0.948	0.852	0.856	0.678	0.709	0.723	0.025

at 0.05 significance level

Table 1. Empirical study data

As one can see from the p-value, the difference in model completeness is significant at the 0.05 level. Additional tests on the *means* (Student-Newman-Keuls range test) have shown that there is no significant difference among the models developed using V-elicit, or among the models developed using the other tools. However, there is a significant difference (at 0.05 level) between the models developed using V-elicit and the models developed using the other tools: the average completeness measures are higher in the case of V-elicit than in the case of the other tools. Thus, the models developed using V-elicit are more complete than the ones developed using the other tools.

5 Conclusion

From the results of this empirical study, we conclude that, in general, the models developed using a view-based approach (V-elicit) are more complete than the ones developed using other elicitation approaches (or tools), as stated in our initial hypothesis.

We believe that this difference comes from the fact that by allowing the elicitor to focus on one view at a time during the modeling process, more information can be extracted from the process.

---

[4] ANOVA test is the one to be used when the experimental design is a "randomized complete block design". An equivalent non-parametric test (Friedmen) has also been used, with similar results.

The results of this study are encouraging. However, note that this study is perhaps the first one of its kind, and therefore, additional experimentation or replication is important.

References

1. J.-M. Aumaitre, M. Dowson, D.-R. Harjani, "Lessons Learned from Formalizing and Implementing a Large Process Model", Proc. of Third European Workshop on Software Process Technology, Villars de Lans, France, Springer-Verlag, LNCS #772, February 1994, pp. 227–239.
2. S. Bandinelli, A. Fuggetta, L. Lavazza, M. Loi, G. P. Picco, "Modeling and Improving an Industrial Software Process", IEEE Trans. on Software Engineering, vol. 21, no. 5, May 1995, pp. 440–454.
3. A. Broeckers, C. Differding, G. Threin, "The Role of Software Process Modeling in Planning Industrial Measurement Programs", Proc. of Third International Metrics Symposium, Berlin, Germany, March 1996.
4. J. Galle, "Applying Process Modeling", Proc. of Second European Workshop on Software Process Technology, Trondheim, Norway, Springer-Verlag, LNCS #635, September 1992, pp. 230–236.
5. C. R. Hicks, "Fundamental Concepts in the Design of Experiments", 4th edition, Saunders College Publishing, 1993.
6. P. J. Kawalek, "The Process Modeling Cookbook Orientation, Description, and Experience", Proc. od Second European Workshop on Software Process Technology, Trondheim, Norway, Springer-Verlag, LNCS #635, September 1992, pp. 227–229.
7. M. I. Kellner, G. A. Hansen, "Software Process Modeling: A Case Study", Proc. of 22nd Annual Hawaii International Conference on System Sciences, vol II – Software Track, IEEE CS Press, January 1989, pp. 175–188.
8. M. I. Kellner, P. H. Feiler, A. Finkelstein, T. Katayama, L. J. Osterweil, M. H. Penedo, H. D. Rombach, "ISPW-6 Software Process Example", Proc. of First International Conference on the Software Process, Redondo Beach, California, IEEE CS Press, October 1991, pp. 176–186.
9. E. Koutsofios, S. C. North, "Editing graphs with Dotty", technical report, AT&T Bell Laboratories, Murray Hill, New Jersey, June 1996.
10. N. H. Madhavji, "The Macroscope Project – Software Process Engineering and Evolution", research proposal submitted to CRIM, McGill University, June 1991.
11. C. L. McGowan, S. A. Bohner, "Model Based Process Assessment", Proc. of 15th International Conference on Software Engineering, Baltimore, Maryland, IEEE CS Press, May 1993, pp. 202–211.
12. Nazim H. Madhavji, Dirk Höltje, WonKook Hong, Tilmann Bruckhaus, "Elicit: A Method for Eliciting Process Models", Proc. of third Int. Conf. on the Software Process, October 1994, pp. 111–122.
13. R. A. Radice, J. T. Harding, P. E. Munnis, R. W. Phillips, "A Programming Process Study", IBM System Journal, 24(2), 1985, pp. 91–101.
14. Dieter Rombach, "Practical Use of Formal Process Models: First Experiences", Proc. of eight Int. Software Process Workshop, Dagstuhl, Germany, March 1993, pp. 132–134.
15. I. Sommerville, G. Kotonya, S. Viller, P. Sawyer, "Process Viewpoints", Fourth European Workshop on Software Process Technology, 1995, pp.2–8.

16. J. Turgeon, N. H. Madhavji, "A Systematic, View-Based Approach to Eliciting Process Models", Proc. of Fifth, European Workshop on Software Process Technology, Nancy, France, LNCS #1149, October 1996, pp. 276–282.

17. J. Turgeon, "A View-Based System for Eliciting Software Process Models", Ph.D. Thesis, McGill University, September 1999.

18. M. Verlage, "About Views for Modeling Software Processes in a Role-specific Manner", Proc. of the Workshop on Viewpoints, San Francisco, California, ACM Press, October 1996.

Structuring Complex Software Processes by „Process Landscaping"

Volker Gruhn, Ursula Wellen

University of Dortmund, Department of Computer Science, Software Technology,
44227 Dortmund, Germany
{gruhn,wellen}@ls10.cs.uni-dortmund.de

Abstract. Process Landscaping is a method, which supports modelling of related processes. These processes can be modelled on different levels of abstraction. Interfaces between processes are considered as first class process entities. It prevents loosing an overview of the whole framework of processes and ensures that decisions about processes are not burdened out by an overwhelming amount of details. In this article we discuss the approach of Process Landscaping by developing a real-world software process.

1   Introduction

Modelling of software processes can have various purposes like documentation, analysis and improvement of software process models [Gru92, BFG93, CW95], software process improvement [ABC96, BJ95, SNT98] and software process execution [DG98, EAD99]. Independent of the concrete purpose most process modelling projects have to identify the core processes and define their chronological order of modelling. Furthermore, they have to identify and specify the interfaces between processes.

To ensure that the overall context of process modelling does not get lost one should concentrate on a small number of core software processes and distinguish between processes with and without direct interfaces to customers (internal and external processes) [HC93]. It becomes obvious that interfaces have to be modeled already on an abstract level (that means at the very beginning of a modeling project) when a number of processes has to be modeled and when the involved process modellers cannot easily identify how these processes are related. Additionally, the lack of manager's understanding of the purpose and benefits of process modelling sometimes requires modelling processes on different levels of detail. It is important to abstract from details of certain processes or even from certain processes as a whole to keep in view the whole process framework.

The salient features of the method of „Software Process Landscaping" are

- identification of the core software processes and their positioning on a top level view of a process landscape,
- explicit modelling of interfaces between software processes,
- switching between different levels of refinement,
- extension by process model details only where needed.

Especially the second feature differentiates process landscaping from other process modelling methods like those based on event-driven process chains [MS96], Petri Net-like languages and data flow diagrams, where interfaces are not first class entities. Therefore corresponding software process modelling tools do not provide mechanisms for checking interface consistencies.

In section 2 we discuss the process landscaping method in terms of key activities carried out. In section 3, the development of a real software process landscape is discussed. Section 4 sums up our experiences with applying process landscaping to real world software processes and gives an overview of our future research directions.

2   The Process Landcaping Method

A process landscape describes how software process models are related. Figure 1 gives a schema of a process landscape on the most abstract level. On this level, we do not identify individual process models, but we deal with clusters of process models which are logically related (for example, because all of them describe processes from the area of configuration management). The clusters are related by cluster interfaces represented on this level by two-headed arrows. To each of these clusters the method of process landscaping can be applied again. Based on refinements of this kind, we start from high level descriptions. We can add details about all entities of process models (like activities, object types, tools, etc.) wherever needed.

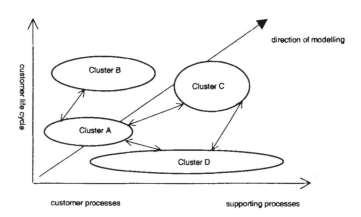

Fig. 1. Schema of a process landscape

We put a process landscape into a system of coordinates. The x-axis ranges from processes with direct interfaces to customers (called customer processes in the following) to supporting processes. The y-axis describes the dimension of the customer life cycle. It starts when a customer comes into life and terminates when the customer relationship terminates. The term "customer" is used in a rather general sense here; the "customer" of a software house is somebody who purchases software, the customer of an internal software development department is the software user.

At least one of the processes identified in a process landscape is supposed to be a customer process, otherwise all activities of all processes are exclusively devoted to internal work without any impact on the real world. Each customer process may depend on an arbitrary set of supporting processes. Each of these may itself depend on other supporting processes. The further away from an interface to the customer, the further to the right on the x-axis the process is allocated. The later in the customer life cycle the further up (on the y-axis) the process is allocated. Process clusters which contain processes starting immediately after first contact to the customers and living until the end of the customer life cycle are identified as background processes. They are depicted as clusters on the bottom of a process landscape (compare process model cluster "Project Management" in figure 2). The allocation of process model clusters in a process landscape is not meant to convey a formal notion of when to start with a process model cluster and when to terminate it. It is supposed to illustrate the context in which processes take place. All details needed to understand when to start and terminate processes are given on the lower level of process models. Based on these simple agreements, the process landscape immediately shows how processes are related and which role they play in the concert of all processes of a software company.

According to the two dimensions of distance to customers and customer life cycle, there is a natural direction of process modeling. It starts with processes which deal with new customers arriving. Processes which directly support these processes and customer processes which are carried out next are modelled afterwards. This modelling direction ensures that details about other processes (e.g. from the upper right corner of our landscape) are not described, unless it is obvious that they are actually needed. Without a clear modelling direction there is the danger to start modelling in a rather unfocused way. The results could be fragments of process models which do not fit and which perhaps are not needed. Thus, process landscaping does not only serve as an important means for orientation during modelling, but it also helps to spend modelling effort in a focused and goal-oriented way.

Process landscaping contains the following steps:

1. Identification of process model clusters
2. Identification and description of interfaces between clusters
3. Refinement of clusters
4. Acquisition of knowledge about processes
5. Process model release and change control

These steps are discussed in the following section in more detail. They are explained along an example of a software development process.

3   Developing a Software Process Landscape

In this section we discuss the development of a software process landscape which covers all processes concerning a complex software development project. In this example we use FUNSOFT nets [GU98] (high level Petri nets), but we could use any other modeling languages which supports the definition of interfaces between processes as for example SLANG [BFG93], SOCCA [EG94], Little-JIL [SOS98]. For this article it is sufficient to know that we use Petri nets; it is not necessary to know any details about FUNSOFT nets.

Following the direction of modeling of the process landscaping method, we start the development of the software process landscape with processes concerning the preparation of a project plan. Then we continue with starting the software development activities. In parallel to software development activities, several quality management tasks have to be carried out. When the first software components are released, configuration management can start.

Subsections 3.1 to 3.5 explain the different steps during the development of a software process landscape, each illustrated by an example.

3.1 Identification of Process Model Clusters

We identify process model clusters by interviewing those persons who either consider themselves as process owners for specific processes or who are claimed to be process owners by executive managers. Talking to these people usually gives a quick impression about the core processes to be considered. Of course, this quick and immature impression is not definitive, but it serves as a good starting point. If a refinement or a summary of a cluster seems to be necessary at a certain time, this can be done easily (see section 3.3).

The customer life cycle oriented approach taken in process landscaping results in the following process model clusters:

- Project Management
- Software Development
- Quality Management
- Configuration Management

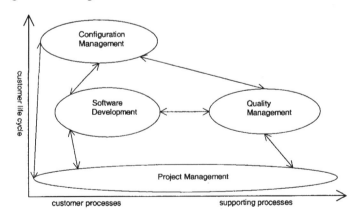

Fig. 2. Software Process Landscape

Figure 2 shows the top-level representation of the software process landscape. We start with the overall cluster "Project Management" because it contains processes very closely related to a future user as well as background processes of the software house. This cluster also affects the whole customer life cycle. In the graphical representation we find it in the bottom part ranging over the complete x-axis. To receive and to check the order to develop a software system is one of the processes of this cluster. When the order is received, the development of the software system can start. Once the requirements for a software system are identified, the processes from the area of quality management and further project management processes become active. These are processes which do not deal with users directly. When the system design has been defined and some software components are implemented, configuration management processes become more and more important. Configuration units have to be identified and a release plan has to be developed. Installation checks have to be carried out in co-operation with the quality management and at least the system delivery has to be prepared. The delivery process itself is again a process closely related to the user (within the cluster "Configuration Management").

The two-headed arrows already depict some cluster interfaces which exist obviously. The way how to identify them all and how to describe them will be discussed in the following section.

3.2   Identification and Description of Interfaces between Clusters

Two clusters are connected if there is at least one information exchange between processes of both clusters (compare to the notion of an interface refinement illustrated in figure 3). Key interfaces between clusters become obvious in the same way as clusters do, simply by asking people to tell the types of information which are exchanged.

On the most abstract level the purpose of cluster interfaces is just to indicate that both clusters contain process models which share at least one interface. For a more detailed description we use circles (called channels), named like the type of data which has to be exchanged. Directed edges indicate from where to where information is exchanged.

Figure 3 shows an example of an interface agreement between two process model clusters, namely between cluster "Software Development" and cluster "Quality Management". It shows that there are six channels between these two clusters and it shows which types of data are passed from one cluster to another. The example shows that some guidelines for development activities are passed from quality management processes to software development processes and that results are returned. The programming guidelines and the specification guidelines are mentioned explicitly, other types of guidelines are omitted in figure 3. Single-headed arrows denote the flow of information between clusters. Sometimes pairs of channels are used to show the type of information which is passed into one direction, processed in the destination cluster and returned back. For example, the software code which has to be tested (see figure 3, interface B) is sent back from cluster "Quality Management" to cluster "Software Development" through channel C (tested software code) when it has been tested.

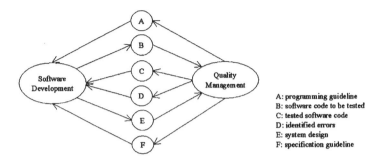

A: programming guideline
B: software code to be tested
C: tested software code
D: identified errors
E: system design
F: specification guideline

Fig. 3. Refined interfaces between process model clusters "Software Development" and "Quality Management"

3.3 Refinement of Clusters

After the identification of the core processes the concerning clusters have to be refined. To get a more detailed knowledge about the internal structure of each cluster we need a complete list of all activities belonging to such a cluster. These activities either can be so coarse-grained that they are described as a cluster (which itself needs further refinement) or they can be so fine-grained, that they can immediately be described by a process model.

Figure 4 illustrates the relationhip between the refinement of a core process and its mapping on the several levels of the software process landscape.

Each core process is described as a set of process models either directly or after one ore more subclustering steps.

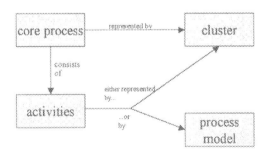

Fig. 4. Relationship between core process and cluster, activities and process models

If we apply the way of refining a cluster to our software development example, the cluster "Software Development" can first be devided into five subclusters, namely

- Requirement Definition
- Requirement Analysis
- Software Specification
- System Design
- Implementation

Figure 5 shows this refinement together with interfaces to cluster "Quality Management" and cluster "Configuration Management". While the interfaces to cluster "Configuration Management" are not refined, single-headed bold arrows show how interfaces between cluster "Software Development" and cluster "Quality Management" are used in the refinement of cluster "Software Development". They are connected with subclusters of cluster "Software Development". This shows how interface refinements and cluster refinements are composed. The subclusters of cluster "Software Development" also have interfaces between each other. They are indicated as two-headed arrows in figure 5 and can be refined in a further step.

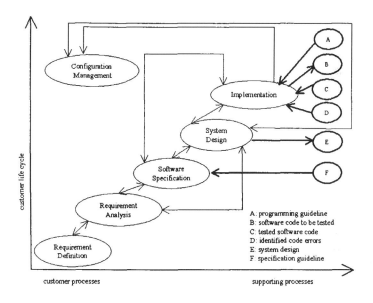

Fig. 5. Subclusters of cluster "Software Development" with refined interfaces to cluster "Quality Management" and interfaces to cluster "Configuration Management"

The cluster "Project Management" is refined directly to a set of process models (see figure 6), namely "prepare project plan", "review project plan", "cost control", "post mortem analysis". Each of these process models is then described by means of a software process modelling language, in our example by FUNSOFT nets (not depicted here).

Fig. 6. Process models within the cluster "Project Management"

3.4 Acquisition of Knowledge about Processes

Knowledge acquisition starts with interviews and with careful reading of available documentation. To obtain more detailed information about processes, we deploy process scenarios dealing with customers with different perspectives and objectives. A scenario describes a typical process situation and identifies processes used to cope with this situation. Scenarios start from high level descriptions. A process owner and a process modeler use a scenario for a step-by-step walkthrough. For each activity, details are added (which exceptions may occur, what is the type of input information needed and of output information produced, who is responsible, which tools are used, which guidelines are to be applied). The result is a detailed process model which can be refined in the same way.

In our example we did knowledge acquisition for one process model out of the cluster "Configuration Management". This cluster has been refined by a set of process models directly. The process models used the FUNSOFT net semantic as basis.

Figures 7a and 7b represent the process model "Release System" which belongs to the cluster "Configuration Management". Figure 7a shows the complete process model, whereas figure 7b illustrates a refinement of the activity "release" within the process model "Release System". The arrows within the two FUNSOFT nets indicate data and control flow.

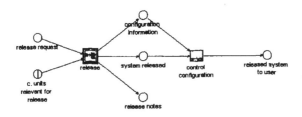

Fig. 7a. Process model "Release System" of cluster "Configuration Management"

When a release request comes in, the activity "release" needs information about the configuration units relevant for a new release. This information will be sent via a process model interface of the cluster "Quality Management" depicted as channel"c. units relevant for release" (see also figure 4, interface C).

The activity "release" itself consists of several tasks like the identification of configuration units to be exchanged and the adaptation of altered configuration units (compare to figure 7b). As results of the release activity we get the released system, detailed configuration information and release notes (see channels in figure 7a, 7b). After the integration of all exchanged and adapted configuration units the configuration will be under control of the configuration manager. He can now deliver the released system to the user. This fact is illustrated as activity "control configuration" and the outgoing channel "released system to the user".

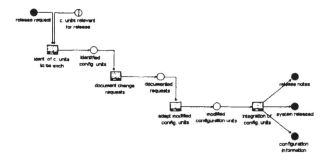

Fig. 7b. Refinement of activity "release within the process model "Release System" of cluster"Configuration Management"

3.5 Process Model Release and Change Control

Once stable process models have been obtained, they have to be released and "change-managed". This means, that the process model is made available to all people interested and that from then on change requests are handled in a formal way. Internal details of a process model are checked by the process owner. If he/she decides that everything is properly modelled, then one precondition for a model release is satisfied. The other precondition is that changes of process interfaces have to be agreed on by all owners of processes using these interfaces. The mechanism for doing so is a common meeting with the owner of the process whose model is about to be released and with the owners of all other processes with interfaces to the model which is to be released. These meetings are moderated by the process owner of the process model concerned. The goal of such a meeting is to present process details (in order to raise understanding for the structure of the process) and to finally agree on interfaces. Once this is done, new versions of process models can be released.

3.6 Process Model Release and Change Control

Figure 8 depicts the software process landscape as it was developed in the previous subsections. It doesn't depict the complete landscape because this would go beyond the limits of the figure. The overall view is just to get a feeling of how a complete landscape could look like and how different representations on different levels of abstractions are related.

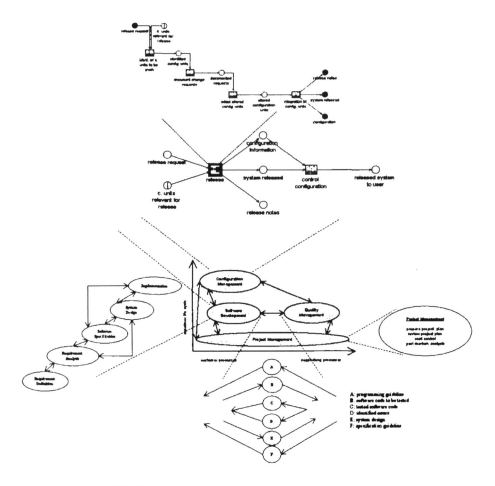

Fig. 8. Overall view of the software process landscape

In the center of the overall landscape we find the most abstract clusters representing the core processes. They are arranged into a system of coordinates as it was introduced in section 2, figure 1 (see bold lines in figure 8). All refinements of either a cluster, an interface or a process model activity are indicated by two broken lines leading from the abstract entity to its refinement.

Starting from the very top of the landscape we refine the clusters by subclusters, and/or process models. The cluster "Software Development" is refined into five subclusters (left side of figure 8). Their interfaces to each other are depicted as two-headed arrows analog to the most abstract level of the landscape. The overall cluster "Project Management" is refined into four process models without subclustering previously (right side of figure 8).

The cluster "Configuration Management" is refined into subclusters neither. One of its process models, namely the process model "Release System", is depicted as a FUNSOFT net (see also figure 7a). This type of Petri nets enables further hierarchical refinement of process model activities. The activity "release", depicted as rectangular symbol, is refined this way (see also figure 7b).

Figure 8 also shows a refinement of the interface between the two clusters "Software Development" and "Quality Management" (see bottom of figure 8, see also figure 3). The list of the objects to be exchanged is not complete, but it shows how the two-headed arrows, indicating the data flow relation, has been refined to one-headed arrows.

For cluster "Project Management" it is indicated that details are given by four process models, called "prepare project plan", "review project plan", "cost control", "post mortem analysis". These process models are described by FUNSOFT nets in the next step. In figure 8 we omitted some details about the composition of refinements, because the composition rules have already been illustrated in the previous subsections.

Figure 8 might appear overly complicated, but the different notions of refinement turned out to be useful in structuring complex software processes. Obviously, it is not reasonable to apply all kinds of refinement in a small example (as given in figure 8). This example is only meant to illustrate the interplay of the different notions of refinement.

4   Conclusion

We applied the method of Process Landscaping to software processes in various telecommunication and insurance companies as well as in software houses. The experiences we made in modelling software processes show this method is useful in most cases. Only small modelling projects could be handled in a more efficient way without Process Landscaping.

There are two particular strengths of Process Landscaping: One is the focused modelling of core processes where information details are only modelled, when there are relevant. Otherwise their depiction will be avoided. The other one is the communication support on different levels of abstraction. The top level view of a process landscape is useful to discuss with managers, details can be discussed on lower landscape levels with software developers.

In its current state, process landscaping supports checking of predefined consistency conditions. Our future research with respect to consistency conditions will be focused on user-defined consistency conditions and support for their automatic evaluation. Our future work will also be focused on the integration of process modelling tools into the process landscaping method. This will ensure us to avoid unnecessary re-implementation of process modelling tools and it will easily allow to benefit from process landscaping in projects which already fixed a particular software process modelling language and/or tool.

References

[ABC96] D. Avrilionis, N. Belkhatir, P.-Y Cunin, Improving Software Process Modelling and Enactment Techniques, In: C. Montangero (ed.), Software Process Technology – Proceedings of the 5th European Workshop, Nancy, France, Oct. 1996, appeared as Lecture Notes in Computer Science No. 1149, pages 65-74

[BFG93] S. Bandinelli, A. Fugetta, S. Grigolli, Process Modelling in-the Large with SLANG, In:Proceedings of the 2nd International Conferenceon the Software Process – Continous Software Improvement, Berlin, Germany, Feb. 1993, pages 75-83

[BJ95] J.G. Brodman and D.L. Johnson, Return on Investment (ROI) from Software Process Improvement Measured by US Industry, In: Software Process Improvement Practice, John Wiley and Sons, Pilot Issue, Volume 1, August 1995, pages 35-48

[CW95] J.E. Cook, A. Wolf, Automating Process Discovery through Event-Data Analysis, In: Proceedings of the 17th International Conference on Software Engineering, Seattle, Washington, US, 1995, pages 73-82

[DG98] W. Deiters, V. Gruhn, Process Management in Practice - Applying the FUNSOFT Net Approach to Large Scale Processes, In: Special Issue on Process Technology / Automated Software Engineering, Nr. 5, 1998, pages7-25

[EAD99] J. Estublier, M. Amiour, S. Dami, Building a Federation of Process Support Systems, In: Proceedings of the International Joint Conference on Work Activities and Collaboration WACC '99, San Francisco, California, Feb. 1999, pages 197-206

[EG94] G. Engels, L. Groenewegen, SOCCA: Specifications of Coordinated and Cooperative Activities, In: A. Finkelstein, J. Kramer, B. Nuseibeh (eds.), Software Process Modelling and Technology, John Wiley & Sons, London, England, 1994, pages 71-100

[Gru92] V. Gruhn, Software Process Simulation on Arbitrary Levels of Abstraction, In: A. Sydow (ed.), Computational Systems Analysis 1992, Elsevier, Amsterdam, Netherlands, 1992, pages 439-444

[GU98] V. Gruhn, Urbainczyk, Software Process Modeling and Enactment: An Experinece Report Related to Problem Tracking in an Industrial Project, In: Proceedings of the 20th International Conference on Software Engineering, Kyoto, Japan, Apr. 1998, pages 13-21

[HC93] M. Hammer, J. Champy, Reengineering the Corporation, Harper Business, New York, US, 1993

[MS96] S. Meinhard, F. Sänger, R/3 Deveolopment Processes as Framework for Successful Projects (in German), HMD 33 (192), 1996, pages 100-112

[SNT98] K. Sakamoto, K. Najakoji, Y. Takagi, N. Niihara, Toward Computational Support for Software Process Improvement Activities, In: Proceedings of the 20th International Conference on Software Engineering, Kyoto, Japan, April, 1998, pages 22-32

[SOS98] B. Staudt Lerner, L.J. Osterweil, S.M. Sutton Jr., A. Wise, Programming Process Coordination in Little-JIL, In: V. Gruhn (ed.), 6th European Workshop on Process Technology, Weybridge, UK, Springer, Heidelberg, Germany, 1998, appeared as Lecture Notes in Computer Science No, 1487, pages 127-131

Keynote on "Experimental Software Engineering"

Victor R. Basili,
University of Maryland, College Park MD, USA

Abstract:

This presentation offers a view of software development based upon building knowledge through model building, experimentation, and learning. It treats the study of software engineering as a laboratory science. To this end, various abstraction techniques, experimental designs, and learning methods must evolve to support this paradigm.

To support experimental software engineering research, we need to provide a framework for building relevant practical Software Engineering knowledge that will increase the effectiveness of individual experiments. To support the practitioner, we need to provide a better basis for making judgements about selecting and tailoring processes and organizations integrate their experiences with processes.

An example of knowledge evolution will be given: the evolution of software reading from early reading versus testing experiments to the development of focused tailored reading techniques based upon feedback from experimentation and application in practice. The example will be used to demonstrate a mechanism for organizing sets of related studies so that experiments can be viewed as part of common families of studies, rather than isolated events.

Common families of studies can contribute to higher level hypotheses that no individual experiment could achieve. Then the replication of experiments within a family of studies can act as the cornerstone for building knowledge in an incremental manner. A mechanism is suggested that motivates, records, and integrates individual experiments within a family for analysis by the community at large.

The example studies are used to demonstrate that:

(1) techniques that are procedurally defined, document and notation specific, and goal driven can be effectively designed and studied,

(2) a procedural approach to a software engineering task can be more effective than a less procedural one under certain conditions (e.g., depends on experience), and

(3) a procedural approach to reading based upon specific goals will find defects related to those goals, so reading can tailored to the environment.

Software Process Technologies and the Competitiveness Challenge

Giovanni A. Cignoni

Cesvit SpA
Via G. del Pian dei Carpini, 28
Firenze, ITALY
`cignoni@cesvit.it`

Abstract. Competitive quality is a need for the progress of the Information Technology sector. For enterprises, *process* is the starting point of all the approaches in the achievement of competitive quality. Despite these widely accepted hypotheses, we fail to demonstrate that Software Process Technologies are really adopted by enterprises. In this position paper we want to stimulate the discussion about the practical adoption of process technologies proposing two issues. First, following the demand for quality, work in the field of process technologies must be directly addressed to quality achievement. Second, if we want to "sell" process technologies, we have to propose to enterprises an incremental approach that minimises investments and promises quality results in the short term.

Introduction

Information Technology (IT) is one of the key sectors, probably the most important one, that will drive technological and economical progress in the next century. Research and practical applications will contribute to new infrastructures for social interaction, scientific research, industrial production, and business activity [1].

IT enterprises have to transform research achievements in products and services able to satisfy the needs and the expectations of the market. It is a great business opportunity, but it is also a hard challenge: enterprises have to compete keeping low prices and offering better quality.

Software Process Technologies (SPTs) collect the results of a wide research area. Up to now, many proposals for formal definition, evaluation, and partial automation of the development process, were suggested by the SPTs research community. Can such results become useful tools for the enterprises engaged in the competitiveness challenge?

Demand for Process, Product, and Project Quality

Process quality is an axiom of the Total Quality Management approach. Such imperative is explained by the natural remark that good results seldom arise from bad processes. More practically, when production has industrial dimensions a (good) process is needed to organise and control the development activities.

Process quality is the focus of many initiatives aimed to assess and improve the capabilities of the enterprises. The ISO 9000 standards define the requirements of a specific structure inside the enterprise organisation – the *quality system* – that imply the definition and the control of all the enterprise processes. The next revision of the standards, foreseen for late 2000, will be even more process-focused [2]. In the IT sector, and particularly in software production, *Software Process Assessment & Improvement* (SPA-I) methodologies were defined with a twofold goal: customers use them to assess and select their suppliers, suppliers use them to improve their organisation. From the original CMM [3] to the almost defined ISO 15504 standard [4], SPA-I methodologies are the most practical tools for the application of the TQM concepts in the software production.

However, competitiveness of enterprises is proportional to the value/cost ratio of their products – where products are both goods and services. Value/cost is the most practical way to define *product quality*. In this perspective, process quality is functional to achieve product quality. Effective processes reduce defects and improve the value of products; efficient processes decrease costs; flexible processes let the enterprise successfully face the demand for innovation and the changes in the market.

Another way to approach competitive quality is to look at *project quality*. Process quality focuses on its correct definition, on compliance to standards, on application of best practices. Such issues aim to give confidence of the enterprise capabilities. Project quality focuses on management of resources and activities, on control of costs and schedule, on result verification and risk prevention. Project quality aims to detect and timely solve the problems that may lead to a project failure.

Process, product, and project quality are different ways to approach quality as a way to be competitive. Process quality is not a silver bullet [8], however, seems to be a common factor and a needed requirement in all the perspectives. Suppliers have to show good processes to demonstrate their capabilities to customers (and this is pure process quality). Then they have to show a faultless project management, but, because projects are instantiations of the enterprise process, process quality is necessary for project quality. At last, suppliers have to deliver results fully compliant with the customer requirements; again, timely quality control requires a well defined and correctly applied process.

All these arguments lead to consider the process as the starting point in the competitiveness challenge. As TQM gurus say and European funding initiatives propose, enterprises have to invest in their processes, to understand them, to define them, to assess them, to improve them, but most of all to use them to set up sound projects and deliver better products.

SPTs Technologies and Quality Achievement

Several proposals and solutions have been developed in the field of SPTs. Description, evaluation and control are the main approached issues: using this perspective we can classify research and applicable results in three different areas:

- *process definition and enactment*; this is the software process modelling area, which general aim is to formally define the process and to provide enactment environments that execute the process program controlling development tools and delivered products;

- *process assessment and improvement*; this is the SPA-I standard and methodologies area, which main aim is to define a capability framework to assess the processes and define improvement paths;
- *project planning and management*; this is the area devoted to tools for project support, which comprehends tools for planning and tracking of activities, resource allocation, cost control, and automation of documentation management and flow.

Besides their goals and specialisation, these areas are also characterised for their typical contexts. Each of them is the result of a different path that often reached its maturity without much sharing with the other areas. Process definition and enactment has its typical context in the research community. The latest results in process assessment and improvement belong to the context of the international standardisation bodies. Project planning and control, including workflow and document management (read *version & configuration control*, when applied to software development), is a field well covered by continuously evolving commercial tools.

The idea of joining the efforts is natural and already discussed. We have to fill gaps between different areas, to develop common concepts and principles, to exploit the achievements of each others. Several good motivations to these goals were proposed in [5]. Here we want to add to the discussion a new perspective that aims to facilitate the introduction of SPTs in the enterprises.

Rather than classify SPTs from the perspective of historical evolution, we propose six *technology levels*. The idea is to propose to enterprises a defined improvement path in the adoption of available technologies. The order we propose follow the natural availability and maturity of specific SPTs and aims to maximise the return-of-investment for the enterprise. At the lower levels there are technologies that are more suitable as the first ones to be adopted in an enterprise. Higher level technologies are to be introduced later so that they can take advantage of the already established lower technologies. Table 1 defines the levels: for each technology level we identified the possible direct benefits in terms of quality achievements.

At level 0 there are the tools for activities support. Tools for basic workflow, version and configuration control, documentation management, and personal scheduling do not address the process, they just support and partially automate simple activities. However, their integration and customisation capabilities can be exploited in the process perspective. Tool customisation, often requiring not trivial programming efforts, is the first attempt of formal process definition that is a move toward level 1: adoption of languages to define, to understand, and to argue about the enterprise processes. Level 2, process measurement, has now to be seen as the marriage of the process formalisation with the assessment goal. In the new perspective, a formal assessment is not an audit performed by severe assessors, but a measure taken on a process definition. At level 3 the formal definition of the process is used to instantiate the enterprise projects giving actual values to deadlines, efforts, and resources. Level 4 introduces automatic control of project critical parameters as a valuable tool for decision support. Last, level 5 is the final goal of the SPTs area: enacting environments that completely control the process and automate manual activities.

While adopting the 0-5 mystic range, we do not refer to the classical process maturity scale. However, there is an underlying idea of increasing maturity, both in the perspective of the adopting enterprise and in the complexity of the technologies themselves.

Level	*Technology*	*Benefits*
0. support tools	tools that automate and support basic activities	• more efficiency • better control of activities
1. process languages	languages for formal process description	• better comprehension and training • more customer confidence
2. process measurement	formal measurement and assessment of the process	• better compliance to standards • more customer confidence
3. project templates	automated instantiation of processes in projects	• better planning and resource allocation • higher standardisation
4. project control	automated verification of costs and schedule	• early detection of problems • budget and schedule control
5. automated enacting	automation of manual activities	• implied correctness of performed activities • more efficiency

Table 1. Levels of Software Process Technologies

Up to now there exist technologies at all the levels, but low levels are better covered: there is a wide offer of commercial support tools – and commercial means used. Several process formalisms were defined, and, at the moment, UML is probably the best runner. Many SPA-I methodologies were proposed, and an international standard is upcoming. Some tools for project planning offer features similar to project templates. While tools for controlling costs and resource allocation do exist, enactment environments are still research prototypes.

Unfortunately, we lack, for instance, a process language useful for formal ISO 15504 assessment, that can be interpreted by personal schedulers naturally integrated in an enacting environment that exploits configuration management tools and fully supports project instantiation and control. In fact, neither the ISO standard is completely defined.

Marketing Conclusions

The challenges of the IT sector in the next years and the demand for quality seem good reasons for IT enterprises to invest in the adoption of SPTs to improve their processes. However, experience shows a completely different situation.

We directly participated in a survey about software process in the enterprises of Central Italy [6]. A similar survey was performed at European level [7]. Both surveys show enterprises that have grown as their main goal, but score low maturity levels and display very scarce intention about SPTs investments. European funding initiatives are successful, but the absence of spontaneous investments shows that IT is a sector in which enterprises want to be subsidised for improving their organisation.

A possible reason is that customers do not push for quality: they are forced to accept the delivered quality because the IT market is still captive. Suppliers at the moment have benefits from such situation, but they have to face the risk of a quick change – as already happened in other sectors – with strong customers and new smart competitors.

Technologies have to follow the demand for quality: we must be very conscious of this issue and accordingly direct the research if we want to "sell" our SPTs. Moreover, we have to propose the application in the enterprises following an incremental approach that requires affordable investments and promises quality results in the short term.

Acknowledgements

This work is partially funded by CESVIT SpA in the context of the TOPS project, ESPRIT No. 27977. Some of the issues presented in the paper originate from discussions had with Letizia Jaccheri and Tor Stålhane. Vincenzo Ambriola contributed to the paper with some useful suggestions.

References

1. President's Information Technology Advisory Committee, "Information Technology Research: Investing in Our Future, Report to the President", February 1999.
2. "ISO 9000 revisions", *ISO News*, Vol. 8, No. 3, May/June 1999.
3. W.S. Humphrey, "Managing the software process", Addison-Wesley, 1989.
4. "ISO/IEC TR 15504:1998 Information technology – Software process assessment – Parts 1-9", International Organisation for Standardisation, 1998.
5. R. Conradi, A. Fuggetta, M.L. Jaccheri, "Six Thesis on Software Process Research", Proceedings of the 6th *European Workshop on Software Process Technology*, LNCS 1487, Springer Verlag, 1998.
6. G.A. Cignoni, "Rapid Software Process Assessment to Promote Innovation in SMEs", Proceedings of the *European Software Day at Euromicro 99*, 1999.
7. T. Stålhane, "SPI - why isn't it more used", Proceedings of the *EuroSPI'99 Conference*, October 25-27, 1999.
8. J. Voas, "Software Quality's Eight Greatest Myths", *IEEE Software*, Vol. 16, No. 5, September/October 1999.

Test Management Automation: Lessons Learned from a Process Improvement Experiment

Giuseppe La Commare[1], Griselda Giraudo[1] and Paolo Tonella[2]

[1] Sodalia SpA, via V. Zambra, 1 - 38100 Trento - Italy
[2] ITC-Irst, 38050 Povo (Trento) - Italy

Abstract. Test management aims at organizing, documenting and executing test cases, and at generating execution reports. The adoption of a support tool for such activities is expected to improve the current practice. ITALO is a European project devoted to the evaluation of the benefits coming from test management automation.

In this paper the experiences collected and the lessons learned during ITALO are summarized. An experiment was designed to measure the effects that are produced by the new test process complemented with the introduction of the support tool. Pilot projects were conducted to measure the benefits obtained from tool usage and process modification.

1 Introduction

The goal of ITALO (Improvement of the Testing Activities for the Development of Object Oriented Software), the ESSI PIE (Process Improvement Experiment) European project n. 27912, is to improve the component testing phase in Sodalia, by adopting automatic tools to complement and help programmers.

The area of component test which was perceived to need prior improvement and for which commercial tools are available is *test management*. The DESMET method, described in [2], was followed in the selection of the tool to be adopted within the ITALO project [3]. The result was TestExpert, a test management tool by Silicon Valley Networks.

The general approach to the component test process was enhanced, so that it can be performed with the support of the selected tool [1]. Main changes involved a reorganization of the testing activities and artifacts, to allow their production by exploiting tool facilities.

An experiment was set up to apply the new testing process and evaluate the related benefits. This paper describes the activities performed within the main phases of such experiment and reports some general lessons that could be learned from this experience.

The paper is organized as follows: Section 2 describes the experimental design developed to evaluate the effects of tool adoption on three pilot projects, while the results of the experiment execution are given in Section 3. A discussion of such results can be found in Section 4, and a list of lessons learned is provided in Section 5.

2 Experimental design

The aim of the experiment is to demonstrate that the adoption of tools helping programmers during component testing enables to promote a higher software quality with decreasing or constant human resources. It also contributes to making the development process repeatable, by introducing a standard and uniform way of organizing, documenting and managing test sessions.

The improvement in the *test case organization* consists of a uniform hierarchical structuring of all test cases defined for a component. In the current practice, the only opportunity for test case organization is the use of a proper structure of directories, while documentation is generally provided by means of comments in the test scripts and README files.

As regards *test case execution*, the selected tool supports the automatic execution of a given scenario, consisting of a sequence of test cases from a test suite. Automation in the execution phase is now achieved by defining ad hoc test scripts.

Report generation permits the automatic production of individual test execution logs and summaries. In addition, the final documentation on the component test activity is automatically filled in. According to the current practice the final report is written manually and detailed reports are not considered mandatory.

The *state variables* are the factors that can influence the results of the experiment. The coverage of the most typical values for the state variables is a precondition to obtain general and valid results on the experimental hypothesis. The most important state variables for the pilot projects are the following:

1. Programming and testing experience of the developers.
2. Application domain of the tested component.
3. Functional area of the classes involved in the tested component.
4. Familiarity of the developers with other tools.
5. Scale of the project.
6. Size of the project team.
7. Number of iterations previously completed.

In order to check that pilot projects are selected with features that are typical of Sodalia, subjects were asked to fill in a pre-questionnaire.

To evaluate the results of the experiment on the pilot projects, the following measures strictly related to the experimental hypothesis were collected:

1. Component construction effort.
2. Defects found in component test.
3. Defects found in integration/system test, associated to an isolated component.
4. Component size in LOC (Lines Of Code).

Comparison data were extracted from the historical data base from a previous iteration on the same component or from projects with similar characteristics.

Objective quantitative measures were complemented with subjective evaluations on the usefulness of the test support tool, collected through a post-questionnaire. The purpose of the questionnaire is also to evaluate the medium to long term effects of tool adoption, that cannot be otherwise captured given the short time scale of this experiment.

3   Results

The first pilot project was a re-engineering project aimed at restructuring the REULIB component, which merges the functionalities of two previous components, ULIB and COMMONLIB. The analysis of the pre-questionnaires for the pilot project suggests that the collected data are meaningful.

	ULIB	COMMONLIB	REULIB
Size (LOC)	7038	4504	6678
Effort (pd)	20	79	109
Defects (CT)	7	N/A	4
Defects (I/ST)	8	12	5
Effort per kLOC	2.84	17.5	16.3
Defects (CT) per kLOC	0.99	N/A	0.59
Defects (I/ST) per kLOC	1.13	2.66	0.74
User projects	2	3	2

Table 1. Measures collected for the pilot project.

Since REULIB is an evolution of both ULIB and COMMONLIB, the latter were used as *baselines* against which response variables are evaluated. Both baseline projects have features making them similar to REULIB, but the interventions performed for COMMONLIB make it a slightly better reference point.

Table 1 gives the collected measures. Effort was measured in person/days (pd). Defects were counted both during Component Test (CT) and Integration/System Test (I/ST). Measures are normalized with respect to the size of the component, to make them comparable. The last line of the table gives the number of user projects that included each component, and thus exercised it during their integration and system test.

The normalized effort is substantially unchanged (actually, slightly decreased) with respect to COMMONLIB. The increase with respect to ULIB is due to the different kind of modification required by the REULIB. In fact, the maintenance performed on ULIB was corrective, while it was basically adaptive, perfective and preventive for both COMMONLIB and REULIB.

As shown in Table 1, the normalized defects found during component test are less than those detected for ULIB, while the COMMONLIB value is not available. The decrease with respect to ULIB can be explained by the different kind of intervention performed on the two components.

REULIB entered the integration and system test phase with a lower number of residual defects than both ULIB and COMMONLIB. Such improvement in the quality of this component may be due to a more effective component test phase. The number of user projects that exercised REULIB during integration and system tests is the same as ULIB and lower than COMMONLIB. The presence of 1 more test project for COMMONLIB can only partially explain its higher number of defects found, thus suggesting that an increased quality of component test may be the reason for the remarkable difference between the two projects.

Tool support	Score (median)
Organization and documentation	*somewhat–much*
Execution	*somewhat*
Report generation	*much*
Effort reduction	*little*
Defect removal increase	*little*
Medium-long term documentation	*much*
Medium-long term regression check	*much*

Table 2. Subjective scores given by the REULIB team. The adopted ordinal scale consists of five levels of support: *not at all, little, somewhat, much, very much.*

Table 2 contains the subjective tool evaluations collected through the post-questionnaire. Since scores on the tool support were given on an ordinal scale, the median is provided as a summary of the evaluations.

Qualitative data are more pessimistic than the quantitative ones, as regards the short term effects. Only a little support to effort reduction and defect removal increase was perceived by the subjects involved in the experiment. This may be due to the difficulties encountered when the tool is adopted for the first time.

The evaluations of the tool intrinsic features range from *somewhat* to *much*, thus showing that they are generally satisfactory, even if not particularly good. The lower score for the execution support is due to the peculiarity of the REULIB project, which required the possibility of execution under 9 configurations.

The medium to long term impact of tool adoption was judged very positive, with regard to the possibility of obtaining good documentation and of effectively and efficiently performing regression check.

4 Discussion

The selected tool for test management automation was successfully introduced within a pilot project. The experimental hypothesis was confirmed by this first experiment, since an increased defect removal was obtained without any substantial change of the effort.

Moreover, initial costs, related to importing existing test cases into the tool database, finding an appropriate organization, customizing the tool to satisfy specific needs, and solving problems in the tool functions, are expected to disappear in the next usage of the tool within the same project.

Several positive effects of tool adoption are not apparent from the quantitative data. The test case organization was judged very satisfactory. A new software engineer charged to test the component is expected to be able to understand it in a short time. Test case documentation is another important achievement.

The component test process resulted improved in general, since test case management and execution is now a reproducible activity, independent of the personal choices of the programmers, even in presence of complex multi-version structures. The tool was considered of interest also for the successive testing phases, namely integration and system test, thus extending the associated benefits to a wider portion of the software life cycle.

The answers to questions associated to medium and long term effects suggest that regression check, test case reuse, documentation and organization are expected to find substantial support from the tool, thus reducing the effort during the future testing iterations. The deeper regression check is also expected to increase the defect removal level.

5 Lessons learned

Reduced effort and increased quality are goals that often drive the selection and adoption of support tools. Nevertheless, unavoidable problems are related to the culture of the people, the need to customise the tool, the learning phase, and the modification of existing practices. Therefore managers and project leaders should be aware that a start up difficulty may be encountered.

Ideally tool introduction and process formalisation should be conducted in parallel, so that the new activities can be directly coupled with the tool features. A common situation is that the current practice is already somewhat structured, and the migration requires the possibility to import old artifacts, together with a modification of the user's perspective on their organization and execution. For a successful tool introduction both activities need specific support.

A consequence of the above considerations is that the role of tool expert, possibly different from the tool administrator, is an essential one. A person has to be responsible for helping people to deal with practical problems, to make decisions on the overall organization of the artifacts and the overall approach to tool use, and to customise the tool according to specific needs.

To import existing test cases into the tool database, a re-design activity may be necessary. In fact, the organization and operations provided by the tool could not always be directly mapped into the existing structure. The result in our experiment was a higher standardisation and quality of the inserted test cases.

References

1. G. Giraudo, P. Tonella, G. La Commare: Component Test Guidelines. ESSI PIE 27912 - ITALO - Deliverable D2, September 1998.
2. B. Kitchenham: A method for evaluating Software Engineering methods and tools. Technical Report TR96-09, DESMET project UK DTI, 1996.
3. P. Tonella, G. Giraudo, G. Antoniol, E. Mambella: Tool Selection Feature Analysis. ESSI PIE 27912 - ITALO - Deliverable D1, August 1998.

The Introduction and Evaluation of Object Orientation in a Company Developing Real-Time Embedded Systems

Colin J Theaker, Neil Blackwood, Robert Mason

Terrafix Limited, 23c Newfield Industrial Estate,
High Street, Tunstall, Stoke-on-Trent, England, ST6 5PD
cjt@terrafix.co.uk

Abstract. This paper considers the practical experiences of a commercial company when undertaking the move to an object oriented paradigm, and the impact that the paradigm shift has entailed, both in terms of the product quality, and the process for software development. The context for the work is outlined, in particular identifying the demanding nature of the company's product development.

A significant aspect of the move to object orientation was the selection of appropriate technologies and tools to support the development, and the adaptation of the toolsets to suit the company context. A rigorous evaluation of the move was undertaken as part of an ESSI Process Improvement Experiment - PIOJAVA, and the initial experiences of collecting process and product metrics are described.

Introduction

Terrafix is a UK company that produces leading edge command and control systems, specifically involving vehicle location, data communication and control room management. The main application areas are for the emergency services and other organizations that require a command and control capability, including facilities for mapping and vehicle tracking. These systems are highly software dependent, with tight constraints that involve complex real-time, multi-tasking, distributed and communications intensive requirements spanning diverse platforms.

The customer base is also distinctive, and this impacts on the specific functionality of the systems, which are tailored to the individual user requirements, and the needs to support thousands of individual mobile/portable units. This has obvious implications on the maintainability of the system components, and particularly on the ability to upgrade as new technologies are introduced. It has also been noted that clients often request software related changes to the functionality at short notice.

To meet these market needs, the company must be responsive to this very specialized market, and consequently the ease of software production and change is of significant importance to the business. At the same time, high quality, reliability and performance in the most cost-effective way are all expected, particularly as many of the systems are safety-critical, and system failures in areas such as the ambulance services have a very high visibility [London Ambulance Service, in Flowers 1996]. This imposes particular constraints on the quality of the delivered product, and the needs of the company to provide systems of auditable quality.

Historically, the software development process at Terrafix has been defined and managed by written procedures, which the software engineers are required to observe. Quality assurance is also very paper based and manual. It is obviously in the interests of the company to move towards more automated forms of quality management.

Most existing code is written in C and has been modified at frequent intervals for over a decade. This has resulted in highly functional but difficult to maintain and modify software modules. Portability across platforms is also a problem.

The company has recognized the need for a radical change in its software approach and to this end, the company decided to review its software engineering processes, and to adopt object oriented techniques within its development programmes. Support for this change has come from a number of sources, including the UK Department for Trade and Industry, and an assessment of the impact of the change is part of a Process Improvement Experiment, PIOJAVA, funded by the European Union.

Changes being introduced within the company

It was envisaged that a move to an object oriented paradigm for both design capture and development would have an impact in terms of both the development process (particularly with respect to module reuse and distribution) and to the products themselves. New design techniques and languages would have to be introduced, and this would entail staff training and also a learning curve as the software engineers gained experience in the techniques.

The choice of precise language and design notations was relatively straightforward. Java was seen as the most attractive language, particularly as many of the company products are based on mobile computing applications and platforms. The rationale was that Java is designed to be modular (due to its enforced object oriented structure), multi-tasking (due to its user controllable multi-threading capability), platform independent (due to a fixed strict binary interface and virtual machine approach) and tightly structured (being defined in such a way that some of the vagaries of C and C++ are not allowed). It can be compiled onto diverse platforms for speed advantages, and processors directly running Java byte-code are available and could be incorporated into the company products. It is becoming the de-facto standard for mobile and SMART card applications, and most importantly, provides the capability to integrate simply with communications networks. The potential for code reuse between the mobile systems and the workstation-based command and control stations was of particularly interest and is one of the aspects of the paradigm change that is being measured.

In terms of the design notations, the scope of the techniques in UML [Rumbaugh, Jacobson and Booch 1999] was attractive, particularly as it includes mechanisms such as State Transition Diagrams and Sequence Diagrams, which are of particular interest for real-time software development. Extensions to provide timing behaviour, as described in [Douglass 1998] were also positive points. The greatest weakness was seen as the development process itself, and many of the techniques appeared disjoint and created the impression that the process lacked cohesion. Better documented processes are now starting to emerge [Jacobson, Booch and Rumbaugh 1999]. A further strong point in support of UML was the availability of industry strength development tools at affordable prices. The Artisan toolset [Artisan 1999] is now being used within the company for the design process.

Rather than just introducing the new technology and effectively following the hype that has accompanied object orientation, it was decided that the migration to the new paradigms should essentially be treated as a tightly controlled experiment for which the impact could be measured. As the company falls within the SME category (approx. 40 employees), a rigorous approach to this was feasible.

Two further pieces of the jigsaw puzzle needed to be in place. The first was related to the quality assurance processes and the reliance on manual and paper-based techniques. This was addressed by the introduction of a configuration management system. After evaluation of a number of systems, the one chosen was Perforce [Perforce 1999]. The second issue was concerned with how the measurement process would be addressed, and in particular, what would be measured and what tools would be used. This is considered within the later sections of this paper.

The overall evaluation process

A number of questions relating to the paradigm shift were identified as being important for the Company in meeting its objectives for undertaking this change:

a. Would the introduction of object-oriented Java improve the software development process.
b. Is the resulting code implementation more maintainable and re-usable.
c. To determine whether code reliability improves, as assessed by monitoring the iterations needed for "fixes" on functioning code and failure rates attributable to the software.
d. To determine the ease with which software professionals adopt object orientation and Java when starting from a "traditional" non-object-oriented way of thinking.
e. To validate relationships between good code structure and development costs, as assessed by comparison of structure metric data with cost data.

From a business perspective, these factors affect both the technical performance of the software (a, b and c above) and commercial performance in terms of product costs, time to market and market share (a, b, c and d above). Although these may be seen as adventurous goals with very far reaching implications for the Company, they are all of interest when assessing the impact of such a major paradigm shift.

The evaluation process effectively has two dimensions that result from the change in paradigm: firstly that the 'quality' of the product was expected to change with the introduction of object orientation; secondly that the productivity would change.

For the product quality, there are relevant measures that can be taken relating to code structure (relevant for a, b and e above), component re-use (b), bug fixing and failure rates (c). For productivity, this would have a longer-term impact on the cost effectiveness (a and e) of the staff. In particular, the staff involved in the development would have to assimilate object-oriented concepts and learn the new languages and tools used in the software development (d).

The assimilation process, in particular, is quite a complex one to assess. Crude milestones relating to qualification or certification are not effective as they are too closely aligned to the training activities rather than the application of the knowledge. Consequently the view was taken that one of the best indicators was relating the impact of the paradigm shift to the change in the programming style of the developers as they used it (in reality/anger) and as they gained experience with it.

Again, this could be related to the quality measures, and particularly the object-oriented characteristics of the product and the change in those measures over time. Effectively, therefore, the assessment of the 'quality' of software components as they were being produced would provide much of the information for identifying if, how and at what rate the take up of object orientation was having an effect.

The results would determine if the measurable gains arising from the use of object orientation do indeed also have an impact on development costs and in the longer term such aspects as reliability and maintainability. In addition, it was anticipated that issues regarding the performance of Java in an intensive real-time and mobile environment would be highlighted.

The experimental structure

It was decided that the monitoring was to take place over a period of approximately 18 months, during which time, a new baseline product for the company was being designed and implemented. This involved the development of an advanced command, control and communication system, addressing the mobile/portable element used for vehicle and person location, data messaging and database functions.

Metrics would be collected at all stages of this development, relating specifically to product quality and productivity. As closely as possible, the same measures and metrics would be applied to existing company products with similar functionality, thereby providing a reference datum. This has led to an experimental structure, as illustrated in figure 1. The experimental process therefore includes both a comparison with a 'control' (Reference Data Set) and also monitoring of the development over time.

There were a number of practical considerations that could potentially have had a significant impact. In particular, the introduction of a metrics programme accompanying the paradigm shift could have been viewed with scepticism by the personnel in the company. However, as the ethos within the company was that the programme was aimed at process and product improvement, rather than culpability, this turned out not to be an issue.

As probably the most significant impact of the paradigm shift is on the developers themselves, staff training would play an increasingly important role as product development takes place. This provides an opportunity to monitor the impact on the developers of experience gained at different stages of the development. That is, one would expect observable differences in 'quality' in components developed immediately after initial training to those produced after, say, 12 months experience.

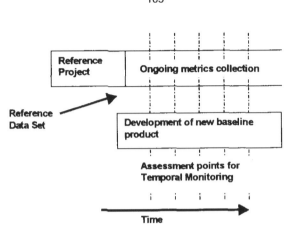

Fig. 1. Experimental Structure

As the new baseline product is being generated using UML for design notation and Java as the implementation language, it was decided that metrics would be collected, from the outset for both the design and implementation processes, and this in as automated a way as possible. Transparency of data collection was considered important to ensure that the measurement process did not interfere with the development activity, thereby perturbing any experimental results.

The development of the baseline product would be performed under the strict regime of the configuration management system identified earlier. This would be used for all aspects of the new product (documentation, design, implementation, etc.). As the integrity of the Company's products is a major factor, the traceability of the design and implementation is of high priority from a commercial and marketing point of view. However the benefit of this approach is that it provides an opportunity for configuring and extending the chosen suite of configuration management software to enable the collection of metrics on the development process. The primary extensions were to date-stamp all system developments, and to provide a (constrained) rationale of the nature of all changes, and logging of the development staff involved. This would allow the temporal analysis to be performed and was also the primary way of noting changes/bug fixes and re-use.

Choice of metrics and metrics tools

The 'quality' of the software components being developed has been identified as the major item in assessing the success of the paradigm shift. Although this could be quantified using metrics such as failure rates and bug fixes, these metrics are of most use once a product is established, in use and being enhanced. They provide little information during the early stages of development when the software components are just becoming established. For this reason, it was decided that an attempt should be made to assess the attributes of the software and to relate these to what is generally regarded as good software engineering practices. The later information that would be collected as components were used in real applications would help to confirm whether the theoretically good characteristics of well-engineered software did, in practice, reflect improved quality.

Four important software engineering characteristics were identified. These are:

- **Structural.** This is sometimes referred to as *Structural Complexity.* Although the primary traditional use of metrics relating to this is in cost estimation, such as within Putnam's Model [Putnam 1978], COCOMO [Boehm 1981], Jensen's Model [Jensen 1984] and COPMO [Conte 1986], there is also a quality dimension to this, as brought out in [Pfleeger 1991].
- **Module Complexity.** This is generally accepted as a major factor in software quality, as it affects the testability and overall manageability of the software components. In contrast with the structural complexity, which is primarily concerned with the external relationships of components, the module complexity focuses on the internal characteristics of the software. The Cyclomatic Complexity metric proposed by McCabe [McCabe 1976] is the de-facto standard, and is one of the few metrics for which accepted norms are published (< 10 is considered good).
- **Cohesion.** This property is concerned with the functional relatedness of software units. It is acknowledged that software may have increasing strengths of cohesiveness (seven categories have been identified in [Constantine and Yourdon 1979] (and reproduced in many software engineering texts) namely increasing from coincidental to logical, temporal, procedural, communicational, sequential and finally functional). It is generally accepted that high cohesiveness is a desirable property.
- **Coupling.** This is a measure of interconnection amongst modules. Loose coupling is generally regarded as a desirable property. Again subcategories of coupling have been identified, covering content, common data, control, and stamp/data coupling. These are described in [Pfleeger 1991].

There is an obvious danger, of which the authors are very aware, of trying to compare different systems using metrics and ultimately arriving at the conclusion that the systems simply are different. What is needed is a stronger impression as to how and why they are different. This is the problem when comparing software developed with two very different paradigms and languages, in that quality metrics appropriate for one paradigm may be inappropriate for another. This is the case when comparing the Reference Data Set software with the new baseline system being developed in Java.

It was decided that appropriate collection tools should be identified that could give function or method metrics for all the sample code (C or Java) in both the reference and new baseline systems, and class oriented metrics that could be applied to the Java code. Furthermore, the metrics would be chosen to help in assessing the software engineering characteristics identified above. The rationale and justification for these metrics is presented elsewhere [PIOJAVA 1999a].

The metrics chosen for functions or methods were:

Structural complexity
Method Metrics
  SLOC – Source Lines Of Code per Method;
  EXEC – Number of executable statements;
Class Metrics
  SLOC – Source Lines Of Code comprising a Class;
  CSA – Class Size in Attributes;
  CSO – Class Size in Operations (Methods);
  NOCC – Number Of Child Classes;
  DIT – Depth of Class Inheritance Tree;
  NOAC – Number of Operations Added by a Class;

Module complexity
Method Metrics
  V(G) – Cyclomatic Complexity;
  OC – Operational Complexity;
  CONTROL – Number of control statements;
  BRANCH – Number of Branching Nodes;
  NEST – Maximum Number of Levels;
Class Metrics
  WMC – Weighted Methods per Class;

Cohesion
Method Metrics
  NION – Number of Input / Output Nodes;
  CALLS– Number of Calls;
Class Metrics
  NOCC – Number Of Child Classes;
  LOCM – Lack Of Cohesion of Methods;
  NOOC – Number of Operations Overridden by a Class;

Coupling
Method Metrics
  CALLS– Number of Calls;
  NP – Number of Parameters per Method;
Class Metrics
  PPPPC – Percentage of Package, Public and Protected members in a Class;
  CBO – Coupling Between Objects;
  PA – Public Accessors;

It is acknowledged that some metrics appear under more than one category, and in practice, the major indicators for each of the four software engineering characteristics may only be one or two of the metrics identified. However, as the collection process is largely automated, there is some justification in collecting all and applying filtering at the analysis stage.

A number of tools from different tool suppliers were assessed for their suitability for this task. Considerable variability was observed, often with different tool sets yielding widely variable results for supposedly the same measures applied to the same piece of software. Eventually a reliable, coherent and consistent tool set was identified, being based on the Krakatau metrics package produced by Powersoftware [Krakatau 1999].

Initial analysis

As this is an on-going programme, results are emerging as the development proceeds. The current findings, particularly with respect to the object-oriented metrics, represent a snapshot taken at the time of writing this paper - around six months into the new product development.

The architectural design has identified a number of high level components that are being developed independently. The focus of development is on the tracking system, which includes the processing of GPS data, communications interfaces, and map management functions. A general GUI interface is also under in hand for data base enquiries, and prototyping of a speech recognition component is being undertaken. The first completed JAVA component is the GPS server, which has the characteristics shown in Table1. This has been used for the initial comparisons.

PRODUCT	NUMBER OF SOURCE FILES	NUMBER OF METHODS	NUMBER OF CLASSES	SOURCE LINES OF CODE
J-GPS Server	10	108	14	1123

Table 1. Software products developed in baseline project

Three sets of analyses have been undertaken. These relate to:

1. An assessment of the reference data set and the new product software. This is effectively an ongoing comparison of software providing similar functionality but implemented using different paradigms.
2. A comparison of the new product software with other JAVA packages. In addition to being a useful check on the metrics collection, it also would provide an indication of how typical the new product might be, and in fact, whether there is a 'typical' style.
3. An assessment of the JAVA code generated during the different periods of the product development. This is to indicate if the style is changing as programmers become more experienced.

Analysis of the reference data set

The reference data set comprises software from existing Terrafix products, including both application level software and deeply embedded software. The six software products that make up this set have been developed in the C or C++ programming languages and comprise 159 modules and over 1300 functions or methods.

The software has been implemented in a number of ways, in a mixture of formal and informal approaches. The approaches taken have been found, pragmatically, to be appropriate to the mixture of applications and interfaces being used. There is little data concerned with the design process of the reference software, as it has evolved over many years. Measurement of appropriate metrics for the design, while not impossible, is difficult to carry out consistently on non-computer-system-based data. Consequently the main metrics to be derived from the reference data relate to the implementation of the software components.

Although the main role of the Reference Data Set is to provide a benchmark for comparison, an initial analysis of the software characteristics has been performed in order to identify whether the different categories of software (embedded or workstation based) exhibit distinctive characteristics. It is a hypothesis, drawn from the philosophy that underpins languages and support environments, such as for Java, that such distinctions should no longer exist within modern software system environments. This dimension is being investigated as part of the experimental evaluation.

The first four products contain embedded code; whilst the remaining two are non-embedded applications. Table 2 summarizes the basic content of these software products.

	OPERATING SYSTEM	LANGUAGE	NUMBER OF SOURCE FILES	NUMBER OF METHODS	SOURCE LINES OF CODE
EMBEDDED					
IIU	RTOS	C	20	198	14853
MIP	RTOS	C	10	63	3176
CIU-CHANNEL	RTOS	C	6	39	2638
CIU-CONTROL	RTOS	C	8	84	4741
NON-EMBEDDED					
DGPSSERVER	Windows NT	C/C++	17	157	3978
BASESTAT	DOS	C/C++	98	809	29421

Table 2. Software products used for the reference data set

Software metrics were initially applied to this data to check the accuracy of the method metrics collection and to provide reference metrics for comparison with the new JAVA code. A number of different analyses were performed on the data collected, based on standard statistical calculations.

The mean values of metrics reflecting structural complexity and module complexity are shown in figures 2 and 3.

Considering the reference data set in isolation, a significant difference is observable between the embedded and non-embedded aggregate groups. This has been verified using statistical techniques [PIOJAVA 1999b]. The structural complexity and module complexity for the embedded software was noticeably higher, and one must conclude that this relates to the programming style of the software engineers developing the embedded applications.

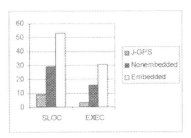

Fig. 2. Structural complexity metrics for reference data set and new JAVA software.

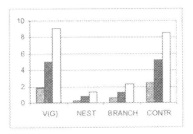
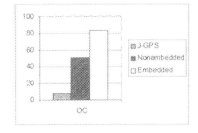

Fig. 3. Module complexity metrics for reference data set and new JAVA software.

When the JAVA software is included in the comparison, further 'simplicity' with respect to the complexity measures can be seen over both the embedded and non-embedded reference data sets. One might infer that this is a desirable product characteristic that should lead to more reliable software systems.

The mean values of metrics relating to coupling and cohesion are shown in figure 4. The number of input/output nodes (NION) would appear to be not a significant differentiator, but the metrics relating to CALLS and NP (Number of Parameters) would indicate a more cohesive structure within the JAVA code.

A summary of the statistical analysis performed on these results is shown in table 3. To evaluate the differences between the JAVA and the embedded and non-embedded groups of the reference data set, Student's "t" tests were applied with a significance level of $p < 0.5$. Significant differences are shown as **"D"**.

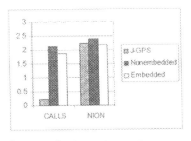
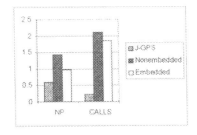

Fig. 4. Cohesion and Coupling metrics for the reference data set and new JAVA software.

	Structure		Module Complexity					Cohesion		Coupling	
	SLOC	EXEC	V(G)	OC	NEST	BR	CONT	CALL	NION	CALL	NP
EMB	D	D	D	D	D	D	D	D	N	D	D
NON	D	D	D	D	D	D	D	D	D	D	D

Table 3. Significance table for reference data set and new JAVA software.

Comparison with existing JAVA software

Some software modules from published Java products were also evaluated. These products are summarized in Table 4.

PRODUCT	NUMBER OF SOURCE FILES	NUMBER OF METHODS	NUMBER OF CLASSES	SOURCE LINES OF CODE
JCVS	17	130	18	2426
CVCS	21	432	19	8639
J-EMAIL	116	1148	239	10301

Table 4. Software products used for JAVA comparison

This allowed the investigation of the application of metrics to Java based software, as a forerunner to the evaluation of the new software products, and in practice, was an important step in verifying the use of the metrics collection package.

In addition to the method metrics applied to the reference data set, class metrics appropriate for object oriented code were also applied to the JAVA products. The mean values of metrics relating to structural complexity are shown in figure 5. For both the method and class metrics, considerable variability was observed between the different JAVA products, indicating that there is probably no such thing as 'typical' JAVA programs. In the context of this experiment, the new JAVA products were very similar to most of the existing code. Few classes exhibit much depth of inheritance (DIT) or have child classes (NOCC), although there is some evidence that these metrics are closely related to the total number of classes in the product.

The module complexity measures are indicated in figure 6. Again, there is some notable variability between the different JAVA products, with the new JAVA product being apparently less complex.

The coupling and cohesion metrics did not indicate any significant variability. An exception was within one of the products, where all class attributes had been declared public, thus producing a distortion of the PPPPC value. In general, the JAVA methods had few parameters and calls, particular with respect to the reference data set.

As with the reference data set, a statistical analysis was used to compare the new JAVA with the existing JAVA products. This comparison is represented by table 5, where significant differences are shown by "**D**".

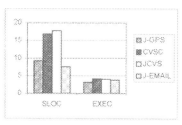

Method Metrics

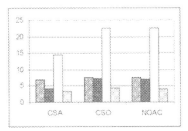

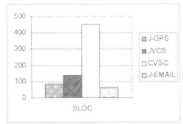

Class Metrics

Fig. 5. Structural complexity metrics for JAVA products

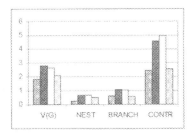

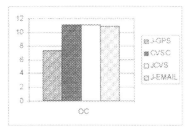

Fig. 6. Module complexity metrics for JAVA products

	Structure		Module Complexity					Cohesion		Coupling	
	SLOC	EXEC	V(G)	OC	NEST	BR	CONT	CALL	NION	CALL	NP
JCVS	**D**	N	**D**	N	**D**	**D**	**D**	N	N	N	**D**
CVCS	**D**	N	**D**	N	**D**	**D**	**D**	**D**	N	**D**	**D**
MAIL	N	N	N	**D**	**D**	N	N	N	N	N	**D**

	Complexity							Cohesion			Coupling		
	SLOC	CSA	CSO	NOCC	DIT	NOAC	WMC	NOCC	LOCM	NOOC	PPPPC	CBO	PA
JCVS	N	N	N	N	**D**	N	N	N	N	N	N	N	N
CVCS	**D**	N	**D**	N	N	**D**	**D**	N	**D**	**D**	N	N	N
MAIL	N	N	N	N	N	N	N	N	N	**D**	**D**	N	**D**

Table 5. Significance table for existing JAVA products and new JAVA software.

Initial temporal analysis

Table 6 shows the pattern of development of the new JAVA product over a six month period. Certain aspects are very obvious from the table, namely that although the number of classes produced has been the same, on average they comprise far fewer methods, each of which is bigger. It is recognized by the authors that this is based on quite a small sample.

STAGE	NUMBER OF SOURCE FILES	NUMBER OF METHODS	NUMBER OF CLASSES	SOURCE LINES OF CODE
0-3 months	6	75	7	651
3-6 months	4	23	7	362

Table 6. Software products developed in baseline project

A detailed analysis of the code, particularly focussing on the object oriented class metrics did not reveal any significant difference between the code produced in the first 3-month period and that subsequently. The experiential learning of the developers is obviously quite small, and this would be expected to increase significantly over the forthcoming months as the coding effort increases.

In this initial period, there did not appear to be a significant adoption of the constructs that would characterize an object-oriented approach to development, for example, with significant use of inheritance or child classes. It is anticipated that this would increase as the experience and volume of software produced within the new product increases.

Conclusions

Although the Process Improvement Experiment is still progressing and data on the software development is being gathered, a number of conclusions can be drawn from the metrics collected so far.

Analysis of the reference set of data was both surprising and revealing, showing that the embedded software tended to have far larger methods and be less well structured than its non-embedded counterpart. The JAVA code being developed in a similar application area was also seen to have smaller methods and be considerably better structured than either of the C/C++ code in the reference data set, and had much better cohesion and coupling.

Within the Java group, there was considerable variability observed between the JAVA from different sources. As a control point, the JAVA being developed as part of the base line project of the experiment was similar in many respect to other JAVA products. Consequently there was a strong view formed that the style of JAVA development was not untypical.

Little information was gained from the object-oriented class metrics, which tended to indicate that many of the object-oriented characteristics were not being exploited within the JAVA products examined. This aspect is being monitored further within the new product development.

The collection of metrics over a time period, using the configuration management system to monitor the software development, has yet to yield sufficient data for extensive analysis. It is anticipated that the design and implementation styles of the software engineers would change as they become more experienced with object oriented concepts and practices. This has still to be verified.

With respect to the overall objectives of the Company, as identified as being the rationale for changing paradigms to object-orientation, the software engineering measures of complexity, coupling and cohesion are indicative of an improved product quality. This was related within the paper to a number of the Company goals. The monitoring of the software development that is coming through the use of configuration management tools is expected to deliver further measures on the re-use of components and on the maintainability. This will become apparent as the base line development project progresses and enters use.

It has been observed that the Java software developed at the start of this project is exhibiting the desirable characteristics that were anticipated for object-oriented software, and consequently, the Company has already gained confidence that .object-oriented development has technical and commercial benefits.

Acknowledgements

This work was supported by the UK Department of Trade and Industry under the auspices of the Teaching Company Directorate, via a collaborative programme in conjunction with Staffordshire University.

The evaluation work was undertaken as a European Systems and Software Initiative (ESSI), Process Improvement Experiment, No 27719 – PIOJAVA.

The authors would also like to acknowledge the efforts of David Leigh in the collection and evaluation of the metrics, and of the staff at Powersoftware for assistance with the Krakatau metrics tool set.

References

Artisan 1999, http://www.artisansw.com

Boehm BW, *Software Engineering Economics*, Prentice-Hall 1981.

Constantine L L and Yourdon E, *Structured Design*, Prentice-Hall, 1979.

Conte S D, Dunsmore H E and Shen V Y, *Software Engineering Metrics and Models*, Benjamin-Cummings 1986.

Douglass B P, *"Real-Time UML – Developing Efficient Objects for Embedded Systems"*, Addison Wesley, Object Technology Series 1998, ISBN 0-201-32579-9.

Flowers S, *"Software Failure - Management Failure"*, John Wiley and Sons 1996, ISBN 047195137.

Jacobson I, Booch G, Rumbaugh J, *"The Unified Software Development Process"*, Addison Wesley, Object Technology Series 1999, ISBN 0-201-57169-2.

Jensen R W, *A comparison of the Jensen and COCOMO schedule and cost estimation models*, Proceedings International Society of Parametric Analysis, 1984.

Krakatau 1999, http://www.powersoftware.com

McCabe T, *A Software Complexity Measure*, IEEE Transactions on Software Engineering Vol 2, No 12, 1976.

Perforce 1999, http://www.perforce.com

Pfleeger S L, *Software Engineering: The production of quality Software,* Macmillan 1991.

PIOJAVA 1999a, *PIOJAVA Experimental Plan,* ESSI project report, 1999, http://www.terrafix.co.uk/essi

PIOJAVA 1999b, *PIOJAVA Reference Data Report,* ESSI project report, 1999 http://www.terrafix.co.uk/essi

Putnam L H, *A General Empirical Solution to the Macro Software Sizing and Estimating Problem,* IEEE Transactions on Software Engineering, Vol 4, No 4, 1978.

Rumbaugh J, Jacobson I, Booch G, *"The Unified Modeling Language Reference Manual",* Addison Wesley, Object Technology Series 1999, ISBN 0-201-30998-X.

Descriptive Process Modeling in an Industrial Environment: Experience and Guidelines

Ulrike Becker-Kornstaedt[1] and Wolfgang Belau[2]

[1] Fraunhofer Institut für Experimentelles Software Engineering (IESE),
Sauerwiesen 6, D-67661 Kaiserslautern, Germany
becker@iese.fhg.de
[2] DaimlerChrysler Aerospace AG, Space Infrastructure Division,
P.O. Box 28 61 56, D-28361 Bremen, Germany
Wolfgang.Belau@ri.dasa.de

Abstract. Process modeling is a key activity in process improvement to understand the software process, to detect weaknesses in the process and to allow estimation. A major problem when process modeling is done in industrial environment is obtaining access to the information needed. This paper describes experience from descriptive process modeling in an industrial environment and reports problems and difficulties encountered in acquiring and formalizing that knowledge. From the experience, guidelines for descriptive process modeling activities, especially for process knowledge acquisition, are derived.

1 Introduction

A key component for any measurement program is a description of the actual software process [FP96]. In order to be useful as a foundation for measurement programs the process model has to be accurate (i.e., it has to capture the development process as it takes place and not as it *should* take place [BFL+95]). Descriptive software process modeling is concerned with capturing and describing software processes as they actually take place in an organization. Much research has been conducted in the area of process modeling, most of it focused on technical and tool-related aspects [Ros99]. There are only few examples of methods aiming at developing accurate descriptive software process models (see for instance [MHHB94]).

Little experience has been reported from applications of process modeling to large and complex real-world processes. While a lot of experience exists on how to formalize software process knowledge into a model, little experience has been reported on how to obtain the process knowledge that is needed to develop a process model. This paper reports experience on an application of process modeling that was done at the Space Infrastructure Division of DaimlerChrysler Aerospace AG (Dasa RI) with a focus on process knowledge elicitation. Dasa RI develops and operates manned and un-manned space infrastructure systems. Process modeling was done under relatively tight schedule constraints, within a short calendar time, and with limited access to process experts.

The remainder of the paper is structured as follows: The following section describes the environment in which the process modeling took place. This includes a brief characterization of the organization and its processes, the scope of the modeling activity, and the general strategy followed for modeling. Section 3 describes how the strategy was followed at Dasa. Section 4 presents lessons learned and guidelines for descriptive software process modeling, Section 5 lists research issues to be addressed in the future.

2 General Context of the Process Modeling Activities

For a better understanding of the overall work this section gives an overview of the general context in which process modeling took place. This includes a short description of the organization and its process and a sketch of the general strategy followed.

2.1 The Target Organization and its Processes

Process modeling took place in a subdivision of the Space Infrastructure Division of DaimlerChrysler Aerospace (Dasa). The subdivision is responsible for avionics and has about 100 employees in software development. Dasa is involved in the development of the Columbus Orbital Facility (COF), the space lab of the International Space Station. COF is to be shipped to NASA in 2002. Columbus space lab to be docked onto the planned International Space Station (ISS) in 2003 or 2004. The project responsibilities for COF and the ground-support system are within Dasa RIO. The focus of the process is on the Columbus ground support (CGS) system.

Since software development in the European space industry is characterized by contracting and subcontracting between different partners the software development process at Dasa is characterized by a high number of both organizational interfaces (external to other partners from the consortium or to subcontractors, and internal within the project organization or development departments), and product interfaces. The software development complexity is increased by factors such as long durations of the project life cycles, the integration of various COTS products, or restrictions in hardware components and programming language selections for the software.

This leads to the situation that extremely large amounts of the software process are event-driven, in order to react to changing requirements, interfaces, or changes in the hardware.

The focus for the improvement program was on the software process of CGS as a representative process for Columbus development. The official process for the Columbus software – a tailored version of the ESA PSS-05-0 standard [ESA91] – is described in an official process handbook. The Columbus software development standards were published in 1993. The standards describe different types of software life cycles that were expected in the COF, various documentation standards, development methods, coding standards, and various project procedures for different project disciplines, including configuration management and product assurance.

At Dasa RIO a software process improvement program had been established. During the improvement program several goals had been defined. One of these was the establishment of a basic measurement process, defining core metrics that could be tailored for supporting different improvements on project management level. Therefore, process modeling had to provide a framework for effort estimation and comparability across projects. It was also expected that process elicitation would yield a better understanding of the process actually performed – as compared to the software life cycles documented in the standards. In this context, a goal was to detect discrepancies of the actual and the official process. Hence, typical activities, artifacts, and roles in the software life cycle phases were to be captured.

2.2 General Strategy Followed for Process Modeling

This section outlines the general framework followed for descriptive process modeling. The general framework in which process modeling was performed is an 8-step approach as depicted in Figure 1. This framework had been applied in previous process modeling cases (see [BHV97]) and was further refined for the Dasa process modeling activities.

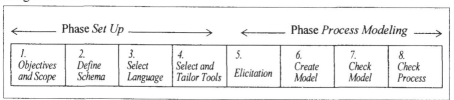

Fig. 1. The 8-Step Process Modeling Approach

The eight steps are grouped into a "set-up" phase, where the general and organizational issues have to be clarified for a process modeling project and a "process modeling" phase, which deals with performing process modeling in development projects. The eight steps are the following:

1. **State objectives and scope**: In this step, the scope of the modeling activities, the characteristics of the model, and the organizational context of the modeling activities have to be settled. Here the granularity of the model and the intended users of the process model have to be specified. The scope and the granularity of the process model to be developed depend on the purpose of the model and its intended users. Different people usually have different expectations and needs regarding detail, contents, and degree of formality depending on their role in the process. In this step, the organizational details should be clarified. These include access to relevant artifacts or process documents, or process experts. It is helpful to determine a contact person in the target organization. This contact person can serve as the major communication point in the organization.

2. **Select or develop a process modeling schema**: Such a schema should identify and structure the information to be captured by the process model and the relationships between these information entities. The schema has to take into account the objectives and scope defined in the first step. If, for instance, the objective of the process model is to support a measurement to capture effort for activities, the schema should provide concepts such as attributes and values to allow effort data collection.

3. **Select a process modeling language**: A process modeling notation in which the process model has to be 'written down' has to be selected. It is likely that a single language is insufficient to capture all aspects needed, and a set of process modeling formalisms is needed to cover the aspects described in the schema. A formal process modeling language allows for analysis on a formal basis. This helps to identify deficiencies in the process model to be investigated by the Process Engineers [BFL[+]95].

However, when selecting a language, it also has to be considered that learning a complex language which is new to the organization can involve significant overhead.

4. **Select and tailor tools**: Depending on the process modeling language(s) decided upon in the previous step, tools to support the formalism have to be selected. These do not necessarily have to be process modeling tools: Graphical notations, for instance, can be well supported by drawing tools. In practice, the process modeling notation and the tool are often selected together.

5. **Elicit process knowledge**: The goal of elicitation is to acquire all information needed to describe the software process. The sources of information include interviews, observation, and analysis of organizational documents and process products. ([Sea99] gives a nice overview on collection methods for qualitative data in software engineering.)

6. **Create model**: The information obtained is classified, sorted, and interpreted to create a process model. The Process Participants are asked to review the process model. Corrections may be made to the process model. It is very likely that several cycles of creation, modification and review will take place until all Process Participants agree upon the process model. It may be possible that different views of the process must be created in order to fulfil the objectives of the process modeling activity or to conform to the needs of various roles. A view is a subset of the overall process model, described in a view-specific notation.

7. **Analyze the process model**: Process models are checked for completeness, correctness, and structural consistency (i.e., static analysis), and for behavioral aspects, such as possible risks, critical paths, or cost overruns. [RV95]. Again, the scope of the model determined in the first step determines what the process model should be analyzed for.

8. **Analyze the process**: The descriptive model is used to check the process itself for fidelity during performance.

Often, the organizations in which process modeling is done are unfamiliar to a Process Engineer who develops the process model. Therefore Process Engineers should familiarize themselves with the organization, its structure, and the development processes in general during the early steps.

3 Procedure Followed at Dasa

This section describes how these steps were followed in the case of Dasa. Especially we focus on the details of process elicitation and model creation at Dasa.

3.1 Set-up Phase

To set the **scope** for the process model and to select the **schema**, we had agreed upon the following:

- For the activities we had to find a level of granularity that on the one hand would yield enough effort data to allow for cost estimation and on the other hand would not be too detailed to keep effort for the data collection itself low. For the improvement program at Dasa we had agreed to include in the final process model only the activities with an effort of at least four hours per week (on average) – this level of granularity seemed feasible to get a good understanding of the overall process without impeding daily work. For these activities it was necessary to have a description of what tasks they comprised in order to obtain valid measurement data.

- The artifacts to be captured in the process model were the major artifacts described in the official process handbook.

The process modeling activities were performed by a Process Engineer from Fraunhofer IESE. The Process Engineer was supported by a contact person at Dasa who was part of a process improvement team at Dasa. The contact point coordinated many of the process modeling activities at the Dasa site. This was especially important since the target organization is located at some distance from Fraunhofer IESE, so that the contact person could handle a large amount of the local organization. The modeling activities were hindered by the following constraints:

- The process improvement activities should interfere as little as possible with the everyday work of the experts. Therefore, interviews could be conducted with only eight Process Performers. Each of them was guaranteed to be available for two interviews of two hours each. Thus, the limited availability of experts had to be taken into account and any interaction with process experts had to be planned carefully.

- Due to the geographical distance between the target organization and Fraunhofer IESE, we had to plan for few but very intensive direct meetings on site, the rest had to be done via email, phone or video conference.

- Since the process model was the starting point of the improvement program, it was the 'bottleneck' for the following activities. The overall calendar time for the development of the process model had to be less than two months.

For the **process modeling language** and **tool** we had agreed upon the following:

- A formal process model was not necessary. The final process model was to be used by Process Performers at Dasa. Hence, we had decided on a natural language description of the process, no formal approaches were employed. The tool we selected was Framemaker.

3.2 Process Modeling Phase

3.2.1 Preparation and Familiarization

Due to the limited availability of the process experts we had decided on structured interviews as a major information source. Interviews allow to obtain information about situations that occur only infrequently or happened in the past. In a structured interview, questions are quite specific, allowing to focus on specific aspects. Other advantages of structured interviews are that they are rather time-efficient, and the data obtained is easier to analyze than data obtained otherwise (see for instance [JSK90] for an overview). In order to perform a structured interview, the Process Engineer needs a lot of background knowledge of the matter studied [Coo94]. Thus, the Process Engineer had to familiarize with the process. In order to prepare for the interviews, we took a look at the official process [BFL+95]. The development standard in use is derived from ESA-PSS-05-0 [ESA91]. The official process documentation had been devel-

1.1. ... Phase

Name of interviewee:
Role:
Entry Criteria for phase:
Exit Criteria for phase:
Activities/Artifacts:

Activities \ Artifacts	Requirements Doc	:	:	.. Doc.	.. Plan							
Requirements Analysis ...												
...												
System Design												
...												

Alternatives/Variations of phase:

Roles involved:

Fig. 2. Excerpt from an interview template

oped some 10 years before and during the process modeling activities it showed to be outdated in some places. For instance, it asked for special development techniques which were no longer employed and where no tool support was available.

In addition we examined some process artifacts (requirements documents and architectural design) and organizational documents (project plan). It showed that it was very difficult to understand these documents and their relationship to the overall process without extra explanation. Informal (telephone) discussions with our contact person helped answer some general questions regarding the official process. From the official process handbook plus the additional information we developed interview templates. The structure of the interview templates was oriented towards the concepts of the conceptual schema described in [WB97], providing slots for the major activities, artifacts, roles, entry, and exit criteria for the relevant phases, taken from the standards. An excerpt from the interview template is shown in Figure 2 (actual names replaced by '...' where necessary to ensure confidentiality).

We decided to interview different roles involved to obtain process information from several viewpoints and at different levels of granularity. This was useful in developing a rich picture of all the processes and their interactions. We talked to Project Leader, Department Heads, Quality Assurance, and to the people who are responsible to set up the bids. In addition to their roles we wanted to sample interviewees according to their experience with different subprojects in order to cover a wide variety of different project types. Here, the contact point helped select interview candidates according to our selection criteria and could provide the Process Engineer with a lot of background information about the interviewees and their experience with the Dasa process, such as the projects they had been involved in. He could also schedule interview dates. Due to our own tight schedule and the limited availability of the process experts we could not influence on the order of the interviews.

The local contact person also served as a coordination point within the target organization, as he provided information about the process improvement program and the process modeling activities to the interviewees and scheduled the interviews. He therefore served as an entry point and 'gate opener' on the Dasa site. This was not only needed to obtain access to interviewees but also for documents. The documents are in a repository with limited access and the contact point had to negotiate access to the documents.

3.2.2 Process Knowledge Elicitation

To make interviewing as efficient as possible we had decided on structured interviews based on the templates shown in Figure 2. We had sent these interview templates to the interviewees and had asked them to go through them to be prepared for the interviews. Together with the templates we had sent a debriefing document that provided general information about the process modeling activities and assured Process Performers that any information provided would not be used against them.

The interviews took place during three consecutive days at the Dasa location. All of the interviewees had gone through the templates thoroughly, most of them had already filled out the slots. Each interview was conducted by one Process Engineer and involved one Dasa staff member. The interviews started with questioning about past projects and experience. These questions served as warm-up making interviewees feel comfortable with the interview situation. In addition, this background information helped verify the interviewees' background, gave a better idea of how to rate their experience, and clarified their viewpoint of the process. Especially later, this information helped us resolve some 'inconsistencies' in the answers. (As it turned out later, these inconsistencies were mainly due to the fact that interviewees had taken very different roles or had been involved in very different types of projects. In the case of Dasa it showed that different views on the process were due to the fact that people had been involved in different project types but not due to the different roles people had taken in the project. However, this is not generalizable, as experience from a different process modeling project indicates that different views on the process are mainly caused by different roles [Ver98].) This also showed that a certain variety in interview partners does give a richer picture of the overall process.

During the main parts of the interview we walked through the templates, filled them out and wrote down additional information that came up during the interviews. Sometimes the discussion would drift off to concrete situations from a previous project. Often interviewees presented example documents used in order to clarify issues, or to show exceptions or the general structure of those documents. This included documents which were produced as activity outputs (such as requirements documents) as well as organizational documents (e.g., a project plan). It was effective to have interviews in people's offices where they had direct access to example documents. We found it useful to capture concrete examples because it helped us to better understand the process and often the concrete examples helped us probe answers.

It was helpful to capture as much information as possible, even if it was not clear that this knowledge would not be incorporated into the final process model. We faced the problem that a lot of the knowledge obtained through interviews is difficult to formalize or to relate that knowledge directly to the process or parts of it. There is a danger of losing that knowledge. However, it was often this non-formalizable knowledge which increased the Process Engineer's general understanding of the process. It is therefore strongly recommended for process modeling activities to also capture informal knowledge and to provide some mechanism to attach this knowledge to the model.

In one interview, a Process Performer openly said that the official process (and thus the interview template derived from it) did not reflect his way of understanding the process. In that particular case, the interview structure was changed to an open interview without the template structure. Comparing the notes from this interview with other interview transcripts revealed that the interviewee had described the same activities, tasks, artifacts, roles, and relationships, but his overall conceptualization of the process differed. There are two important lessons learned and from this particular interview experience which should be taken into account when setting up requirements or guidelines for descriptive modeling: First, it is not sufficient to use the official process as a basis for improvement activities, because Process Performers may not understand it or may not view it as the process actually performed. Second, this shows the importance of having external Process Engineers, since this type of information might not have been provided to a person from the same organization.

Often it was necessary to distinguish between experience the interviewers had second hand and personal experience. Here again it was helpful to ask for from concrete example situations or documents in order to have their structure explained. This also helped discuss the relationships between different activities, the document, and when and how the document was allowed to be modified. It also turned out that a lot of information was implicit in people's minds and could only be elicited using very specific and detailed questions. One particular question to focus the discussion on was: 'If you were asked to change the standard, what are the three items you would like to keep? What would you like to have removed from the standard?' As an answer to this question Process Performers usually explained which activities prescribed in the standard were performed in reality and which activities were not.

Altogether, seven single interviews were performed since not all process experts were available during the interview week. Interviews were scheduled for 90 minutes, but more time was allowed. It showed, that longer interviews affected the performance of both interviewer and interviewees. From that experience interviews should not exceed two hours, otherwise fatigue effects occur on the interviewer's and the interviewee's side.

In between the interviews, a break was very useful to allow the interviewer to compare notes with results from previous interviews and cross-validate them, to recover, and to prepare for the second interview. It also avoids that information from different interviews gets confounded. From the Dasa experience, no more than two interviews a day should be conducted per (active) interviewer, if possible.

Since the process modeling activities interfere with the everyday development activities of Process Performers, a major problem for scheduling interviews the limited availability of the Process Performers. Some interviews had to be postponed, and one interview even had to be cancelled because the Process Performer had to attend an important review meeting.

In parallel with the interviews, detailed analysis of process artifacts from the document repository took place. Besides the general structure of these documents, organizational information (e.g., when the document was written, reviewed, or modified, and by whom) was helpful to elicit process knowledge.

3.2.3 Model Creation and Analysis

The information from all interviews was collected in a text file and information regarding the same activities compared. (In this step each piece of information still had the name of the interviewee attached to it. This facilitated the resolving of inconsistencies.) For the majority of these inconsistencies it turned out that different people had used the same terms for different tasks, or that the tasks had been described at different levels of granularity.

Then the information fragments were combined into a natural language description by grouping similar tasks and activities into a higher-level activity where needed. For instance, the final description of the higher-level activity *Coding and Module testing* comprised tasks such as analyzing the requirements and the design documents, the coding activity itself, or the development of the individual development environment, module testing by the developer. Some of these tasks are only performed by certain roles.

When summarizing the interview results it turned out in most cases that the roles could describe the parts of the process in which they were involved in a lot of detail, but could only give an overview of other parts and that the strategy to cover a large variety of roles and projects had been beneficial.

We found that a lot of information we had obtained in interviews could not be directly integrated into the process model, e.g., information regarding organizational procedures, what additional tasks were performed or not performed in special project types, or general guidelines.

The Dasa process model covered six phases of the development process. For each phase it contained the major activities, roles, artifacts, and milestones. For each activity, a detailed description was given to facilitate the collection of effort measurement data. The overall model contained the 20 major artifacts, the 26 most relevant activities, and the major roles involved. Behavior was not captured for the activities, but on phase level.

The first version of the resulting model was sent to the contact person who provided feedback by phone. This feedback was incorporated into the model and the new version sent to interview partners for review. We found that it was a rather difficult task to discuss a process model over the phone, since any visual interaction was missing. Then, in a second round of interviews, feedback for the model was incorporated.

Since the model was written in natural language it could only be checked manually. The process is checked for fidelity during the execution of the measurement program. In general, many of the interviewees openly said that they appreciated the process improvement program and the process modeling activities. Consequently they were willing to contribute and give their time and provide information during the interviews. Especially when Process Performers will have to make use of the process model afterwards it is crucial to involve them from the beginning to increase their acceptance and to develop a model that matches their experience. This stressed the importance of involving process participants in the modeling activities.

Analyzing the process and process model was mainly done by comparing the results to the official process. The following major issues were detected:

- Across different software development teams many **variants of the process** exist. Often, it was difficult to map life cycle definitions, as defined in the official standard, to an actual development process.

- **Co-occurrence of generic activity types** in different phases. Comparing the activities/tasks of the various phases it showed that activities/tasks which are characteristic for a certain phase may be performed in other phases. A good description of this phase overlap can be found in [Nat91]. Often in the actual process the boundaries between different phases are fuzzy.

- A **major document** that was identified as important was **not described in** the **standard**. Software development plans, defining specific project and process tailoring were identified (and mentioned by all interviewees) as relevant documents. However, in the standard, these are not covered, nor are there any rules or guidelines what they should look like.

4 Lessons Learned

This section presents the lessons learned in the Dasa process modeling activities and proposes some guidelines which should be followed for descriptive modeling. These guidelines are based on the experience of the Dasa project.

When reviewing the process technology literature only very limited information about process elicitation can be found. There is a need for a deeper research in that area and knowledge transfer from social sciences. It is suggested to borrow techniques for process knowledge elicitation that have already been successfully applied in other areas and adapt them to the specific context of software process modeling. For the overall process modeling activities some checklist or some guidelines would have facilitated our task.

The experience from Dasa showed clearly that a single type of information source would not have been sufficient to develop a descriptive model of the process. Existing process documentation on its own is not suitable as the only information source for a descriptive process model to support measurement programs. First, they are not detailed enough insofar as it does not specify when a certain process step begins or ends. Second, there is no guarantee that it matches the understanding of the Process Performers. This leads to the following guidelines:

For an accurate model **different information sources** must be used. This includes **artifacts** (process artifacts as well as organizational documents), **interviews** with Process Performers, and the **official process documentation,** if available. ([PSV94] report that Process Performers' perception of the process differs considerably from the actual process and therefore suggest **observation** of process participant as information source.)

When interviewing process experts, interviewees should cover a wide range of **different roles** and – if possible – a wide range of projects, in order to give a rich picture of the process. A Process Engineer must have a clear idea of the viewpoints of the respective interviewees.

Often, sensitive information is provided in interviews, e.g., a process expert explained that the official process did not match his or her understanding of the process. People providing process knowledge must not fear that the knowledge is used against them. Confidentiality is therefore important. Hence, the following should be considered:

If **group interviews** are conducted, these should be **role oriented**.

Developing a descriptive model should be done by a **neutral person**, e.g., an outside Process Engineer.

The overall experience showed that the effort spent by Process Performers in interviews can be largely reduced when the Process Engineer has the possibility to get a very good overview of the process beforehand, e.g., by analyzing existing process documents and artifacts, and by having a contact person who can already solve a lot of questions beforehand. More than half of the overall effort was spent on familiarization and preparation. In that context, it is recommended to conduct two different types of interviews in two phases of the process modeling activities: the first type of interview should be conducted in the preparation phase in order to get an overview, then in a second phase, detailed interviews elicit the details of the development process. The usage of interview templates which the Process Performers had received beforehand showed to be very helpful in structuring the interviews. Thus, the following should be taken into account:

Interaction with Process Performers should be planned and conducted in an **efficient** way. Process Performers are willing to share their experience, but their time is very limited.

Plan for **flexibility in the information sources**. Process experts or process artifacts may not be available in the order planned or may not even be available at all.

In our case, using a natural language representation of the process model had the benefit that it could be easily understood by Process Performers during review or for the measurement program. However, the natural language description did not allow for formal consistency checks and analysis, which would have been helpful. No tool was available that had consistency and analysis functions and could provide a textual description. Due to the time constraints we only developed a textual version of the model and abstained from a formal model. We recommend to use a formal language or schema for organizing the questions of the interview, but prefer to avoid formalization during the sessions. Therefore, the following guidelines should be respected:

The resulting process model must be written in a **notation that is easy to understand** by its intended users (this may even result in several models, e.g, one model for the Process Engineer and another one for the Process Performers).

In the Dasa project the **contact point** played a crucial role. He did not only provide access to information sources, but could also help answer a first set of questions. This probably made the process modeling activities more efficient.

The Dasa experience showed that for descriptive process modeling a tool would facilitate the modeling tasks, but is not mandatory. However, the following **features of a tool** would make process model creation easier:

- **Tags for sources of information**: During process model creation it was helpful to determine the source that certain information came from to help resolve inconsistencies. What is needed are specifications of where the respective information came from, attached to single objects or parts of the process model.

- **Bottom-up aggregation**: In the beginning of the model creation the information resulting from the interviews appears like pieces of a jigsaw puzzle. An editing function like "aggregate selected activities to a new process on the next higher level of abstraction" would support gluing together the pieces. Most modeling tools only support top-down approaches.

- **Modifications 'on the fly'**: This allows to continue working with an updated version of the model and get fast feedback. Especially the review phase could be made more efficient, if the process model can be altered at the customer's site.

- **Provide different views of the process**: This includes different subsets of the information shown in the process model, different representation styles, or even different granularity.

From the perspective of Dasa, process modeling provided the following benefits:

- The process modeling activities **increased** the **understanding of the overall process**. However, it has to be noted that it was not so much the resulting model, but rather the process elicitation which triggered a lot of discussions, allowed a better understanding of the process.

- Based on the process modeling activities, effort collection forms were proposed and usage scenarios for a basic measurement program were developed. The effort data collected allows to derive **effort distributions of generic activities**. Process elicitation had been necessary to allow for comparability across projects.

- **Fine-grained process modeling** remains a problem, since at that level the process is not stable enough or has too many project-specific variants. Process models have been developed on a very detailed level for tool-supported software configuration management for a certain project. These process model capture development state transitions, project roles, and responsibilities. Adaptability of these models to other projects is still a problem.

5 Summary and Outlook

This paper presented an eight-step strategy for descriptive software process modeling. This strategy was employed for developing an accurate process model for measurement support under relatively time and effort constraints. It showed that the front-end activities, such as familiarization with the environment and obtaining a general overview of the process are crucial for the development of a descriptive process model, especially in situations where experts' availability is limited.

Experience is reported about the design of the interviews. The interviews should be planned to be role-specific and should be well prepared by the Process Engineer in order to minimize experts' time. A major benefit is to have support by someone familiar with the process who can interpret results, translate terminology, and assess relevant information.

The Dasa process modeling experience raised a number of research questions that should be addressed in future process modeling activities:

- Sampling of interviewees raises the need to define rules for selecting the right interviewees. This is crucial for the success of the whole modeling program. Access to important people is limited and scheduling problems are likely to occur.

- What additional support can be provided to the Process Engineer? Systematic evaluations should uncover needs for better tool support.

- What abstraction and structuring mechanisms are needed in a process modeling language to support specifically the creation of models? More study of complex processes is needed in order to identify mechanisms which help to manage the descriptions of such processes.

- Estimating the process modeling effort is necessary in improvement programs. Little has been is reported on experience from which estimates could be derived. It should be investigated what the cost drivers are (i.e., what are the factors controlling the process modeling effort).

- How can fine-grain dynamic modeling be addressed? Where should modeling stop?

- How can process with much overlap be captured in a model?

A general method, checklists, or heuristics for descriptive process modeling should be formulated by the community. Many of the lessons learned in this project will be of benefit in future projects. A lot of the strategies applied here already came from past projects. The experience reported in this paper should also trigger further discussion and exchange. We hope that the experience reported in this paper will be helpful for other Process Engineer performing similar tasks.

Acknowledgments

The authors would like to thank the people involved in this study, especially Peter Lux and Norbert Schielow. The interviewees contributed by their openness and cooperation. We would like to thank Dirk Hamann and Martin Verlage for many helpful discussions.

6 References

[BFL+95]   Sergio Bandinelli, Alfonso Fuggetta, Luigi Lavazza, Maurizio Loi, and Gian Pietro Picco. Modeling and improving an industrial software process. *IEEE Transactions on Software Engineering*, 21(5):440–454, May 1995.

[BHV97]   Ulrike Becker, Dirk Hamann, and Martin Verlage. Descriptive modeling of software processes. International Software Engineering Research Network (ISERN) Technical Report ISERN-97-10, Fraunhofer Institute for Experimental Software Engineering, 1997.

[Coo94]   Nancy J. Cooke. Varieties of knowledge elicitation techniques. *International Journal of Human-Computer Studies*, 41:801–849, 1994.

[ESA91]   ESA (European Space Agency). *ESA Software Engineering Standards PSS-05-0*, February 1991.

[FP96]   Norman E. Fenton and Shari L. Pfleeger. *Software Metrics: A Rigorous & Practical Approach*. International Thompson Computer Press, London, 1996.

[JSK90]   Charles M. Judd, Eliot R. Smith, and Louise H. Kidder. *Research Methods in Social Relations*. Harcourt, Brace, Jovanovich, 1990.

[MHHB94]   Nazim H. Madhavji, Dirk Höltje, WonKook Hong, and Tilmann Bruckhaus. Elicit: A method for eliciting process models. In Dewayne E. Perry, editor, *Proceedings of the Third International Conference on the Software Process*, pages 111–122. IEEE Computer Society Press, October 1994.

[Nat91]   National Aeronautics and Space Administration. Manager's handbook for software development. Technical Report SEL-84-101, NASA Goddard Space Flight Center, Greenbelt MD 20771, 1991.

[PSV94]   Dewayne E. Perry, Nancy A. Staudenmayer, and Lawrence G. Votta. People, organizations, and process improvement. *IEEE Software*, 11(4):36–45, July 1994.

[Ros99]   Simo Rossi. Moving Towards Modelling Oriented Software Process Engineering: A Shift from Descriptive to Prescriptive Process Modelling. In *Proceedings of PROduct Focused Improvement of Embedded Software Processes 99*, pages 508–522, 1999.

[RV95]   H. Dieter Rombach and Martin Verlage. Directions in software process research. In Marvin V. Zelkowitz, editor, *Advances in Computers, vol. 41*, pages 1–63. Academic Press, 1995.

[Sea99]   Caroly B. Seaman. Qualitative Methods in Empirical Studies of Software Engineering. *IEEE Transactions on Software Engineering*, 1999.

[Ver98]   Martin Verlage. An approach for capturing large software development processes by integration of views modeled independently. In *Proceedings of the Tenth Conference on Software Engineering and Knowledge Engineering*, pages 227–235, San Francisco Bay, CA, USA, June 1998. Knowledge Systems Institute, Skokie, Illinois, USA.

[WB97]   Richard Webby and Ulrike Becker. Towards a Logical Schema Integrating Software Process Modeling and Software Measurement. In Rachel Harrison, editor, *Proceedings of the Nineteenth International Conference on Software Engineering Workshop: Process Modelling and Empirical Studies of Software Evaluation*, pages 84–88, Boston, USA, May 1997.

SDL Based Approach to Software Process Modeling

Ivana Podnar[1], Branko Mikac[1], Antun Caric[2]

[1] University of Zagreb, Faculty of Electrical Engineering and Computing
Department of Telecommunications
Zagreb, Croatia
{ivana.podnar, branko.mikac}@fer.hr
[2] Ericsson Nikola Tesla, Design Centre
Zagreb, Croatia
antun.caric@etk.ericsson.se

Abstract. The paper presents a Specification and Description Language (SDL) based approach to software process modeling. A brief review of other process modeling languages is given and the advantages of the ITU-T standardized SDL for formal model development are outlined. Further on, it is shown how software process entities are modeled using SDL. Software maintenance process performed in a large telecommunications company is used as a case study. The software maintenance practice is first described informally, followed by a formal SDL software maintenance model. Finally, the SDL model simulation and verification results are presented, and an overall assessment of SDL applicability for software process modeling is discussed.

1 Introduction

Software processes performed during software development and evolution are becoming rather complex and resource-intensive. They involve people who perform actions with the primary goal to create quality software in accordance with the previously set user requirements. Only defined, carefully guided and documented software processes can lead to the stated goal.

Constant monitoring and improvement of software processes is therefore of a significant interest for organizations performing software development and maintenance. In order to improve the process an objective description and evaluation of the existing process is needed. Formal process modeling, analysis, and simulation can lead to software process improvement [1].

The paper presents a Specification and Description Language (SDL) based approach to software process modeling. SDL is a standard language for specifying and describing systems [6]. It provides means for formal modeling of software processes by supporting concurrency and object-orientation. Software process inconsistency and incompleteness can be investigated through model simulation and verification. SDL supports hierarchical and modular system specification that decreases the complexity of software processes modeling and increases model changeabilty and evolvability.

The paper reports experiences in modeling of the software maintenance process in a large telecommunications company. SDL process model has been developed in order to understand, describe, and analyze the existing maintenance practice, with the goal of identifying process deficiencies and bottlenecks. SDL provides a rapid and cost-effective means for describing, analyzing and documenting software processes. It has been developed and standardized by ITU-T, and is as such used in the telecommunications community. It needs to be noted that process documentation is used by a large number of process participants. The unambiguous and formally correct process documentation is extremely valuable for software organizations, especially if it requires no additional training. More over, SDL provides graphical representation, which makes it user-friendly. Tools for developing and analyzing SDL specifications are commercially available.

Software process modeling is a diversified field of study. Various modeling approaches have been developed and proposed, depending on the purpose of modeling. Different degrees of formalization are used, ranging from descriptive [3] [10], almost informal, to strictly formal [2], [4]. Formal modeling is the necessity for environments that support software development activities. Such environments are called process-centered software engineering environments (PSEEs). They exploit process languages in order to support process analysis, simulation and enactment. Most of the existing PSEEs are mainly oriented toward providing enactment assistance [7], while, in practice, the most demanding property of the modeling approach is support for process description, comprehension, analysis and documentation. SDL is suitable for earlier phases of the process modeling lifecycle since it is a formal specification and description language. SDL can therefore be used as a process specification language due to its expressiveness and support for analysis [1].

The paper is organized as follows: Section 2 introduces SDL as a process modeling language. In Section 3, the applicability of SDL to process modeling is illustrated through the selected case study. Section 4 assesses the applicability of SDL for process modeling. Section 5 concludes the paper.

2 SDL as a Process Modeling Language

Process modeling languages (PMLs) are used to express software process models formally. Formal notation improves process comprehension and documentation, enables process analysis and provides the means for process enactment in PSEEs.

One class of PMLs is based on Petri nets [2], [8]. Petri net is a modeling formalism for the description and analysis of systems whose dynamics are characterized by concurrency, synchronization, mutual exclusion, and conflict, which can be regarded as the features of interest for software process modeling. Since Petri net has a graphical form, it is easy to comprehend, as long as the net is relatively small and simple. The weakness of Petri nets is the inadequacy of the formalism for describing model entities. Modeling language SLANG [2], which is based on Petri nets, uses object-oriented techniques in order to solve the problem.

The other class of PMLs is based on programming languages with a precise syntax and semantics [4]. Software process is represented as a process program that can be executed automatically. It has been noted that language approach is better than graph formalism approach for modeling software processes in detail due to software process complexity [4].

The investigation of currently used PMLs has shown that the approach to software process modeling should enable the following:

- Process model should be formal since formalism ensures model consistency and unequivocalness.
- Process model should be easy to understand since it is the part of process documentation used by process participants.
- The approach should enable modeling of concurrent activities since concurrency is inherent software process property.
- Process model should adequately describe process entities. Object-oriented paradigm has shown successful in constructing complex systems.

SDL satisfies all of the previously stated properties and can therefore be used for software process modeling. In contrast to most formal languages, it has a graphical representation in addition to the commonly available textual representation. Graphical representation makes the specification language user-friendly and easy to use. Special tools for developing, maintaining, analyzing, simulating and verifying SDL specifications are commercially available.

SDL is designed to model real-time communicating systems composed of concurrent processes. It is designed to describe system's structure, behavior, and data and the communication between the system and its environment. Software processes have characteristics similar to real-time systems, since a timely response to external stimuli is required. The difference between a real-time system and a software process is that in a real-time system the computer generates responses, while in a software process, human agents produce answers. Thus, software processes comply with soft real-time system characteristics. In this context, "soft real time", means that nothing catastrophic happens if project deadlines are missed. Nevertheless, customer satisfaction can be seriously deteriorated and project costs significantly increased.

SDL supports hierarchical structuring that improves readability of complex systems. The system is specified as a set of interrelated diagrams showing different levels of detail, from the general overview to detailed design. The top abstraction level is called *system*. It is built of blocks that communicate with each other and the system environment. System specification specifies the overall behavior of the system. *Block* contains one or more process. *Process instances* exist in parallel, modeling the dynamic behavior of the system. They are concurrent and may influence each other by exchanging signals that carry information.

Formally, SDL process instances correspond to communicating extended finite-state machines. Process instance is either in one of its states (waiting, inactive) or performing a transition between two states (active). A transition is initiated by the consumption of a signal that has previously been sent to the process instance by another process instance.

In 1992, SDL has been extended with object-oriented concepts. SDL 92 supports objects and classes, called instances and types for historical reasons. SDL defines *system type*, *block type*, and *process type*. Types can be placed into packages and used across several specifications. Object-oriented concepts of inheritance and specialization have been implemented through specialization of types.

The SDL syntax and semantics is too extensive to be presented in this paper. An interested reader is referred to the handbook on SDL [6].

3 Representation of Software Process Entities

The basic requirement for a process modeling language is the representation of software process entities that incorporate activities and products of the process, and clearly define roles and responsibilities of process participants. Process model consists of many different entities that have been classified as organizational, technical, and communicational [8].

Organizational entities determine the interaction and coordination of process participants during the software process. Roles and teams are used to represent organizational structure of software processes:

- *Roles* are assigned to process participants granting them a bounded area of responsibility. It may be noted that one person may have several different roles and a single role may be associated with several people.
- *Teams* consist of a number of process participants that have been assigned to certain roles. Teams usually have one team leader and a number of team members.

Technical entities are related to the creation and transformation of process artifacts, such as specification, documentation and source code. Technical entities of interest for software process modeling include activities, documents and tools, where:

- *Activities* are actions performed by process participants. Activities create and modify documents.
- *Documents* are the results of process activities. They are used to exchange information between process participants.
- *Tools* are software or hardware resources used by process participants in order to assist the enactment of the software process.

Communicational entities depicts the interchange of information between process participants. They are vital for the successful enactment of the software process since they enable process coordination and cooperation of process participants.

SDL representation of software process entities is based on SDL process instances. SDL process instance has the characteristics of an object. The data describing the instance is hidden inside its structure, either by its state or by defined process variables. Process instance acts on received input signal by performing actions, and produces the output signal, or it simply changes its current state. The details of modeling specific software process entities follow.

A role is modeled by an SDL process type, which describes the flow of activities performed by a particular process participant. For example, a maintainer receives input tasks from its team leader, makes decisions, utilizes resources and changes the state of produced documentation. Note that a role is assigned to one imaginary person by instantiating a process instance from the process type. SDL does not support multiple inheritance and it is therefore not possible to assign multiple roles to one process instance. This is the limitation of SDL role representation. Persons are not explicitly modeled since SDL enables process description without support for process enactment.

A team is modeled as a block that consists of process instances. Each process instance represents one process participant whose behavior is specified by its role process type. For example, maintenance team is modeled as a block, which comprises two process types describing the role of a team leader, and the role of a maintainer. During the system simulation one team leader process instance, and the predefined number of maintainer process instances is created. Hierarchical structuring of SDL systems allows a flexible representation of organizational entities.

An activity is performed by a process participant. It belongs to a particular role process type. An input signal starts the activity, while the output signal ends it. The activity may require a certain decision point that will guide the process through different activities.

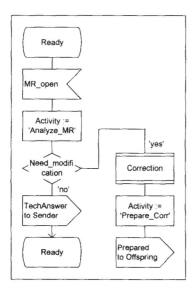 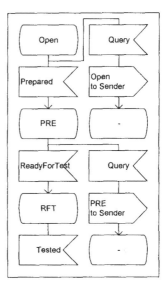

Fig. 1. SDL specification of activity Analyze_MR

Fig. 2. SDL specification of document Correction

Fig. 1 shows a fragment of role specification which describes the activities performed by a maintainer. It models the activity Analyze_MR, which is initiated by the consumption of the signal MR_Open. The objective of the modification request (MR) analysis activity is to decide weather the request can be solved without modifying the code of the system or a correction of the code is necessary. This is modeled by a decision point. If no need for code modification exists, the activity ends by sending the answering signal TechAnswer to the process that has initiated the activity. If the correction of the code is necessary, a new process instance that models the correction is created. New activity Prepare_Corr is subsequently carried out and the signal Prepared is sent to the process instance of type Correction.

A document is modeled by an SDL process type, which describes the set of document states. Document is a passive process entity that can not perform activities.

The state of the document changes as result of human activities. It can be considered as a database entry containing information about the current document state. Fig. 2 specifies the part of document Correction and its states Open, PRE (prepared) and RFT (ready for test). The state of the document changes due to received input signals. The information about the current document state can be obtained by sending the Query signal to the Correction process instance.

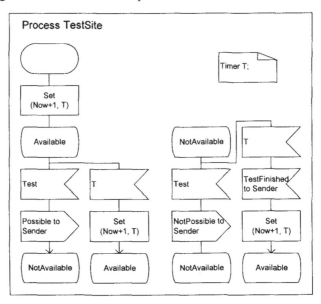

Fig. 3. SDL specification of the tool TestSite

A tool is also specified by an SDL process type. The property of interest for tool specification is availability. At a given time point, the tool can be either available or not available. The tool is modeled as a passive process entity with two states: Available and NotAvailable. The notion of time can be introduced by applying SDL timers. The timer will trigger the change of state and simulate the time period for the tool utilization. Fig. 3 shows the SDL specification describing a testing site. The testing site may be in one of the two states. If a request for testing arrives when the site is available, a positive answer is sent to the process requesting testing and the state of the testing site changes into NotAvailable. If a request for testing arrives when the site is unavailable, a negative answer is sent and the state of the testing site remains unchanged. Timer T is used for simulating the duration of the testing procedure. When a timer signal is consumed, the testing procedure ends and the testing site is again available for further requests.

Finally, the communication between process participants is modeled by signals that carry information between SDL process instances. A signal contains a message and the address of the sending process instance and invokes a transition, which changes the system state.

4 Case Study

Software maintenance is a customer-invoked repetitive software process performed during system operation [10]. Customer reports problems, called modification requests (MRs), which need to be answered in an acceptable time period. MRs enter the maintenance organization, where they wait for maintainers to provide them with a desired service.

The case study reports experiences in SDL modeling of the maintenance process performed in a telecommunications company. The model is based on the information acquired by interviewing the maintenance personnel and by analyzing data repository and process documentation. It needs to be noted that software maintenance is especially demanding in large-scale telecommunication systems. The maintenance team is responsible for corrective maintenance of a large number of software products. The products are similar because they are bound to a particular part of a telecommunication software system.

The objective of the maintenance process modeling is twofold: to acquire the understanding and to analyze the process in order to find process deficiencies and bottlenecks. These objectives are the first step towards maintenance practice improvement, which can enhance company's service performance and increase customer satisfaction.

4.1 Maintenance Practice Description

Maintenance practice under study involves three types of departments: *Registering office* responsible for accepting reported incidents from the customer, *Maintenance office* performing the maintenance, and *Acceptance office* that approves solutions proposed by the Maintenance office. The Registering and the Acceptance office may, in practice, be the same department.

The process of maintenance is initiated by a customer who detects a problem in the field. The incident is reported to the Registering office that investigates the problem. If the incident is considered to be caused by a software fault, it is reported to the department responsible for the maintenance of the subsystem causing the problem. Maintenance expert analyses the MR determining if the cause of the problem is indeed a software fault. If the incident was mistakenly reported, the request is rejected. If the solution of the problem already exists, i.e. if there is a released correction or the request is made due to misunderstanding of function, *technical answer* is created and sent to the Acceptance office. However, a number of MRs needs a correction. The process of creating a correction follows the precisely defined rules. It is performed by handler who designs, implements, and tests the correction. The tested correction is reported to the expert who, in the case of approval, sends a technical answer to the Acceptance office for final approval and subsequent delivery to the customer.

The described procedure is depicted in Fig. 4. It describes the life cycle of a single MR. Based on this representation, one could conclude that the maintenance process comprises sequential activities. The real process, however, consists of concurrent, parallel activities that process a number of MRs simultaneously.

197

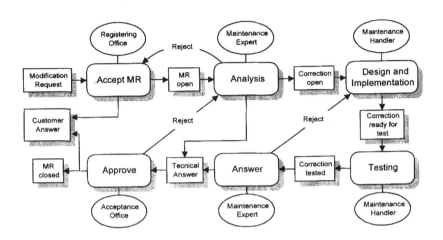

Fig. 4. Description of the maintenance process under study

The number of MRs in the system varies with time since the arrival pattern of MRs is the random process. The representation used in Fig. 4 can not adequately model the dynamical behavior of the maintenance process. SDL modeling offers means for investigating such behavior.

4.2 SDL Software Maintenance Process Model

SDL system of the software maintenance process is composed of three blocks: Registering block, Maintenance block, and the Resources block. The SDL system is depicted in Fig. 5. It shows the structure and communication channels of the model.

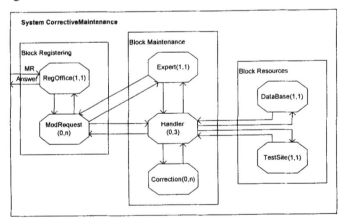

Fig. 5. SDL system of the corrective maintenance process

Registering block models the behavior of the Registering office, which accepts MRs from the environment and creates one entry for each request. Registering block consists of two process types: RegOffice and ModRequest. RegOffice models the activities of the Registering office that opens a new MR entry after it receives a signal MR from the environment. Signal MR simulates customer's incident report that initiates one cycle of the maintenance procedure. For every MR signal, RegOffice creates a new ModRequest instance, which models the MR. In the example (Fig. 5), only one RegOffice instance is created during system simulation, while the number of ModRequest instances depends on the number of requests arriving from the environment.

Maintenance block models the behavior of the maintenance team. It consists of the following process types: Expert, Handler and Correction. Expert models the activities of the team leader who performs the preliminary analysis of the arrived MR and sends it to an available maintainer. Handler models the activities performed by a maintainer who produces corrections to received requests. Corrections are modeled by Correction process type. The total number of Correction instances in the system varies in time.

Resources block models the hardware and software resources. It contains two process instances: DataBase and TestSite, where the former models the data base storing information about MRs and corrections, while the latter models the testing site.

Note that RegOffice, Expert and Handler represent roles in the context of software processes. ModRequest and Correction are documents, while DataBase and TestSite are tools.

Each of the listed process entities is modeled by a collection of appropriate SDL constructs as described in Section 3. The process is modeled imitating the real maintenance procedure. MRs and corrections are used for the exchange of information between process participants in the real process. By analogy, ModRequest instances and Correction instances are used for the exchange of messages between process actors and to store information about the process execution. Process instance RegOffice keeps records of created MRs and is used for coordination of process activities. Process instance Expert is used as a coordinator of activities performed by Handler instances. Expert distributes incoming requests between Handler instances taking into consideration the number of available Handler instances. The complete SDL model of the maintenance process can be found in [11].

The system under study has been modeled applying the SDL Development Tool (SDT) developed by Telelogic AB. SDT has the capabilities to design, modify, simulate, and verify SDL systems.

Maintenance process simulation is visualized using the Message Sequence Chart (MSC) tool. MSCs are used for monitoring interprocess communication. System simulation shows the dynamic behavior of the modeled maintenance process. A simulation run executes a sequence of process activities initiated by signals that invoke transitions and change SDL model states. MSC is a valuable tool for monitoring the progress of simulation. A fragment of a simulation run is presented in Fig. 6. The simulation shows a large number of interactions between process participants for a single modification request. The process is highly dependent on the number of MRs in the system and on the number of maintainers performing the process. Testing site has been identified as one of the possible points of congestion.

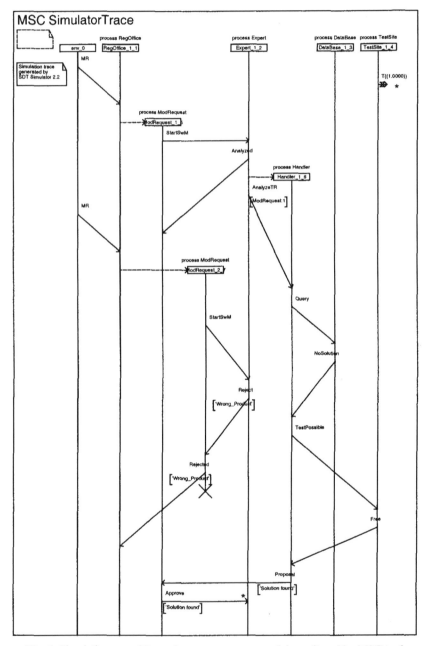

Fig. 6. Simulation run of the maintenance process model monitored by MSC tool

SDT incorporates a tool for system verification, which enables the investigation of concurrent system properties such as liveness, deadlock and conflict. The tool has been used for the investigation of the maintenance process model properties. The property of particular interest for software processes is liveness. The verification procedure detected no deadlocks in the process. However, feedback loops enabling endless process executions were discovered. The first loop is caused by the obligation of the expert to approve the solution proposed by the handler. The second loop is caused by the need for Registering office approval of the proposed solution. It can be noted that time control should be included into the model in order to avoid endless process execution.

5 Assessment of SDL Applicability for Process Modeling

The assessment of SDL applicability for process modeling is performed based on the assessment grid introduced in [1]. The proposed assessment grid has been reduced to topics covering the PML technology evaluation, since other categories are not applicable to our modeling approach. The following topics covering the PML technology have been considered for the evaluation of SDL applicability for software process modeling:

- *Scope of coverage*: SDL can be used to improve process comprehension and documentation. Support for formal analysis through process simulation and verification is available. SDL can therefore be used as a process specification and process design language.
- *Linguistic paradigm*: SDL is a specification language that supports concurrency and object-orientation.
- *Modeling of process entities*: SDL is not specifically designed for process modeling. It has no predefined process-specific constructs for modeling process entities. However, as it has previously been shown, SDL constructs can adequately specify process entities (Section 3). The object-oriented paradigm makes it possible to describe process roles, documents, and tools. Parallel and concurrent activities are modeled quite easily since SDL process instances may run in parallel. The exchange of signals between process instances makes it possible to model communication and coordination between process participants.
- *Modularity, composition, and reuse*: SDL has a hierarchical structure (system, block, and process instance) that shows process views at different levels of detail. Reuse is enabled by the usage of system, block, and process types that can be integrated into packages and used across specifications. SDL supports inheritance.
- *Mechanism for process enactment and evolution*: Since SDL is not a programming language, it can not be used for implementing and enacting software processes.
- *Cooperation and concurrency control*: Asynchronous cooperation is enabled by modeling a person, e.g. team leader, who stores the information about the state of other process participants and coordinates their job assignments. The exchange of signals between process instances and the control of availability of process tools enables concurrency control.

- *SDL tool support*: Tool support for designing, modifying, analyzing, simulating and verifying SDL systems is available. Visualization of system specification is enabled by graphical SDL constructs. Message Sequence Charts enable the visualization of communication between process instances.

Based on the above SDL characteristics, it can be concluded that the advantages of SDL approach to software process modeling are effortless process comprehension and unambiguous process documentation, process analysis through simulation and verification, user-friendly graphical notation, and visualization of the process flow. In addition, SDL is a standard language used in the telecommunications field. Hence, no additional costs for the training and tool development are needed, assuming that the company uses SDL during software development. The limitation of SDL approach to software process modeling is the incapability of the language to be used for process implementation and enactment. SDL models can not be used for the quantitative analysis of the software process.

6 Conclusion

The paper has demonstrated the applicability of SDL for software process modeling. SDL is a specification and description language that supports concurrency and object-orientation, the language paradigms necessary for modeling software processes. SDL has shown to be suitable for modeling the real industrial software process. It proved useful for process comprehension and analysis through simulation and verification. Model simulation can be used to identify process flaws, deficiencies and bottlenecks, to estimate the impact of potential changes to the process and to compare alternative process models without putting the new process into practice. SDL process specification is a cost-effective method for modeling the dynamic behavior of the software system. It needs to be noted that it can not be used for process implementation and enactment.

Future work will be directed to the development of support for quantitative analysis and assessment of software processes. Qualitative analysis offers means for identifying critical points of the process, and investigating their potential causes. Quantitative process assessment enables comparison of different process configurations, and the capability of identifying an improved process design. The development of the process simulation tool is necessary in order to investigate different process configurations without putting them into practice. SDL software process model offers the necessary information for the design of the simulation tool.

References

1. Ambriola, V., R. Conradi and A. Fuggetta, Assessing Process-Centered Software Engineering Environments, *ACM Trans. on Software Eng. and Methodology*, 6(3), July 1997, pp. 283-328.

2. Bandinelli, S., A. Fuggetta, L. Lavazza, M. Loi, and G. P. Picco, Modeling and Improving an Industrial Software Process, *IEEE Trans. on Software Eng.*, SE-21(5), May 1995, pp. 440-453.
3. Briand, L., Y. M. Kim, W. Melo, C. Seaman and V. R. Basili, Q-MOPP: Qualitative Evaluation of Maintenance Organizations, Processes and Products, *J. of Software Maintenance: Research and Practice* 10(4), July-August 1998, pp. 249-278.
4. Chen, J.Y., CSPL: An Ada95-Like Unix-Based Process Environment, *IEEE Trans. on Software Eng.*, SE-23(3), March 1997, pp. 171-184.
5. Curtis, B., M.I. Kellner and J. Over, Process Modeling, *Comm. of the ACM*, 35(9), September 1992, pp. 75-90.
6. Ellsberger J., D. Hogrefe and A. Sarma, *SDL Formal Object-oriented Language for Communicating Systems*, Prentice Hall Europe, UK, 1997.
7. Garg, P. and M. Jazayeri, Process-Centered Software Engineering Environments: A Grand Tour, *Technical Report*, Distributed Systems Department, Technical University of Vienna, Austria, TUV-1841-95-02, 1995.
8. Gruhn, V. and H. Weber, Understanding and Improving Interpersonal Processes in Software Development, 1992. URL: http://ls10-www.informatik.uni-dortmund.de/
9. Mikac, B., I. Lovrek, V. Sinkovic, Z. Car, H. Pehar, I. Podnar, A. Caric, A. Burilovic, H. Naglic, I. Sinovcic, T. Viskic-Huljenic, Assessing the Process of Telecommunications Software Maintenance, *Proceedings of the combined 10th European Software Control and Metrics conference and the 2nd SCOPE conference* , Herstmonceux, UK, April 1999, pp. 267-275.
10. Pigoski, T.M., *Practical Software Maintenance*, Wiley, New York, 1996.
11. Podnar, I., Software Maintenance Process Analysis, *Master's Thesis* (in Croatian), Faculty of Electrical Engineering and Computer Science, University of Zagreb, 1999.
12. Sommerville, I., *Software Engineering*, Addison-Wesley, Wokingham, UK, 1995.

Achieving Customer Satisfaction through Requirements Understanding

John Elliott and Peter Raynor-Smith

Systems and Software Engineering Centre
Defence Evaluation and Research Agency (DERA)
St Andrews Road
MALVERN
Worcestershire WR14 3PS
UK
[jjelliott, prsmith]@dera.gov.uk

Abstract. Achieving and measuring customer satisfaction is a key aim in systems development. However, widespread customer satisfaction is not normally attained largely due to problems of inadequate 'requirements understanding'. This lack of understanding is a function of a semantic gap that exists between customers and system developers while exploring requirements. What is required is a universal and non-technical customer-oriented process that supports the attainment of customer satisfaction through minimising any barriers to understanding. This paper describes a process improvement theme and a case study that has been directed towards better customer satisfaction through improved through-life requirements engineering and management. The case study examines the suitability and attributes of the 'Dynamic Systems Development Method' which was chosen as a candidate for evaluation as a customer-oriented process.

1   Introduction

One key goal of all businesses is to achieve a continuous and high level of customer satisfaction in the delivery of services and/or products. Such satisfaction is believed to be the basis of long term profitability and business growth. In the sphere of computer based system products, customer satisfaction is dependent on how system development projects evolve to build operational product systems that satisfy the perceived and actual customer need and associated system requirements.

Ultimately, successful customer satisfaction depends upon the depth of 'through-life' understanding about the business need and associated user requirements for a future system, and the ability to communicate those requirements to the system developer. In addition, customer satisfaction and confidence depends upon the level of system assurance offered throughout the system development lifecycle. Requirements understanding problems inevitably lead to poor customer-supplier relationships, unnecessary re-works, and overruns in cost and/or time.

This paper discusses the concepts underpinning customer satisfaction and requirements understanding relevant to software-based system development. In addition, the design of customer-oriented development processes is described together with a process improvement case study and associated experiment. The process improvement experiment was EU project number 23893, REJOICE, whose Final Report [12] can be found at the ESSI VASIE website [13]. The REJOICE experiments and their results have been summarised later in this paper.

The REJOICE experimentation was undertaken by the *Systems and Software Engineering Centre (SEC)*, an autonomous business within the UK's Defence Evaluation and Research Agency (DERA). The SEC has about 200 staff and offers a full range of system and software engineering services; the SEC's emphasis is on researching, developing, demonstrating and coordinating best practice across a wide range of application types and quality requirements. The SEC utilises modern software technology supported by a large supply of ubiquitous computing equipment and software tools.

2   Customer Satisfaction and Requirements Understanding

2.1   Concepts

Customer satisfaction is dependent upon many factors that are associated with the business need, the development project and resultant system product quality. Ultimately the customer is looking for added value to benefit the business operations within a defined timeframe but at an affordable price; hence the customer priority is for an overall *successful business*. The system supplier perspective is to deliver a system within the agreed cost plans to satisfy the customer requirements, thus contributing to the supplier's profit and reputation; hence the supplier priority is for a *successful project*. These different perspectives are typically controlled through inflexible and formal contract management arrangements in the pursuit of a successful project for both customer and supplier. The cornerstone to such *'success'* involves an appropriately rigorous and long-term approach to *'quality'* by customers and suppliers.

'Quality' may be loosely inferred to mean 'satisfying requirements' embracing the provision of added capability (i.e. improved business function and performance) and any associated trustworthiness or integrity (i.e. continuously performs as intended without harmful 'side-effects' on business services). One key aspect of the quality perspective concerns the customer and supplier agreeing upon a required level of quality to be achieved within defined and understood cost and time constraints. In addition, the quality level must be defined and be subject to some agreed measurement to monitor attainment. Figure 1 highlights the various project viewpoints affecting quality. Of these, 'time' is often the more common constraint, usually for operational reasons, and this tends to limit functional and/or quality.

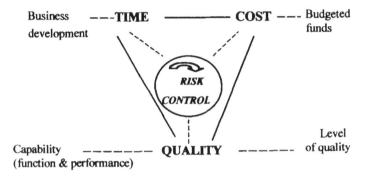

Fig. 1. Balancing the development achievements

The remaining development project consideration is the level of *risk* and *uncertainty* associated with the attainment of the required and agreed quality level; the risk perspective depends upon the available knowledge about the project constraints and their implications. Hence both customer and supplier need to understand the level of risk each is taking within their quality level agreement. In practice, the notion of risk sharing between customers and suppliers is a difficult area that influences the nature of any supporting legally binding contractual arrangements. In summary, both customers and suppliers need to plan and implement compatible quality and risk strategies for the development project. These strategies will need to be reflected in any contractual agreements.

Returning to quality within the customer satisfaction arena, customers need to be assured that defined and measurable final *product quality* attributes demonstrate that their defined needs and associated requirements are satisfied. Achieving defined product quality depends upon 'getting the system requirements right' and then 'building the product right' to meet these requirements. Measuring product quality requires various external and internal system product attributes to be considered; external attributes include its functionality and performance (e.g. speed, reliability, maintainability, safety, security, etc) whereas internal attributes include its architectural structure, portability etc. Different authors such as Fenton and Gillies [2, 3] describe and review different quality models including that developed for the ISO 9126 standard [4]. Achieving defined product quality is not easy to achieve especially within traditional contracting processes that tend to encourage the communication of requirements through formal documents and review activities. This inflexible and formal approach to agreement and communication is often the main reason why customer and supplier teams fail to be effective in achieving continuous levels of understanding, which is sometimes coloured by a culture of disrespect and mistrust.

2.2 Customer Satisfaction Criteria

The necessary criteria for customer satisfaction are provided in Table 1 below to demonstrate the relationship with requirements understanding. Such criteria provide the basis for defining measurement schemes from which to systematically argue and justify whether customer needs and requirements have been adequately satisfied.

Area	Criteria
Need and requirements definition and change management	• The business need for supporting necessary or desirable (process and information) change must be clearly defined. • The system requirements must be clear (and error-free) and related to the business need. • There must be an ability to change the product development as the requirements are better understood and refined (or even changed due to business reasons).
Process definition and execution	• The supplier's development process (for all management, engineering and quality activities) must be consistent with best practice. • The supplier processes must closely interface with the customer's processes in executing the acquisition and system creation activities. • The competence and performance of the supplier teams must be of a high standard. • There must be high visibility of the executing development processes and of the product evolution.
Product quality	• The final system product must be compliant with the agreed and understood requirements. • The final system product must meet defined business needs and added value to the customer's business operations. • The final system product must have high levels of usability and be easily integrated into customer processes.
Product management	• There must be sufficient demonstration regarding the satisfaction of business needs, system requirements and product quality (i.e. overall fitness for purpose). • The agreed project schedule must be met ensuring that the final system delivery and in-service dates are achieved. • The project costs must not be changed without full agreement and justification in customer terms.

Table 1. Customer Satisfaction Criteria

It should be noted that 'requirements understanding' impacts on all these customer satisfaction areas. Initially the understanding of need, as well as requirements, is important, and this will help appreciate and plan for the inevitable (need or requirement) changes that may occur in a system's life. Furthermore, the requirements set the context for quality and risk considerations that drive the development and assurance processes, to be effectively 'product managed' - that also includes ensuring an adequate understanding of requirements is maintained.

2.3 Model of Customer Satisfaction and its Components

Partly derived from the criteria above, the customer satisfaction problem domain mainly depends on four key dimensions:

- *Business need* (i.e. need for new business strategy and change, operations and usability).
- *System requirements* (i.e. includes all aspects: the user/system product definition including quality and risk levels and process criteria and constraints, e.g. interoperability with existing systems, timescales and costs).
- *Confidence in the quality* (i.e. in the development and assurance process capability and people competence with attendant risks).
- *Product quality* (i.e. confidence, demonstration, arguments and evidence about quality and fitness).

These dimensions are the basis of a customer satisfaction model. Figure 2 shows the essential relationships between these dimensions, and the influence on customer satisfaction.

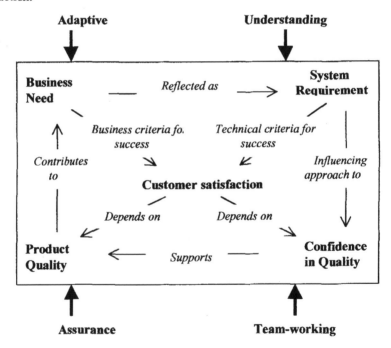

Fig. 2. Dimensions and Viewpoints of Customer Satisfaction

Of significance is the distinction between the need-related business criteria and the requirements-related technical criteria. Also whilst these dimensions are fundamental to achieving customer satisfaction, there are other viewpoints of project success that also need to be considered, see Garrity [1] for example. The following viewpoints, as also shown in Figure 2, complement the customer satisfaction model's dimensions and are necessary for defining a *customer-oriented process*:

- *Understanding* - that both customers and developers throughout an evolutionary-oriented development lifecycle fully and unambiguously understand the business need and requirements.
- *Team working* - that customers and developers work towards the same project goals within a trusting and respectful partnership based on *effective communication, decision making and action.*
- *Assurance* - confidence that the resulting product meets the required level of quality and is fit for its purpose within accepted levels of risk, (derived from 'fit for purpose' arguments and supporting evidence involving assessments and measurements about process (degree of development and assurance rigor) criteria and product (design) criteria).
- *Adaptability* - that the inevitable changes in the customer's perception or situation about the business need and the system requirements are adequately accommodated.

The above dimensions and viewpoints regarding customer satisfaction constitute a framework reference model (customer satisfaction model) that can be used to design and/or evaluate future development processes.

3   Customer-oriented Lifecycle Process Requirements

The aim has been to define a technical strategy based upon the fundamental understanding embodied in the customer satisfaction model. The strategy enhances the level of customer satisfaction through improved customer-developer process design with an emphasis on requirements and their understanding. Based on the concepts described, Table 2 shows the key requirements that need to be considered when designing a new approach to customer satisfaction.

Type	Requirements
Through life Understanding/ Evolution	• *Through-life* treatment of system requirements and business need; this will focus attention on the ultimate project goals and success criteria • Need to embrace the whole system *evolution* lifecycle; this will ensure that systems are not viewed as totally new but rather as add-ons or modifications to existing, albeit larger, systems. • Need to ensure that customers get operational systems as a series of *increments* to meet shorter-term priority needs; this will enable customers to get useful employable systems as a series of incremental deliveries formed within an well-founded overarching business system architecture. • Must be *fast* to react to changing customer perspectives about system requirements; this assists customers to quickly see the impact of their desired changes. • Enable executable system prototypes to be *visible* and allowing user 'play back'; this enables the customer team to see the evolving product in concrete terms and respond accordingly. • Need to be able to *roll* the current system solution both forwards and backwards; this assists the speed at which changes (using new or old perspectives) can be played back.

Adaptability	• Need to be *flexible* to changing customer needs and perspectives; this will encourage effective contracting and working arrangements to be in place that are based on the premise that such change is inevitable and technical agreements will need to change. • Need to manage the customer needs and requirements and their *satisfaction* through a flexible yet controllable approach to system planning and its execution; this will focus both parties on the theme of customer satisfaction and project success by on-going requirements understanding.
Team-working/ communication	• Need for customer-supplier teams to work in *partnership*; this will enable both parties with separate overall business aims to share a more focused and explicit common project goal within a trusted contractual and working relationship that involves more risk and information sharing, and joint decision making. • Needs effective *communication/interfacing* between customer and supplier teams; this enables a common and shared understanding about the business need, system requirements, and the development processes and products. • Need customers and suppliers to be regularly *interactive* about key business and development changes affecting the partnership; this enables an on-going approach to holism, learning and adaptability throughout system evolution. • Need frequent customer *feedback* to design concepts and system increments prior to final acceptance and in-service use; this will ensure that customers declare timely change based on business use perspectives. • All appropriate processes, methods and tools need to be *universally* understandable and accessible to all those involved in the customer and developer teams.
Assurance management	• Need to enable the risk and quality levels to be defined and agreed; this leads to different needs for process, project and people management. • Need to provide effective demonstration and control mechanisms to decide about system *fitness*; this will enable customers and suppliers to understand any arguments based on evidence about risks and fitness prior to operational use.

Table 2. Customer-oriented Process Requirements

4 Proposed Customer-oriented Lifecycle Processes

4.1 Customer-oriented Technical Strategy

The proposed strategy is to:

• Define a customer-oriented lifecycle process with defined attributes; that will place an emphasis on through-life 'requirement understanding' processes.
• Integrate the proposed lifecycle processes into established project, risk and quality management practices; this will involve identifying the tailoring issues

surrounding the introduction of a customer-oriented approach into established software practices and local cultures.

- Propose a set of techniques to support the new lifecycle that is appropriate to a project situation.
- Define a means of measuring the effectiveness of the new lifecycle and supporting techniques in business and project terms; this will focus on the cost-effectiveness using criteria about *identifying need/requirements, communication/interaction* and *requirements control*.
- Ensure that the new customer-oriented approach is focusing on business benefits and be widely applicable; this directs the approach to be geared towards the non-software specialists, needing no specialist tools, knowledge or equipment.

4.2   Customer-oriented Process Overview

The aim is to establish an improved process and set of techniques that will assist customer and supplier to gain a better understanding of initial and changing requirements so that systems are delivered on time, to cost and actually meeting the customer's real need. These techniques will also need to address accomplishing and preserving product quality throughout the product life cycle. The approach combines and utilises techniques from separate strands:

- A *customer-oriented lifecycle* process supported by fundamental system models that describe requirements understanding concepts and system 'fitness' measurement.
- Use of *business analysis* techniques such as those exploited in Business Process Re-engineering (BPR) [6] to guide the way in which the customer's real needs are articulated and understood.
- *Interactive and iterative* approaches such as JAD (Joint Application Development) [5] and RAD (Rapid Application Development) [5, 8] to assist communication and exploration.
- Formalised approaches to capture the statement of *requirements*, support their management and allow traceability, etc.

The customer-oriented lifecycle process has been based on an adaptation of the *Dynamic Systems Development Method* (DSDM) [5, 8 14] framework called the REJOICE process [9]. DSDM offers a generic lifecycle framework that is geared to being more flexible, faster reacting and dynamic practices involving joint customer-developer working. Figure 3 shows the five DSDM-based customer-oriented lifecycle process phases. The proposed process adaptations to DSDM, as used within the REJOICE process improvement case study, combine and refine Phases 1 and 2 activities. The techniques from the various strands above will be incorporated within the implementation of the DSDM lifecycle process.

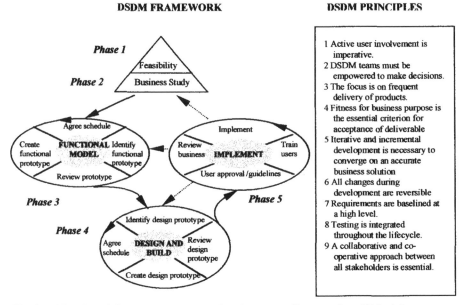

Fig. 3. DSDM Based Customer-Oriented Lifecycle Process Framework and Principles

The DSDM phases are:

- *Phase 1 - Feasibility Study;* An assessment is made as to whether or not the DSDM approach is correct for the anticipated project. [This is not a conventional form of feasibility, i.e. whether the system concept is achievable.]
- *Phase 2 - Business Study;* Provides the foundations on which all subsequent work is based and provides an understanding of the business and technical constraints. [This study is intended to be relatively short with the aim to describe a 'first-cut' high level requirement.]
- *Phase 3 - Functional model;* this activity is broadly equivalent to a functional specification, but expressed using an executable prototype with some documentation support.
- *Phase 4 - Design and build;* this activity is refining the functionality to reflect non-functional and other quality/integrity requirements; the detailed designs are as executable prototypes but with improving quality attributes, supported by essential documentation.
- *Phase 5 - Implement:* this activity is applying the product within a series of systems trials ultimately being accepted in the operational environment.

The essence of this approach is for the customer and developer to work in partnership ensuring that the needs and requirements are well understood by all. The system is allowed to evolve in terms of refining prototypes resulting in useable increments. The strategy is to be flexible and adaptive to changing requirements and to progressively build quality into the evolving product. The customer-development interactions occur throughout allowing for learning, feedback and adapting to influence development directions. The risk of the flexibility offered needs to be countered through the application of sufficient management and quality assurance practices incorporating process and product checks with sufficient traceable documentation. Project control is quite different in DSDM from traditional quality system environments as DSDM projects only generate high level plans, as with requirements, whereas the details are regularly evolved, reviewed and modified as required. Control is focussed on regular short time periods, referred to as 'timeboxes', for which objectives are agreed. A timebox enables detailed activity plans to be defined and undertaken, together with reviewing progress and the results. This approach is to some extent dependent on effective tool-sets, e.g. for prototyping, in order to gain the customer satisfaction benefits.

5   Process Improvement Case Study

A case study to examine the effectiveness of the new proposed approach to customer satisfaction and requirements understanding was undertaken as an EU funded process improvement experiment (PIE), referred to as REJOICE, ESSI Project 23893. The purpose of the PIE was to demonstrate whether the new customer-oriented process could provide the business benefits sought as improvement goals.

There are various elements to the experiment:

- Business context.
- Improvement goals.
- Proposed process.
- Experimental considerations.
- Experimental results.

5.1   Business Context

The experiment was set in the UK Defence Evaluation and Research Agency's (DERA's) System and Software Engineering Centre (SEC). The SEC is an autonomous development and consultancy business that largely serves the defence system businesses within DERA and the UK Ministry of Defence. The SEC is associated with a very wide range of systems for high technology research, system requirements and design modeling, tool development and operational activities. The SEC operates within a highly controlled business management culture (based on the ISO 9000 series) and its activities are regularly subjected to process assessments (e.g. ISO, CMM, SPICE, EFQM-BEM). The SEC has a 'maturing' software culture supported by its DERA Software Practices. The DERA practices incorporate an in-built measurement system.

5.2   Improvement Goals

The SEC is striving to achieve the highest levels of CMM maturity (currently achieving Level 3 in some areas) for all its widespread activities supported by the use of SPICE to develop excellence in particular project domains. There were a number of improvement areas identified from various process assessments. This included those concerned with customer relations and ensuring that the SEC met customer needs and requirements. The relevant, and demanding, 'customer-related' goals to be satisfied through an improved approach to requirements understanding were:

- 20% more customer satisfaction.
- No extra effort on requirements activities.
- 15% decrease in requirements generated problem (i.e. less reworks).

5.3   Proposed Process

The customer-oriented lifecycle process, an adaptation of DSDM, shown in Figure 3, was applied within specific development projects. DSDM's selection was based on its general suitability as a 'customer-oriented process'. REJOICE was, in essence checking whether the customer-orientation of DSDM was in fact well founded, workable and likely to be effective, particularly in support of the SEC's improvement goals defined. The DSDM adaptation was to combine Phases 1 and 2 of DSDM into a single phase, 'User Requirements Study'. The reason was to remove the DSDM suitability analysis (less important to the REJOICE goals than to rapid application development objectives) and to increase the focus on the feasibility and definition of user requirements against a real, and rigorously studied, strategic need for business change. Hence, this new phase focuses on the communication, understanding, elicitation and high level capture of business needs and requirements. In addition, before the adapted DSDM lifecycle process (referred to as the *REJOICE process*) can be applied, further DSDM 'tailoring' considerations need to be addressed:

- How can the flexible proposed process be utilised within a high-control business and quality management culture?
- What standardisation process details should be defined and to what level of detail?
- How do you define the exact process incorporating methods and tools to apply to a specific project?

It should be stressed that the new customer-oriented process represents a major shift in development culture, a major issue for the REJOICE experiment. In support of the new process, a set of specific methods and tools were selected from which the experiment process details were selected. There was an emphasis on business analysis (e.g. BPR), interaction management and facilitation (e.g. JAD), design methodology (e.g. object-orientation) and requirements management support (e.g. procedures and tools).

5.4 Experimental Considerations

The experimentation was divided into four parts:

- Experiment 1 - Defining, tailoring and introducing the new customer-oriented 'REJOICE' process.
- Experiment 2 – Partial Application of the REJOICE process to the development of a Requirements Modelling Tool.
- Experiment 3 - Applying and measuring the impact of the 'REJOICE' process during the development of a DERA Intranet based CMM Self-Assessment Tool.
- Experiment 4 - Comparing the 'REJOICE' process with the existing development process during the development of a DERA Intranet based CMM Self-Assessment Tool.

Each experiment had its own design that included a number of specific hypotheses to be tested and an associated measurement scheme, each of which was linked to the improvement goals. Overall the measurement strategy included maximising the use of qualitative observations backed up by argument based on valuable experience identifying the issues, in addition to collecting quantitative measures. The data collection involved a combination of surveys, interviews, project resource extracts and tracking what processes were being implemented in some measurable detail. The major experimental part was the application of the new process to be applied to two tool development projects. Each project had specific and well-informed customer teams; one project was a requirement modelling tool and the other was a CMM assessment support tool. The outline measurement scheme to examine the new process is shown below in Table 3 (more details are described in [12]).

Goal	Area/Factor	Metrics
20% increase in satisfying customer needs	**Customer Satisfaction:** meet need; confidence in product; confidence in process/people **Product Effectiveness:** product quality claimed; demonstration of quality	Satisfaction (score) with project, product, process, people No. of prototype releases - planned, actual No. of the original satisfied/unsatisfied requirements No of requirements changed No of requirements priority changes No of evolution's of requirements
No change in costs of requirements activity	**Project efficiency:** process definition; process cost; people impact	Time spent in customer interactions Number of customer interactions Time spent demonstrating models/prototypes
15% decrease in problems due to poor requirements understanding	**Project efficiency:** requirement defects; people interaction; process cost impact	Number of requirements not satisfied Effort spent satisfying incorrect requirements

Table 3. Goals, Factors and Metrics

These metrics were partly derived to capture the essence of what happens within evolutionary requirements activities. One key feature concerned the need to decide, negotiate and manage the human-centred development dynamics (i.e. interacting pressures for change) that often tends to get forgotten. Such dynamics are well known as a natural part of software development, but the issue is whether DSDM offers project dynamics in an effective and efficient manner, as set out in the REJOICE goals. One area of interest is whether the savings gained in less reworks through more focused DSDM activities is likely to save money though less late discoveries, with a bigger impact, of requirements orientated software errors.

5.5 Experimental Results

The main results of the four experiments are detailed in the REJOICE Final Report [12] that provides detailed qualitative and quantitative (measurements) evidence presented in a form that argues about the validity of the various customer-oriented process hypotheses. The overall results are now briefly summarised in Table 4 below.

Experiment	Main Results:
Experiment 1 Defining, tailoring and introducing the customer-oriented process.	• Successive levels of tailoring are involved - they are difficult to clearly define • The DSDM based customer oriented framework is 'loosely' defined and requires further refinement and instantiation to be employable • The new DSDM based process does not fit easily with existing Quality Systems • Detailed DSDM based processes cannot be fully prescribed due to the highly iterative processes involved that is dependent on actual product development progress • Detailed project planning cannot be achieved: plans need to stay at a high level or they will lag behind the actual development
Experiment 2 Applying and measuring the impact of the new customer-oriented process: Requirement Tool Project	• The pragmatic use of principles leads to a 'fit for purpose' product • 'High level' user requirements are difficult to resolve and manage contractually • The use of prototyping techniques are very effective • The contract requirements would not have been met if traditional processes used
Experiment 3 Applying and measuring the impact of the new customer-oriented 'REJOICE' process: CMM Assessment Tool Project	• There was good 'buy-in' by the development team • There were high levels of user involvement • There was a high level of user satisfaction with the final product • The users sometimes resented the demands on their time • The team emphasis on development of product means documentation/testing suffers unless control exercised; this may be a problem for longer term customer satisfaction • Any organisation and culture changes are non-trivial • It was difficult to control and plan prototyping • It was difficult to monitor project progress with traditional management techniques • The development team was not used to empowerment and they tended to perceive a lack of direction and management

Experiment	Main Results:
Experiment 4 Comparing the new customer-oriented 'REJOICE' process with the existing traditional development process.	• It is difficult to compare results with 'traditional' methods due to non-equivalence with stages in 'waterfall' and variants • Customer surveys provided evidence of improved satisfaction • The REJOICE process was found to be more efficient than traditional methods in terms of required functionality achieved for developer effort • If the development had followed the existing traditional process, that may have led to the development of an altogether different tool, not taking into account real business need • The longer term customer satisfaction advantages are more difficult to assess • The REJOICE process developed products may be more difficult to maintain and evolve

Table 4. Main Results by Experiment

The collective (both hard and soft) evidence from all these experiments provided a valuable basis for assessing whether the REJOICE DSDM-based approach is likely to contribute to the SEC achieving its improvement goals. The overall conclusions were in support of the hypotheses that the DSDM style of working increases customer satisfaction and it appears to be efficient in the use of resources attributable to 'requirements' activities. The degree of benefit is hard to predict and quantify, given the subject matter, especially when based on a single experiment, but the positive indications were very evident given some caveats, as set out in the lessons in Section 6.

The comparison with the SEC's traditional 'waterfall' or equivalent 'staging' lifecycle styles was studied in terms of the varying size/complexity, effort and the degree of completeness in, as well as changes to and iterations involved with, intermediate and final products. In addition, the evidence assisted in deriving the lessons that were learnt within the overall REJOICE process improvement case study in terms of the technological and business impact of the new DSDM-based REJOICE process. As in the REJOICE Final Report [12], these lessons are now described in terms of these technological and business viewpoints. The reader should please note that the final report has many appendices providing both hard data, and the essential soft information from the experience, and both are necessary when assessing the likely impact across the SEC activities of applying the DSDM-based REJOICE process. Hence the following lessons contain high level advice to others, including SMEs.

6 Lessons Learnt

6.1 Lessons Learnt - Technological Viewpoint

This viewpoint assesses the impact of the new process in relation to current software practices and their evolution. The lessons are:

- Adoption by the SEC of a new, evolutionary yet controlled lifecycle approach (where appropriate to the projects) is expected to lead to improved customer satisfaction.
- DSDM offers a useful set of concepts (sensible principles, flexible requirements philosophy, strong user and end product focus) that will advance the SEC best practices.
- DSDM is not only suitable for 'RAD type' projects but its concepts can be integrated, in full or in part, into more traditional lifecycle approaches.
- The integration of the DSDM based process within a traditional ISO 9000 quality controlled software development operation is non-trivial, unless DSDM is used to do RAD developments only.
- Commonly available tools generally support the basic DSDM based REJOICE process although more model based tools are needed that facilitate effective user-modeling interaction (to study requirements and acceptance testing issues).

Overall, the technological lessons about the DSDM based REJOICE processes are fundamental. More radical software lifecycles are designed to improve customer-developer relations. These require new ways of thinking about project control and tool based cultures. There is clear evidence that the REJOICE process is sufficiently mature and does indeed enhance customer satisfaction, assuming that a joint product-focused management approach is taken by both customers and developers. In short, the REJOICE process offers clear claimed benefits when used in part or in full, but there are a number of non-trivial project and quality management issues to overcome.

6.2   Lessons Learnt - Business Viewpoint

This viewpoint assesses the impact of the new process in relation to business goals and activities. The lessons are:

- Customer satisfaction and the attendant advantages are likely to be achieved by the using the DSDM based REJOICE Process.
- The REJOICE process is likely to provide cost saving gains in the efficiency of requirements-based activities, dependent on project complexity and associated implementation issues.
- The REJOICE process requires a co-operative product focused management approach.
- Definition and management of contractual boundaries will be challenging.
- Cultural changes may be difficult to manage.
- Consider applying DSDM techniques to smaller projects until confidence is gained.
- A REJOICE type process will increase business opportunities through improved customer relations.

Overall, many software businesses, often Small Medium Enterprises, should benefit from the DSDM-based REJOICE concepts, process and techniques in terms of customer satisfaction and requirements efficiencies. However, the degree of success will depend upon the organisation and customer culture, the appropriate application to suitably complex projects and an effective use of available software technologies. In short, the REJOICE process framework is well founded but its success critically depends on the management of people and technical resources during any development project implementation.

7 Summary

This paper has described the underpinnings and development of a customer and requirements focused 'REJOICE' process that has been adapted from DSDM. The underpinning arises from the evolving development of an innovative customer satisfaction and requirements understanding model that has a key system measurement component. The underpinning also provides a basis for defining some requirements for a customer-oriented process, that DSDM was deemed to partly satisfy. Hence, a new customer-oriented lifecycle process (i.e. DSDM) has been defined and examined within an EU funded process improvement experiment, REJOICE. REJOICE has focused on the business impact of a requirements-oriented process improvement geared to improve customer satisfaction; the business goals include improved customer satisfaction and cost effective requirements management. The experimental findings support the main hypotheses that the flexible process should yield the business benefits suggested; however a careful approach to process introduction is required as a new cultural approach to customer-supplier partnerships is critical. If implemented well, both customers and suppliers should reap major benefits.

Acknowledgements and Disclaimers

The authors would like to acknowledge the European Commission for funding the Process Improvement Experiment, REJOICE, Project 23893, supplemented by internal Defence Evaluation and Research Agency funding on the general concepts underpinning requirements understanding.
The views expressed in this paper are entirely those of the authors and do not represent the views, policy or understanding of any other person or official body. Further details can be requested from the Defence Evaluation and Research Agency (DERA Malvern), Systems and Software Engineering Centre, Tel: +44 1684-895161, E-Mail: jjelliott@dera.co.uk.

References

1. Garrity, E.J., Saunders, G.L., "Information Systems Success Measurement", IDEA Group, 1998.
2. Fenton, N. E., Pfleeger S. L., "Software Metrics", 2nd Ed, Thomson Computer Press, 1997.

3. Gillies, A., "Software Quality - Theory and Management", Chapman and Hall, 1992.
4. ISO 9126, "Software Product Evaluation", 1992.
5. McConnell, S., "Rapid Development", Microsoft Press, 1996.
6. MacDonald, J., "Understanding Business Process Re-engineering", Hodder & Stoughton, 1995.
7. Bell, S., Wood-Harper, T., "Rapid Information Systems Development - System Development in an Imperfect World", Second Ed., McGraw-Hill, 1998.
8. Martin J., "Rapid Application Development", New York: Macmillian, 1991.
9. Raynor-Smith, P. M., "REJOICE Process", DERA Report, 1998.
10. DSDM Consortium , "DSDM Manual", 1996.
11. Stapleton J., "Dynamic Systems Development Method", Addison-Wesley, 1997.
12. Raynor-Smith, P. M., Elliott J. J., REJOICE Final Report, Version 1.0, May 1999
13. ESSI VASIE website: http://www.cordis.lu/esprit/src/stessi.htm
14. DSDM website http://www.dsdm.org

Keynote on "Current State and Future Perspectives of Software Process Technology"

Robert Balzer,
USC-ISI, Los Angeles CA, USA

Abstract

This keynote reviews the technical foundations of our field in terms of the rationale for formal process notations and the objectives of explicitly representing processes, analyzing those formal descriptions, monitoring the progress of those processes as they are enacted, and automating portions of those enactments.

It clusters the research in this field into four chronologically ordered technology waves - Process Formalisms, Process Adaptive Tools, Process Centered Environments, and Process Middleware.

It then assesses the state of the art in this field, identifies several remaining challenges, and suggests where the field should be headed.

Finally, it closes with review of what has changed in the last few years.

Customizing the PuLSE™ Product Line Approach to the Demands of an Organization[1]

Klaus Schmid and Tanya Widen

Fraunhofer Einrichtung für Experimentelles Software Engineering,
Sauerwiesen 6, D-67661 Kaiserslautern, Germany
+49 (0) 6301 707 – 158/218
{schmid, widen}@iese.fhg.de

Abstract. It is well-known that software processes need to be adapted to the specifics of the organization, the application domain, and the development techniques of the environments in which they are used. This is particularly important for reuse processes as they impact the whole software life-cycle and the reuse of artifacts creates additional relationships among multiple process instances (projects). Nevertheless the support for tailoring existing reuse approaches is at best weak. As a consequence of this realization we made customization support for the method a first rate objective while developing the Product Line Software Engineering method (PuLSE™).

The technology used for customization is called PuLSE Baselining and Customization (PuLSE-BC). This approach relies on an explicit characterization of the environment and the explicit connection of these characteristics to customizable properties of a process. In this paper, we describe the technical foundations of this approach and illustrate them with an example.

1 Introduction

1.1 Problem

Through our work on software product lines in industrial cooperations we recognized that transitioning a technology to a new environment is a difficult task, especially in the area of reuse technology. Each situation poses its unique requirements to which the technique needs to be adapted in order to be accepted and successful.

Software product lines are a recent development in software reuse. The idea underlying this approach is to systematically develop assets that are engineered to be reused across a line of products. The PuLSE method (Product Line Software Engineering) [3], which has been developed at the Fraunhofer Institute for Experimental Software Engineering (IESE), is a systematic approach for developing software product lines. One aim in the development of this approach is to make it adaptable to a large range of different environments. The underlying problem here is that the method needs to be

---

[1] PuLSE™ is a registered trademark of the Fraunhofer Institute for Experimental Software Engineering (IESE).

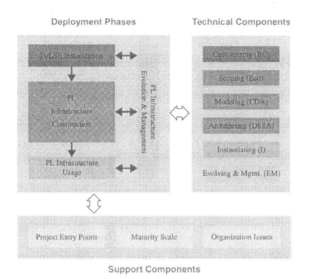

Deployment Phases   Technical Components

Support Components

Fig. 1. PuLSE Overview

adaptable to a variety of different situations, while at the same time it has to be as specific and precise as possible (while not giving inapplicable or badly adapted advice).

The approach taken to address this problem is to make PuLSE customizable and to generate a customized variant of the PuLSE method, which is particularly adapted to the specific situation, prior to its application.

In this paper, we will discuss the technology we developed for customizing PuLSE, which is called PuLSE Baselining and Customization (PuLSE-BC).

1.2 Context

PuLSE-BC was developed in the context of PuLSE and the example used in this paper to illustrate the concepts is taken from PuLSE. Therefore, it is necessary to introduce the PuLSE method.

PuLSE is a method for product line engineering [3]. The goal of PuLSE is to enable the conception and deployment of software product lines within a large variety of enterprise contexts. This requires that PuLSE has a strong alignment with the product centric focus of enterprises and that it is flexible enough so that it can be adapted to meet the specific needs of different enterprises.

Figure 1 presents a decomposition of the PuLSE components and phases. PuLSE is articulated around three main elements: the deployment phases, the technical components, and the support components.

The *deployment phases* are logical stages a product line goes through. They describe the activities performed to set up and use the product line.

The *technical components* provide the technical know-how needed to operationalize the product line. They are used throughout the Deployment Phases.

The *support components* are packages of information, or guidelines, which enable a better adaptation, evolution, and deployment of the product line.

The phases and technical components are described in more detail below.

The Initialization Phase entails the baselining of the enterprise to understand the situation and the adaptation of the PuLSE method based on the baselining results. The process and the technological knowledge for this phase is provided by the PuLSE-BC (Baselining and Customization) technology component which is described in this paper.

The Infrastructure Construction Phase includes activities for creating the reusable product line infrastructure. The technical components that define these activities are PuLSE-Eco (Economic Scoping), PuLSE-CDA (Customizable Domain Analysis) and PuLSE-DSSA (Domain-Specific Software Architectures). PuLSE-Eco defines a method for scoping the reuse infrastructure that shall be developed as part of product line engineering. The method used is based on a description of products and their characteristics and on explicitly relating the reuse support of the characteristics to the business objectives of the organization [5]. PuLSE-CDA describes the process for analyzing the product line domain and creating a domain model, which can be used for design and implementation, and the domain decision model, which enables instantiation of the domain model. PuLSE-DSSA specifies how to develop a reference architecture for the product line. This architecture together with the configuration model is the basis for the implementation and for systematic reuse of the assets [3].

The Infrastructure Usage Phase covers how to use the products created during the Infrastructure Construction Phase to create product line instances. This is the phase where the individual systems are developed. The process for usage is defined by the PuLSE-I (Instantiation) technical component.

Finally, there is the Infrastructure Evolution & Management Phase. This phase maps to the EM (Evolution & Management) technical component. This component plays an important role throughout product line development as it addresses all project management issues. It is also particularly relevant during the evolution stage, as it handles iterations through the other phases based on change requests.

1.3 Solution Approach

The PuLSE technical components capture the core processes of PuLSE. It is these processes that need to be adapted when applying PuLSE.

Our solution to process customization is to define what a process has to provide so that it can be customized and to provide a process for customizing such a process using that information. The underlying idea here is that process customization is domain-specific. Thus, while the specific types of information that are needed can be standardized (cf. Section 2.1), the exact information cannot, but needs to be provided together with the process. Thus, the approach works by identifying factors that describe the situation in which the process shall be enacted and that influence how it shall be performed. These factors are then operationalized in a step-wise manner to a level that is directly meaningful to the process. This is described in a domain-independent way by the PuLSE-BC process. As, using this approach, the technical component processes are customized independently, our approach also handles the integration of these process instances into a coherent PuLSE instance.

Because the PuLSE-BC process is separated from the process it customizes, any process that defines the necessary input can be customized using PuLSE-BC.

In the following section we describe what information must be provided by the customizable process and what the PuLSE-BC process is for customizing a customizable process. In Section 3, we then illustrate the approach with an example. In Section 4, an analysis of the approach is given, discussing its main advantages and disadvantages. In Section 5, work related to PuLSE-BC is described. Finally, in Section 6, we give our conclusions and discuss areas of further work.

2 PuLSE-BC

2.1 Concepts

PuLSE-BC defines what information is needed in order to customize a process using the PuLSE-BC process. This information is separated into different concepts, which are described below.

Customization Decisions and Customization Strategies. First of all, each customizable process must define the points at which the process can vary and how it can vary at these points. This information is captured in customization decisions. For example, the PuLSE-DSSA, architecture development, component has a customization decision which defines that prototyping is an optional activity during architecture development (cf. Figure 5). That is, an instance of PuLSE-DSSA may or may not include prototyping. An instance of the process is attained by resolving all of the customization decisions and adapting the process based on the resolutions.

Customization strategies package the detailed information on how a technical component should be adapted based on a customization decision resolution. Each customization decision has a corresponding customization strategy. The adaptation to the process may show up on the process level or as a refinement of parts of the process. An example for the first case is that the prototyping step may be included or not. An example for the second case is deciding on a specific notation for architecture documentation. This does not change a step, but is used within a step.

Customization Factors and Intermediate Decisions. To support resolving the customization decisions, PuLSE-BC requires that, for each customization decision, the information that may influence the resolution is defined. This information can be at two levels. The first level includes information that can be directly collected from an organization — for example, the skills of personnel and existing development practices. Information at this level is called a customization factor. The second level includes information that itself is influenced by other information and therefore has to be resolved; for example, the level of domain understanding in an organization is a complex factor that is influenced by other factors. Information at this level is called an intermediate decision.

The customization factors capture many different aspects of the situation in which a process will be applied. During the definition of these factors for PuLSE technical components the customization factors were classified into six categories. These include organizational aspects, characteristics of the domain, and project characteristics. The list of the different categories of customization factors is given in Table 1. The purpose of these categories is to provide a structuring of the set of customization factors and thus to structure and simplify elicitation of these factors.

A core set of customization factors is common to all customizable processes. However, each customizable process may have additional impacting information. Thus, the set of customization factors is not fixed, but can be adapted to the needs of each customizable process. The values of customization factors are derived using baselining strategies, those of intermediate decisions using evaluation strategies (see below).

Domain Characteristics	factors which relate to the domain itself and are independent of implementation aspects (e.g., domain complexity which represents how difficult to understand a domain is)
Information Sources	factors that relate to the availability of information about the domain
Implementation Characteristics	factors that influence implementations in the domain
Integratable Software Artifacts	factors that relate to the actual artifacts that can be integrated in a new product line
Project context	factors relating to the specific project that is planned
Enterprise context	factors relating to the enterprise in general

Table 1. Customization Factor Categories

Decision Graph and Evaluation Strategies. The decision graph illustrates all the "impacts"-relations among customization factors, intermediate decisions, and customization decisions (cf. Figure 2). It is a graphical representation that provides an overview of the relations. In addition to the decision graph, each intermediate decision and customization decision has a corresponding evaluation strategy that provides guidance on how the influencing factors may affect the resolution of the decision. Evaluation strategies describe how the values of different factors should be combined to come up with a value for a decision.

The evaluation strategies for the PuLSE technical components have been derived from several different information sources. A major input was current software engineering knowledge (esp. current reuse approaches) as described in literature. Further, initial experiences with applying product lines in industrial practice proved to be an important form of input. Naturally, these strategies are of a preliminary nature only and are supposed to evolve over time as more and more experiences are gained with their application.

Baselining Strategies and Questionnaires. Additionally, each customization factor has a corresponding baselining strategy that provides guidance on how to gather the necessary information. That is, the strategies describes how the corresponding information shall be elicited. An example for a baselining strategy for "domain experience" is given in Figure 4.

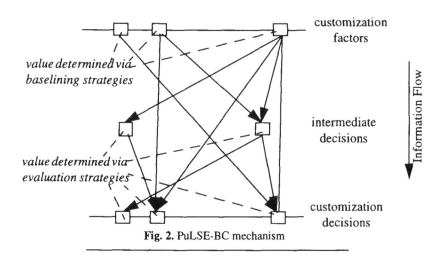

Fig. 2. PuLSE-BC mechanism

As the information collected is very similar to that in assessments, the techniques used for eliciting this information are taken from assessment approaches. Therefore, the baselining strategies for all of the customization factors are consolidated in questionnaires that can be used for gathering the information from a company.

Baseline, Decision, and Customization Profile Library. The PuLSE-BC process is systematically defined to go through gathering information, evaluating the decisions and customizing the technical components. However, the decision graph and evaluation strategies have been developed based mainly on our experiences, general knowledge about the technology, and experience reports in literature with other similar technology. Our goal is that they will evolve over time with more experience. This is enabled through storing each organizations decisions along with the rationales and factors that influenced them. This information, captured in the baseline, decision and customization profiles, can then be analyzed, for example to determine if new factors influenced a decision that could be added to the decision graph. Through this feedback loop, PuLSE-BC supports continuous improvement.

Storing the profiles also enables the systematic evolution of the results. The PuLSE-EM component monitors for changes and would restart PuLSE-BC to evolve the customized process based on changes. Through the traceability provided by the graphs the places where the change might have affects can be determined, and through the rationales coupled with the change request the decision can be reevaluated.

The stored profiles also enable systematic reuse of evaluations and customizations during an application of PuLSE-BC. During evaluation and customization, the stored profiles can be searched for matching profiles based on the gathered information. If appropriate, the existing profile can be reused, as opposed to evaluating all decisions anew.

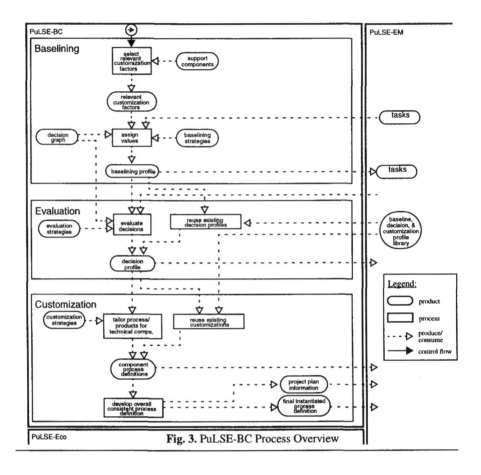

Fig. 3. PuLSE-BC Process Overview

2.2 Process

In this section, the PuLSE-BC process is described. The aim of the process is to produce a customized instance of a process which is appropriately tailored to the situation. To customize a process, the information described above must be available for that process. It is used throughout an application of PuLSE-BC. PuLSE-BC is basically a three-step approach: *baselining*, *evaluation*, and *customization*. A high level view of the process is shown in Figure 3.

Baselining starts with the identification of the customization factors that are relevant in the particular organizational environment in which the process shall be established. For customizing the PuLSE process, the customization factors depend on the technical component(s) that need to be customized and on the support components. The support components provide a gross characterization of the environment (cf. Section 1.2).

Once the customization factors are selected, their values are determined. This information is collected using the questionnaires of *baselining strategies* for the selected factors (cf. Section 4). The values that are elicited using this strategy are recorded in the baseline profile of the project.

Once the baselining profile has been developed, evaluation starts. PuLSE-BC supports two complementary ways for evaluating the profile and developing a customized process instance. The first one aims at developing a customization from scratch. This is depicted in the left-most thread of the process model shown in Figure 3, (i.e., all process steps except *reuse existing decision profiles* and *reuse existing customization*). This approach relies on the *decision graph* and *evaluation strategies*. The decision graph provides an abstract view on what information impacts each decision and the valuation strategies describe how the values of different factors should be combined to come up with a value for a decision.

The second possibility is represented by the remaining two steps in Figure 3: *reuse existing decision profiles* and *reuse existing customizations*. In this case previous customization experience is reused for deriving a process customization. In order to do this the developed baseline profile is matched against the *baseline profile library*. This library contains profiles gathered during previous applications of PuLSE-BC. If a sufficiently similar profile can be found, the customization associated with it is retrieved and is used as a basis for the customization, that is, the customization is reevaluated in the current context and appropriately adapted. This allows to take advantage of experience from previous customizations, where a fine-tuned customization was developed over time

The two approaches to evaluation are complementary, as one is based on customization rules, which have been derived from a conceptual analysis of the customization problem, while the second is based on an experience-driven approach. Reusing previous customization experience does not only save time, it also enables better customizations, as particular cases that were previously encountered, but could not be generalized into evaluation strategies, can be reused.

In both cases, evaluation results in the *decision profile*. This profile summarizes the customization decisions that have been made for every relevant technology component. Based on this, a tailoring of the technical components is performed in the step *tailor process* using the customization strategies. In the case that evaluation is based on the reuse of previous cases, also *(partial) process instances*, i.e., the customization cases from which the experience was derived, are used.

The tailoring step results in the *component process definitions*, i.e., the process models of the respective technology components are adapted with the information derived during tailoring.

So far, adaptation of the individual technical components happened mostly independently. This is sensible, as they were developed to possess clean interfaces and should not be too tightly coupled. However, some aspects connect several components. For example, the particular workproducts chosen for PuLSE-CDA may have an impact on PuLSE-DSSA. Consequently, some additional integration work is necessary in order to come up with a smoothly integrated process definition. This is done in the step *develop overall consistent process definition*. In this step restrictions are propagated among components. This can happen on a syntactical and on a semantical level. In the first case, e.g., the deletion of an output is reflected in another component by the deletion of an input (these are the kind of adaptations that are typically supported by existing process tailoring or evolution environments like Pro-Tail [12, 11]). In the latter

```
How many systems did developers develop prior to this
system? (on average)
     No system: 0; One system: 1; Several systems: 2

How many systems have been developed in-house?
     No system: 0; One system: 2; Several systems: 3

How many systems of this type did developers use(on
average) before?
     <= 1 system: 0; > 1 system: 1

Based on the sum the following results are given:

Domain Experience:0,1:low; 2,3:medium; >3: high
```

Fig. 4. An example of a baselining strategy

case additional semantic information is used to restrict the instantiation of the process, e.g., if the analysis models are object-oriented, than the architectural description language should also support object orientation, in order to enable a smooth transition between the two technical components responsible for these activities. As this step needs a lot of background-knowledge it strongly relies on human involvement.

During these activities, not only information on the processes and products is derived, but also additional information relevant to project management, like a rough break-down of the resources, or the expected number of iterations required for a certain step. This information is captured and forwarded as *project plan information* to PuLSE-EM. It should be noted that this is not a complete project-plan, but merely a collection of constraints on project planning.

In this section we gave an overview of the PuLSE-BC process. PuLSE-BC is actually used during two phases: initialization and evolution. Above we described the process used during initialization, where PuLSE-BC plays its main role. During evolution it may be found out that this instantiation is not or no longer appropriate. Reasons for this might be that the situation of the enterprise changes, that errors were made during baselining, or just that it becomes apparent that the instantiation is inappropriate. In these situations PuLSE-BC is used to perform a re-customization of the method.

In the following section we illustrate the initialization process description of PuLSE-BC with an example.

3 Example BC-Application

In this section, we will describe in more detail how customization of the PuLSE method is performed by giving some illustrative excerpts of an example. First, we will show in some detail how the customization of a single component (PuLSE-DSSA) looks like. We choose PuLSE-DSSA, because its customization is not as complex as, for example, the PuLSE-CDA customization. Therefore we can describe it in sufficient

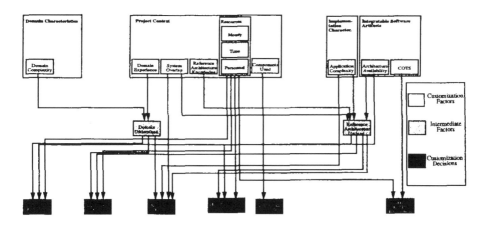

Fig. 5. PuLSE-DSSA Decision Graph

detail in this paper. Then we will illustrate the integration of processes of different technical components.

The decision graph of PuLSE-DSSA is shown in Figure 5. This graph shows the customization factors relevant to PuLSE-DSSA in the top row. In the middle layer some intermediate decisions are identified while at the bottom the customization decisions for PuLSE-DSSA are given. Each factor and decision is described briefly below.

There are eleven customization factors for DSSA. In the category domain characteristics there is only one, *domain complexity*. This factor captures the inherent difficulty in understanding the domain due to the complexity of its content.

In the project context category there are seven factors. Three are combined into a group called resources. These three factors capture the amount of the different resources available for the project. The factor *domain experience* captures what type and amount of experience with the domain exists in the development group and in the organization (cf. Figure 4). The factor *reference architecture knowledge* is similar but for experience with developing reference architectures. The factor *systems overlap* denotes the percentage of total functionality that is expected to be shared by all systems in the product line. The last factor, PuLSE components used, determines to what degree the PuLSE process is being applied.

Only one factor from the category Implementation Characteristics is used: *application complexity*. This factor captures properties of expected systems, such as size and number of modules, or coupling and cohesion.

In the last category, integratable software artifacts, two factors are used. *Architecture availability* captures whether existing architectures exist and can or have to be used. The factor *COTS* is similar for COTS products.

There are only two intermediate decisions in the DSSA decision graph. The first is *domain understanding*, which denotes the extent to which a domain is understood by an enterprise. The second is *reference architecture understanding*, which has an analogous meaning for concepts underlying reference architectures.

The DSSA decision graph has six decisions that affect the DSSA process. *Prototyping* denotes whether or not a prototype will be built and if so, what type of prototype.

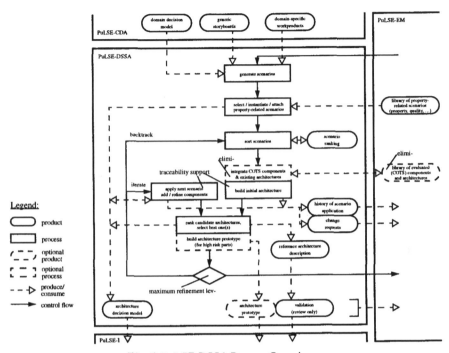

Fig. 6. PuLSE-DSSA Process Overview

Architecture validation addresses the need for validation of products created during the DSSA application. The *number of levels* captures the expected number of iterations through the DSSA process. *Try architecture integration* and *try COTS integration* address the issue of using or combining existing parts into the architecture. Finally, the *architecture traceability* decision focuses on whether links are created to input products from CDA or not.

As shown in Figure 3, PuLSE-BC starts with selecting the customization factors that are supposed to be relevant in the current situation. In our case all customization factors shown in Figure 5 (top row) are relevant. Thus we develop a baseline containing values for all these factors using the baselining strategies of these factors. The baselining strategies describe how to find the appropriate information to determine the value of a specific factor, e.g., the baselining strategy for *domain experience* explains how to assess the existing experience of the project team relative to the domain. Some information can also be gathered directly from the project agenda (e.g., available resources, aimed at PuLSE maturity level). A summary of the resulting customization factor values is given in Table 2.

For the purpose of this example we assume that there is no existing profile in the library that matches the current one sufficiently well to warrant its use. Thus the reuse steps cannot be applied and consequently a customization needs to be developed from scratch. In a first step the values of the intermediate decisions *domain understanding* and *reference architecture understanding* are determined. In order to do so the respective evaluation strategies are applied.They describe how for the relevant node the incoming values are aggregated. An overview of the interdependencies among factors is provided by the decision graph (cf. Figure 6)

Evaluation strategies stem from the common technical knowledge relevant to the decision and from experiences gained from applying the process. Consequently, they can vary widely in complexity. In some cases it is only possible to provide rough guidelines on how to perform the evaluation and a lot of human experience is needed to derive the appropriate choice for the customization decision. An example of this is the decision on the particular workproduct types and their representations, which has to be made for PuLSE-CDA.

On the other hand, in very simple cases the evaluation strategies can be described by a table as is the case with the intermediate decision *domain understanding* (cf. Table 3; vl = very low; l = low; m = medium, h = high, vh = very high). The basic idea behind this is that the higher the domain complexity is, the higher is the level of domain experience which is needed to attain a certain level of domain understanding. The resulting values of the intermediate decisions are given in Table 2.

Using the same approach, the values of the customization decisions are determined. For example, architecture validation is strongly needed (e.g., in the form of an inspection process) if any of: reference architecture understanding ≤ medium, domain understanding ≤ low, resources ≤ medium). In the other cases a simple review of the architecture will be sufficient.

The description given here for the evaluation strategies should not be misinterpreted in the way that this process would be fully automatic. Human expertise is still a necessary ingredient, especially for borderline cases. The values for the customization decisions are summarized in Table 4.

Using these customization decision values (step *tailor process/products for technical components*) an instantiation of the PuLSE-DSSA process is created using the customization strategies. As described earlier the customization strategies describe in more detail how certain values should be mapped onto specific adaptations of the PuLSE process. For example, one customization strategy describes that the decision *architecture integration = no* leads to the elimination of the *try architecture integration* step in the process.

Domain Complexity	low
Domain Experience	low
System Overlap	high
Reference Architecture Knowledge	low
Resources (Money/Time/Personnel)	low
PuLSE Maturity Level	full
Architecture Availability	no arch. available
Application Complexity	medium
COTS	no COTS-products
Domain Understanding	medium
Reference Architecture Understanding	low

Table 2. PuLSE-DSSA Customization Factors

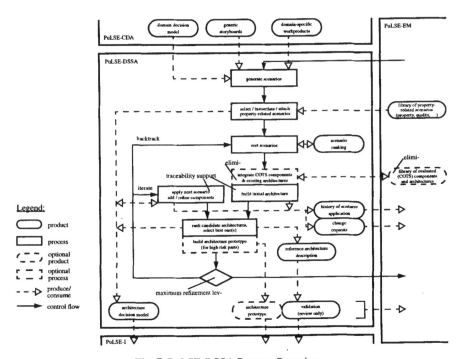

Fig. 7. PuLSE-DSSA Process Overview

The customized process with some annotations is shown in Figure 6. The dashed parts are those that are optional in the generic process. As there was no need for the integration of COTS components or existing architectures, the corresponding process steps were eliminated. On the other hand prototyping support is needed (in a restricted form) as shown in the diagram. The other customization decisions only show up as annotations in this diagram. However, in a more fine-grained process description some of them would also show up as additions/deletions to the process (e.g., traceability support). The resulting process diagram gives us the *component process definition* for the PuLSE-DSSA technical component. Similarly, we apply the steps described above of baselining, evaluation, and customization for coming up with an instantiated PuLSE-CDA process description. This is shown in Figure 8.

Both process instances are raw processes in the sense that the customized processes of the different technical components are not necessarily well-integrated. Their integration is the aim of the step *develop overall consistent process definition*. In our example, the definition of object models during PuLSE-CDA poses a need for integration (cf. Figure 8). Although this object model is a model on the analysis level (i.e., does not describe the software implementation) as opposed to the model on the implementation level as it is developed by PuLSE-DSSA, it should still be clearly traceable to this model (i.e., the reference architecture). Thus, special treatment needs to be given to this model by the PuLSE-DSSA steps *build initial architecture* and *apply next scenario*. In our case this would mean that one would prescribe the usage of an ADL

Domain Experience \ Domain Complex.	vl	l	m	h	vh
vl	vl	vl	vl	vl	vl
l	m	m	l	vl	vl
m	vh	h	m	l	vl
h	vh	vh	h	m	m
vh	vh	vh	vh	vh	vh

Table 3. Evaluation Strategy for Domain Understanding

that supports object-oriented concepts in PuLSE-DSSA and that the initial architecture would be defined as an adaptation of the analysis model.

Further the step *generate scenarios* needs to be particularly adapted to the specific set of workproducts developed in PuLSE-CDA. Usually the influence of such customizations will be minimal as PuLSE was designed to provide clean interfaces between the individual technical components

While so far we did only discuss the adaptation of PuLSE-CDA and PuLSE-DSSA, it should by now be clear how this process extends towards the adaptation and integration of further technology components. As a result of this an integrated PuLSE-process variant which is particularly customized to the requirements of a certain product line project is developed

4 Analysis

In the preceding section we described the PuLSE-BC component, which aims at developing an adapted variant of the PuLSE methodology. This approach consists of three stages: baselining of the situation, evaluation of the impact, and customization of the process.

We see this approach as an important improvement over existing product line and domain engineering approaches as these do not support a disciplined customization approach. Most approaches either do not support customization at all (e.g., FODA [10]) or support it only in a limited fashion, e.g., by giving only an abstract description of how to perform customization (e.g., ODM [17]). In contrast to these approaches PuLSE-BC supports the repeatable and traceable customization of the method to the environment. This entails not only a risk reduction for technology transition, it also enables a systematic re-customization of the method as the project environment changes over time.

Prototype	limited (for high risk parts only)
Architecture Validation	review
Number of Levels	low (≤ 2)
Try Architecture Integration	no
Architecture Traceability	yes
Try COTS Integration	no

Table 4. PuLSE-DSSA Customization Decisions

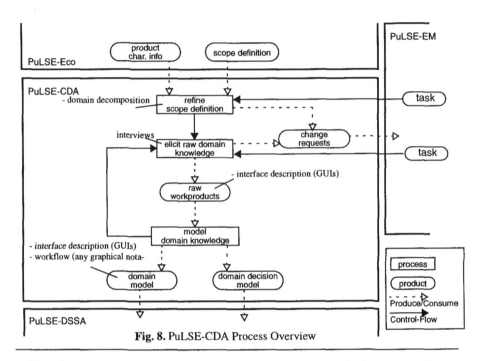

Fig. 8. PuLSE-CDA Process Overview

But the PuLSE-BC is not specific to reuse processes, as it does not make any assumptions on the kind of process that is customized. Thus it provides a general framework for the customization of processes. This generality is due to the fact that the approach relies on a structure consisting of customization factors, decisions, and the evaluation strategies. This structure is obviously exchangeable for different processes. However, as the process has been developed to support the PuLSE product line engineering approach, the current set of factors and decisions is defined for the current technical components of PuLSE.

The work done on PuLSE-BC is heavily linked with work on process tailoring, assessments and baselining, and also work on experience factories, which influenced the integration of experience in the customization process.

While the basic operation of PuLSE-BC relies on a knowledge-intensive approach (that is, characteristics of the environment are explicitly linked to desirable aspects of the process), it also incorporates an experience-based approach. In some situations experience will show that a process configuration derived using the knowledge-intensive approach is not optimal, as it leads to customizations which have previously been found to be non-optimal. For handling these situations PuLSE-BC enables the reuse of experience through the step *reuse existing customization*, i.e., it supports the recognition of these situations and the reuse of process instantiations which were found to be more appropriate.

The process, as it is currently defined, is a starting point for further improvement. The decision graphs and strategies have been developed based on our current understanding of the product line development process. In order to systematically improve the customization process this framework is needed, so that experience can be gathered in an organized fashion. For example, it may turn out over time that some dependencies that are seen between customization factors and process configurations are erroneous. By making this linkage explicit in the *decision graph* it is possible to capture such information. This provides an evolution path for PuLSE-BC itself, too. In order to analyze the appropriateness of the PuLSE-BC process, the validation of the customized process in the environment is important. Here, we will use an approach like the one described in [14] for analyzing the congruence between process and environment.

5 Related Work

The fact that processes must be tailored to the specific environment in which they will be applied in order to be accepted and of maximal use is well-known [2]. Further, some work has been done on determining the congruency between a process and the environment it is used in [14]. However, developing an instance of a process which is specifically tailored to its environment is a very difficult task. Consequently, this problem has been rarely truly addressed. Instead most process descriptions that are supposed to be used across different situations usually stay on a rather general level so that they can subsume the different variants. This is often referred to as a process framework [9].

While this is the general approach, some notable exceptions exist to this. For example the German process standard "Das Vorgehensmodell" [7] offers explicit means for tailoring the standard process model to specific situations. However, this tailoring is limited to the deletion of process elements (products and processes), which overly restricts the customization possibilities. An overview of adaptations that are typically used in process tailoring is given in [12].

In research environments more sophisticated methods of process tailoring have been developed like the ProTail-tool, which supports the semi-automatic tailoring of formal process models using adaptation rules [13]. However, these approaches do not describe a method for deciding on what kind of adaptations have to be made.

In the field of process evolution many approaches have been developed to address the adaptation of process models [11]. However, major differences exist to our approach. First, these approaches aim at the step-wise adaptation to changing environments and not at the tailoring to a multitude of considerably different environments. Further, these approaches do usually not address the selection of adequate adaptations, but focus on the technical issues involved in performing the adaptations, once the selection has been made. However, some exceptions to this exist like [4], but there the selection of adaptations is strongly specialized to specific situations.

The situation in the area of reuse processes is very similar to this general description. In particular the ODM [17] and Synthesis methods [16] try to be adaptable to the specific situation. However, they do this mostly by remaining on a very general level. Especially the Synthesis approach goes as far as refraining from any specific modeling guidelines in order to be applicable with any notation. ODM is more precise on this, but still mainly supports changes in the representation of artifacts, but does not support the addition or deletion of products and process elements.

In the area of process tailoring PuLSE is most strongly related to the explicit tailoring supported by the ProTail-tool. However, contrary to this, PuLSE-BC does not focus on the technical process of adapting the process models, but on the identification of the most appropriate way of adapting the process through its baselining aspect.

Baselining in PuLSE-BC heavily draws on existing work on assessment. This includes work like the Capability Maturity Model (CMM) [8], the reuse adoption guidebook [15], which addresses domain and reuse capability assessment, and the domain scoping framework [6], which centers around the assessment of domains.

As discussed in Section 1.3, the customization approach we chose is based on explicitly deriving required characteristics of the process from specific aspects of the situation. This approach is complementary to the experience factory approach which relies on reusing complete models based on a characterization of the current situation [1]. Therefore, we augmented our PuLSE-BC component with this reuse approach in order to take advantage of its complementary characteristics.

6 Conclusions

In this paper, we described PuLSE Baselining and Customization (PuLSE-BC), a technique for customizing processes, which also describes what needs to be provided in addition to the mere process so that customization can be performed based on environmental characteristics. PuLSE-BC enables traceable and repeatable customization of a method based on information about the situation in which it shall be applied. PuLSE-BC was developed in the context of the PuLSE method. In this paper we presented PuLSE as an example of a process that can be customized using our approach.

The PuLSE-BC method is currently defined at a high level. It is our intention to refine the steps of the method using the experience we gain from applying the customization process on PuLSE. In this sense it should be seen as a first step on an evolutionary path. Without the initial process definition, experience could not be gathered systematically, as there would be no framework for gathering or comparing. Starting with the initial process definition we will apply the process and improve the graphs and evaluation strategies based on the gained experience. In addition we will build up a profile library that can be reused in other customization applications.

In the future, the main task will be to extend and refine the existing framework through practical experience in applying PuLSE-BC to a variety of industrial situations. In the long term we also expect to provide appropriate tool support.

7 Acknowledgments

The authors would like to thank the anonymous reviewers whose input contributed substantially to this paper. We would also like to thank Jürgen Münch, Martin Verlage, and Barbara Dellen for insightful reviews and comments on earlier drafts of this paper.

Our co-workers on PuLSE also contributed a lot: Joachim Bayer, Jean-Marc DeBaud, Oliver Flege, Cristina Gacek, Peter Knauber, Roland Laqua, and Dirk Muthig.

8 References

[1]   V. Basili, G. Caldiera, and D. Rombach. Experience Factory. In J. Marciniak, editor, *Encyclopedia of Software Engineering*, volume 1, pages 469–476. John Wiley & Sons, 1994.

[2]   V. Basili and D. Rombach. Tailoring the software process to project goals and environments. Technical report, University of Maryland, 1986.

[3]   J. Bayer, O. Flege, P. Knauber, R. Laqua, D. Muthig, K. Schmid, T. Widen, and J.-M. DeBaud. Pulse: A methodology to develop software product lines. In *Proceedings of the Fifth ACM SIGSOFT Symposium on Software Reusability (SSR'99)*, pages 122–131, Los Angeles, CA, USA, May 1999. ACM.

[4]   Inderpal Bhandari, Michael Halliday, Eric Tarver, David Brown, Jarir Chaar, and Ram Chillarege. A case study of software process improvement during development. *IEEE Transactions on Software Engineering*, 19(12):1157–1170, December 1993.

[5]   J.-M. DeBaud and K. Schmid. A systematic approach to derive the scope of software product lines. In *Proceedings of the 21st International Conference on Software Engineering*, pages 34–43, Los Angeles, CA, USA, May 1999.

[6]   Department of Defense — Software Reuse Initiative, Version 3.1. *Domain Scoping Framework, Volume 2: Technical Description*, 1995.

[7]   Wolfgang Droeschel. *Das V-Modell. Der Standard fuer die Softwareentwicklung mit Praxisleitfaden*. R. Oldenbourg Verlag, 1995.

[8]   Kenneth M. Dymond. *A Guide to the CMM(sm). Understanding the Capability Maturity Model(sm) for Software*. Process Inc US, 1996.

[9]   Dennis J. Frailey. Defining a corporate-wide software process. In Mark Dowson, editor, *Proceedings of the First International Conference on the Software Process*, pages 113–120, 1991.

[10] K. Kang, S. Cohen, J. Hess, W. Novak, and S. Peterson. Feature-oriented domain analysis (FODA) feasibility study. Technical Report CMU/SEI-90-TR-21, Carnegie Mellon Software Engineering Institute, November 1990.

[11] Nazim H. Madhavji and Maria H. Penedo. Guest editor's introduction. *IEEE Transactions on Software Engineering*, 19(12):1125–1127, December 1993. Special Issue on the Evolution of Software Processes.

[12] J. Münch. Anpassung von Vorgehensmodellen im Rahmen ingenieur-mässiger Softwarequalitätssicherung. In *6. Workshop der GI-Fachgruppe 5.1.1: "Vorgehensmodelle, Prozessverbesserung und Qualitätsmanagement", 19. - 20.04.1999, Kaiserslautern*. To appear.

[13] Jürgen Münch, Markus Schmitz, and Martin Verlage. Tailoring großer Prozeßmodelle. In *Tagungsband des 3. Workshops der GI-FG 5.1.1 - Vorgehensmodelle - Einfürung, betrieblicher Einsatz, Werkzeug-Unterstützung und Migration, GMD-Studien Nr. 311*, number GMD-Studien Nr. 311, pages 63–71, Berlin, August 1997.

[14] Graciela Pérez, Khaled El Emam, and Nazim H. Madhavji. Evaluating the congruence of a software process model in a given environment. In *Proceedings of the Fourth International Conference on the Software Process*, pages 49–62, 1996.

[15] Software Productivity Consortium Services Corporation. *Reuse Adoption Guidebook, Version 02.00.05*, November 1993.

[16] Software Productivity Consortium Services Corporation, Technical Report SPC-92019-CMC. *Reuse-Driven Software Processes Guidebook, Version 02.00.03*, November 1993.

[17] Software Technology for Adaptable, Reliable Systems (STARS), Technical Report STARS-VC-A025/001/00. *Organization Domain Modeling (ODM) Guidebook, Version 2.0*, June 1996.

The Application of Metrics to Industrial Prototyping Processes: An Empirical Study

Keith Phalp[1] and Steve Counsell[2]

[1] Empirical Software Engineering Group, Bournemouth University, Bournemouth, UK. email:kphalp@bournemouth.ac.uk

[2] Birkbeck College, University of London, Malet Street, London, UK. email:steve@dcs.bbk.ac.uk

Abstract. A key problem in the development of information systems is understanding features of the development process. To this end, in recent years, considerable interest has been focused on modelling processes. In this paper, the results of an empirical investigation into the use of prototyping in information systems development is described. Nine prototyping processes across eight different sites of varying size were analysed and data relating to each process collected. The notation of Role Activity Diagrams (RADs) was used to capture each of the nine processes. Analysis of the interactions in each process revealed that the project manager interacted with the prototyper far more often in large developments than in small or medium-sized developments. However, significantly more interactions between the project manager and end-user were found in small-sized developments than for any other sized site. The study demonstrates how measures of business models can aid analysis of the process rather than the product and highlights the need for more empirical investigation into this and other facets of the development process. A number of lessons have been learnt from our analysis; these we also explain.

1 Introduction

Through participation with the end user, prototyping claims to reduce the risk of building the wrong product. Through greater understanding of requirements by the prototyper, it also claims to enhance the quality of the software product.

In this paper, a case study of the prototyping process at eight sites of varying sizes and application domains is described. The modelling notation of Role Activity Diagrams (RADs) [7] was used to model the business processes investigated and data then collected from nine processes containing a prototyping role. A high degree of autonomy and interaction with the end-user was expected of the prototyping role. The underlying motivation for the work contained in this paper stems from a number of sources. Firstly, very little research has been undertaken into the features of the prototyping process; very little is understood about the prototyping process. Secondly, only a small body of quantitative analysis has been carried out using RADs as the modelling tool; using such a notation allows a process modeller to discuss and validate a model with an end-user. This is likely to lead to a more realistic representation of the process. Thirdly, the approach described in this paper lends itself well to future development of measures on the RADs developed; such an approach has already provided interesting conclusions [10].

Results from the analysis contained in this paper indicated that the relationship between project manager and prototyper varied depending on the size of the development site being analysed. Interactions between the two roles at large development sites were considerably greater than between the same two roles at small-sized sites. However, significantly more interactions between the project manager and end-user were found in small-sized developments than for any other size.

One possible implication of these results is that in large organisations, the prototyping process has a more rigid structure imposed on it with specific responsibilities and channels of communication for each role. Small organisations rely more on a flexible structure for the prototyping process with direct communication at all levels (including that between project managers and end-users).

In the next section, we describe the notation of Role Activity Diagrams. In Section 3, details of the application domains and how the data was captured are provided. The empirical evaluation is then described (Section 4). A discussion of some of the issues raised is provided in Section 5. Finally some conclusions and research research aims are given (Section 6).

2 Role Activity Diagrams

Role Activity Diagrams were initially developed for software process modelling [8]. RAD notation lends itself well towards understanding behaviour and interactions of individuals or groups [5] and have been used extensively within process modelling and business process reengineering [6].

Figure 1 illustrates a RAD with three roles: Divisional Director, Project Manager and Designer. A role (depicted as a rounded rectangle) groups together activities which may be carried out by a person, group or machine (an actor or an agent). Activities (shaded squares), allow the role to move from its current state to the next. Roles act in parallel, and communicate and synchronise through interactions (shown as unshaded squares joined by a horizontal line). Interactions are like shared events, in that all roles involved move from their current state to the next state as a result of the interaction. Vertical state lines joining actions and interactions show the thread of control within a role. A role has constructs to depict concurrent or parallel behaviour (known as part-refinement) depicted by a point-up triangle. Choice (known as case-refinement) is depicted by a point-down triangle.

Roles are like *types* or *classes* (as found in Object-Oriented languages) in that they describe a particular kind of behaviour. They are not, however, instances of that behaviour. A role may be assigned to a number of different people and there

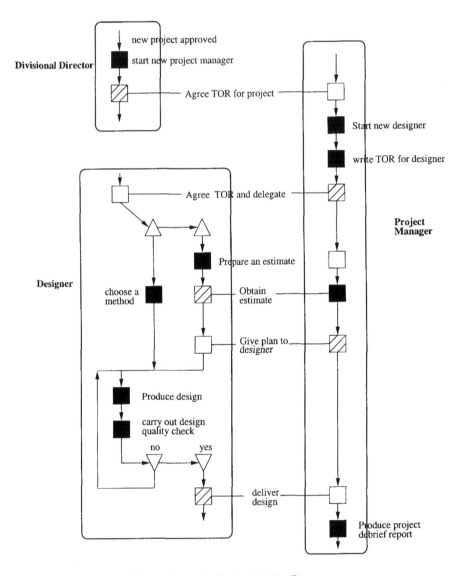

Fig. 1. Example Role Activity Diagram

may be a number of such roles acting in parallel at any given time. For example, in a retail outlet, there might be a number of shop assistant roles, and a number of manager roles. A single role may be acted out by a number of different people at different times. It is therefore useful to think of *instances* of the role.

The RAD in Figure 1 is taken from Ould [7], and it is considered close to the ideal RAD for that process (interaction between roles is kept to a minimum). An aim in the design of RADs would be, typically, to minimise the degree of interaction hence allowing roles to become more autonomous. They then no longer have to synchronise with other roles, giving them the opportunity to complete their tasks more quickly.

Earlier work has shown that RADs can be a useful means of capturing organisational processes [9, 10]. Simple measures can be used to complement and guide expert analysis of process models [10]; process improvement comes from an understanding of the complexities of the process itself. In the next section, we describe details of our evaluation.

3   Evaluation Details

In the software engineering community, empirical evaluation can be used to investigate the association between proposed software metrics and other indicators of software quality such as maintainability or understandability; thorough qualitative or quantitative analyses can be used to support these investigations [3, 2, 1]. Very little research, however, has been undertaken to establish whether empirical evaluation of business process models, as described in this paper, can be used to assess the quality of the process rather than product.

3.1   Data capture

To produce the RADs on which our investigation rests, a number of visits were made to each site to validate models and to conduct further interviews over the course of two to three years. Data collected from interviews was documented on formatted forms for later analysis. Further process evidence was gathered from both documentary sources and observation. The data collected formed the basis of the RAD diagrams reflecting the prototyping and other roles at each of the development sites. Details of the interview process, the interviews themselves and the RADs on which our analysis rests can be found in [4].

3.2   Application Domains

Table 1 contains descriptions of the nine RADs analysed. Altogether, three small projects, three medium projects and three large projects were analysed as part of the investigation. Two of the RADs (from projects 2 and 3) were drawn from the same telecommunications organisation. Drawing the RADs from differently sized projects reduced the threat to the validity of the investigation. One advantage of this was that the results of our analysis were more generalisable.

RAD	Site Size	Application Domain
1. International Banking	large	information system
2. Telecommunications	large	intelligent networking
3. Telecommunications	large	intelligent networking
4. Airway Service	medium	information system
5. Air Traffic control	medium	air traffic control
6. Electronic eng.	medium	circuit testing
7. Software House	small	information system
8. Hotel service	small	staff scheduling
9. Univ. Computer centre	small	network monitoring

Table 1. Descriptions of the nine RADs investigated

4   Empirical Evaluation

Table 2 summarises the roles found in each of the nine processes. Every process contained a management role. RADs 3 and 9 differed slightly from other roles in that they had Design Managing and Managing roles respectively. However, for the clarity of analysis, in this paper all managing roles were considered equivalent in the functions that they carried out. Every role also contained a customer or end-user role (or in some cases both). The customer and end user roles were also similar in function (since they both represented the target domain for the application and were important stakeholders in the system). For the clarity of our analysis therefore, where RAD processes included both customer and end-user roles, those two roles were merged; this occurred in RADs 1, 7, 8 and 9.

RAD	Roles
1.	Project Managing, Prototyping, DBA, Customer, End-user
2.	Project Managing, System Design, Prototyping Component Engineering, Proving, Marketing, External Customer
3.	Design Managing, Prototyping, Proving, Commercial Group, Customer
4.	Project Managing, Prototyping, User Group, End-user
5.	Project Managing, Engineering, Prototyping, Customer/User
6.	Business Board, Project Managing, Prototyping, Marketing, Customer
7.	Project Managing, Prototyping, Customer, End-user
8.	Project Managing, Prototyping, Customer, End-user
9.	Managing, Prototyping, Customer, End-user

Table 2. Roles in each of the nine RADs investigated

Table 3 shows the number of actions and interactions in each of the prototyping roles. It also shows the number of interactions each of the prototyping roles has with the project manager role, together with the number of interactions the prototyping role has with the end-user/customer role. The relatively small number of actions and interactions for prototyping roles 2 and 5 was due to additional roles in those processes which undertook some of the prototypers responsibilities (and hence undertook some the prototypers' actions and interactions).

In RAD 2, a **Systems Design** role provided an interface between the Project Manager and the Prototyping roles. Similarly, in RAD 5, an **Engineering** role provided the interface between Project Management and Prototyping roles.

Prot. Role	Actions	Inter.	Proj. Man. Inter.	End-user/Cust. Inter.
1.	8	13	7	4
2.	1	2	0	0
3.	3	5	3	0
4.	4	14	5	7
5.	1	2	0	1
6.	4	5	3	2
7.	5	3	1	2
8.	6	5	2	3
9.	6	6	2	4

Table 3. Prototyping Role Data

For the three large development sites, there was a clear trend of prototyper roles interacting with the Project Manager role considerably more than with the the End-user/Customer (50% of the prototyping roles' total interactions). The same was not true of medium-sized development sites where the opposite effect can be seen for two of the processes (38% of total interactions). In small development sites, the prototyper interacted less with the project manager for each of the three processes studied (36% of total interactions). This suggested that in large-sized development sites, greater controls were exercised between the two roles than in their medium and smaller-sized counterparts.

Table 4 shows, for each of the project managing roles: the number of actions, the number of interactions and number of interactions with the end-user/customer. Interestingly, it is in the three small sites where interaction between the project manager and end-user was the greatest (76% of project manager interactions were with the end-user compared with 42% at large sites and 37% at medium-sized sites). Considering the results of the previous table, this would seem to indicate that in small sites the project manager role bypassed the prototyping role and interacted directly with the end-user at the expense of communication with the prototyper.

4.1 Further Investigation

To determine the exact nature of the interactions between, firstly, the project manager and prototyping roles, and secondly, the project manager and end-user,

Proj. M. Role	Actions	Total Inter.	User/Customer Inter.
1.	4	12	7
2.	0	3	1
3.	4	9	2
4.	1	6	0
5.	2	7	5
6.	2	6	2
7.	3	8	8
8.	6	5	3
9.	5	4	2

Table 4. Project Manager Role Data

each interaction was categorised. Figure 2 shows the breakdown of interactions between the project manager and prototyper. For clarity purposes, only the four most common interactions are shown. The interactions between the project manager and prototyper were, as would have have expected; to fufil functions such as: obtaining signing off documents, delegating tasks, approving requirements and reviewing/reporting.

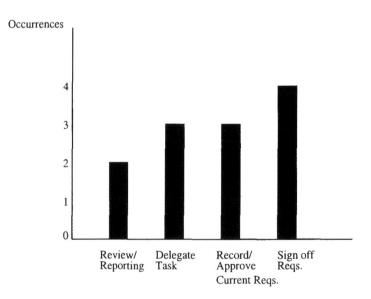

Figure 2: Interactions between project manager and prototyper.

Figure 3 shows the breakdown of interactions between the project manager and end-user. Once again, for the purposes of clarity, only the four most common interactions are shown.

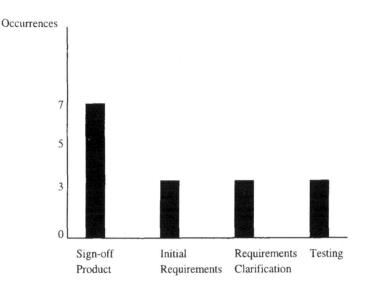

Figure 3: Interactions between Project Manager
and End-user roles

From Figure 3, it would appear that the project manager carried out some of the functions one would normally associate with the prototyping process. For example, *establishing initial requirements* and *requirements clarification*. On closer inspection of the three small-sized development sites, the three interactions for establishing initial requirements were in RADs 7,8 and 9 (the three small sites); similarly for three of the signing-off interactions. RAD 8 contained one of the *requirements clarification* interactions. In the next section, we discuss some of the issues raised from these results.

5   Discussion and Lessons Learnt

The results obtained from analysis of the RADs raise a number of issues. Greater communication between project manager and prototyper in large organisations may be due to a number of factors. Firstly, greater pressure on the prototyping process to succeed may cause more stringent controls by the project manager over the prototyping process. Large sites tend to create hierarchies within development teams and hence, channels of communication which can not be bypassed. In large sites, larger team composition may mean that the project manager has less time to interact with other staff (i.e., end-users). The responsibility in that case rests with the prototyper. In smaller, less formal sites, there are less restrictions. Projects are likely to be on a smaller scale and the project manager has time to communicate with all staff involved. The project manager is able to bypass the prototyper to fulfil tasks without breaking any acknowledged communication channels.

A number of lessons have been learnt from the approach outline in this paper. Firstly, the fact that the result was not unexpected indicates that using RADs as a modelling notation reflects the true picture of the business process. Further research will build significantly on the results of this paper. Secondly, our investigation has highlighted features of coupling between roles. One of the current issues facing the software engineering community is the proper characterisation of software complexity features such as coupling (and cohesion). The Systems Engineering for Business Process Change (SEBPC) research programme [11] highlights the importance of modelling processes as an aid in supporting the evolution of legacy information systems. Finally, the original task of trying to understand the prototyping process in greater detail has only served to highlight the potential for investigating other features of RADs. For example, the evaluation of RAD features common to application domains.

6 Conclusions and Future Research

In this paper, an empirical investigation has been carried out into nine prototyping processes for different application domains at eight sites. Data was collected for each prototyping process, and depicted in the form of Role Activity Diagrams (RADs). Evidence suggests that the project manager interacts with the prototyping role in large development sites far more than in medium or small-sized sites. Small-sized sites tended to incorporate more direct communication between project manager and end-user. From a systems development viewpoint, prototyping in large organisations would seem to be more formalised; small sites tend to encourage communication at all levels. With a view to further exploration of the nine RADs, future research will focus on the analysis of coupling trends in the same eight organisations. Coupling metrics will be used to analyse features of the differently-sized sites. An empirical approach will be taken to establish these features.

Acknowledgements

The authors acknowledge the contribution made by Liguang Chen (University of Bournemouth) to the research contained in this paper in providing details of the RADs on which our analysis rests.

References

1. V. R. Basili. The role of experimentation in software engineering: Past, current, and future. In *Proc 18th ICSE*, pages 442–449, 1996.

2. V. R. Basili, L. C. Briand, and W. L. Melo. A validation of object-oriented design metrics as quality indicators. *IEEE Transactions on Software Engineering*, 22(10):751–761, 1996.

3. L. Briand, L. Bunse, J. Daly, and C. Differding. An experimental comparison of the maintainability of object-oriented and structured design documents. In *Proceedings of Empirical Assessment in Software Engineering (EASE) '97, Keele, UK*, 1997.

4. L. Chen. *An Empirical Investigation into Management and Control of Software Prototyping*. Ph.d. dissertation, Department of Computing, Bournemouth University, 1997.

5. R. Handy. *Understanding Organisations*. Penguin, 1976.

6. D. Miers. *Business Process Re-engineering: myth and reality*. Kogan Page, 1994.

7. M. Ould. *Business Processes: Modelling and Analysis for Rengineering and Improvement*. Wiley, 1995.

8. M. Ould and C. Roberts. Modelling iteration in the software process. In *3rd International Software Process Workshop, Colorado, USA*, 1986.

9. K. Phalp and S. Counsell. Counts and heuristics for static process models. In *Proceedings ICSE Workshop on Process Modelling and Software Evolution, Boston, USA*, 1997.

10. K. Phalp and M. Shepperd. Analysing process models quantitatively. In *Empirical Assessment in Software Engineering (EASE99) Keele, Staffordshire, UK*, April 1999.

11. SEBPC. Systems engineering for business process change, managed research of the engineering and physical sciences research council (epsrc), homepage: at http://www.staff.ecs.soton.ac.uk/ph/sebpc/.

Author Index